We Shall Not Overcome

ROBERT EMIL BOTSCH

We Shall Not Overcome

POPULISM AND SOUTHERN

BLUE-COLLAR WORKERS

The University of North Carolina Press

Chapel Hill

Manufactured in the United States of America

Library of Congress Cataloging in Publication Data

Botsch, Robert Emil, 1947–
    We shall not overcome

    Bibliography: p.
    Includes index.
    1. Labor and laboring classes—Southern States.
    2. Labor and laboring classes—Southern States—
    Interviews. I. Title.
    HD8083.A13B67   305.5′6   80-11567
    ISBN 0-8078-1444-X

To Clyde and Mr. Y

Contents

Preface

QUESTION: *How do you feel about the Medicare system?*

JUNIOR: *Well, I think my momma's on part of it. They don't pay half of what they should pay. They may have their good points, but they got more bad than they do good—bad in terms of not paying enough money. Like good in terms of you can show 'em a card sometimes and it sends the help and other times it doesn't. It's just like it's not all that good.*

QUESTION: *There's been talk recently of a national health care system. How would you feel about that?*

JUNIOR: *Well, they could do that with all the money they waste up there on the moon shots. That'd be fine there. I've got a lot of insurance myself, and it seems like it just don't never pay the whole entire bill. You've got to dig money out of your pockets. . . .*

QUESTION: *Some say this would be socialized medicine. Would this bother you?*

JUNIOR: *Well, in a way—but you sure hear about a lot of people that don't have money to get insurance and dies due to not having money or doctor to see 'em. So, they need to do something!*

QUESTION: *What do you think causes poverty?*

JUNIOR: *Well, they don't either make enough money or they waste what they got, or maybe like a lot of black people. They like to have a lot of kids, five or six. And they don't think: "Well, I got to support them off what I make." They think: "Well, the government's gonna help. They'll build me a house to live in for nothin'," which is the truth! They pay $35 a month toward the electric bill, the heat, and everything else out there in the [public housing] project which to me ain't fair. And the people that's workin' in the same places that we workin' is making as much money as we are and they getting $200 of food stamps for $10 or $15 which ain't fair. They build them this nice Columbia Apartments over here which they rent for practically nothin'! But they take the money that they do make and they set around home and they drink it up and they buy a fancy car that they could do without. And they know when they need a doctor they can get one on credit. And it's just not right. One person can't change all that. And they've tried and tried, now, and they gettin' really aggravated on the food stamps—people gettin' them that don't need them. And they say the government's going to work this all out and check into all these people and find out the ones that really need it that ought to have it and the ones that don't need it ought to have 'em taken away from.*

This book represents my attempt to understand the political attitudes of workingmen such as Junior, who live in small towns all over the South. I have been troubled by their attitudes ever since my own political consciousness developed after moving from the North to a small southern city roughly similar to Furntex, the fictitious name of the town in which Junior lives. There are many of these people; they are angry; they have much to be angry about; but they are politically impotent. They are as likely to vent their anger on each other and on their working brothers with darker skin as they are to direct their frustration toward those who command economic and social power. Even if they are conscious of class-based economic frustrations, they are unlikely to take any political action, even on those rare occasions when the political system offers them relevant choices.

My interest in this subject was triggered by events that took place during my teen years. My father, a member of the middle class who attained a position of employment with professional status without a college degree, held the typical strong feelings that his eldest son should have to work and help earn his way through college. Such work is, of course, believed to have moral as well as economic value. The objects of this great American middle-class ritual presumably learn "the value of a dollar" and something about the likely fate of those who do not go to college.

During my first summer of middle-class socialization through manual labor, I learned how to pace myself digging ditches so I could last the required eight hours. For my successful graduation from a seemingly endless summer of ninety-degree-plus days I give full credit to the black men with long tenure at the job, who taught me many little energy-saving tricks of the trade. No doubt they are still pushing shovels while I am reminiscing and pushing a pen. The next summer's lessons took place in a warehouse, where, after I had survived the customary initiation period when all humor was at my expense, I was taught how to lift and stack without injuring my back or breaking my spirit. The following summer was spent working in the maintenance department of a furniture plant, where self-taught engineers and backyard mechanics showed me how to keep equipment that should have seen its last day working one day longer. The constant heroic acts they performed on old equipment with old tools and older methods under pressure to keep production going earned them little gratitude and less pay. But at least they had mobility and some sense of control over the machines and the production line, freedoms that were denied to the line workers and machine tenders whom I came to know in my daily travels around the plant.

I had assumed that I would return to the plant the next summer, but the college education I had completed through my junior year landed me an intern job with the government in Washington. Toward the end of that summer I received a letter from my parents telling of an accident in the furniture plant. My two immediate supervisors of the previous summer and some men who had come to work there in the year since had been badly burned in an explosion while working in the dust pit (an area where wood dust from machines is blown and stored). Both of my friends of the last summer endured several days of pain and agony before they met an inevitable death. I returned home in time to visit the funeral parlor. Several workers told me of their luck in being outside the pit at the moment of the blast. I thought how lucky I had been. A few expressed belief that the accident would not have happened had the company invested in non-arcing electrical sockets, but the men seemed hesitant to discuss the issue of blame. They became even more reluctant when I suggested that a good union might have seen that the company not allow such conditions to exist. Accidents were not uncommon. I myself had lost several days' pay from an accident when an ancient and much abused chain hoist had broken, fallen, and struck a glancing blow on my head. We were not supplied with hardhats. I became angry and frustrated after these conversations, not understanding why these men would not seize on this incident as a rallying point for collective actions to better their working conditions. The study on which this book is based has helped me to understand. I'm still angry.

The words of Junior, one of the men in the small group I interviewed, give us a preview of the thoughts that were expressed during my discussions with these men. He supports strong and effective government action to deal with personal problems that are beyond his control. Yet he resents government actions that give something for nothing to those he feels are less meritorious than he. For Junior, one large and highly visible group of such people are blacks. But Junior has not been motivated by either attitude to engage in political activities beyond a very occasional political discussion with friends. He has never voted—not even for Wallace, whom he feels had some "good things" to say about both of these sets of issues.

Because the sample is so small, no statistical generalizations can be made, and therefore nothing can be proved. An immediate question that arises is whether anything of value can be learned in a study that uses a sample of fifteen as the central data base.

There are several ways to answer this question. The first requires a leap of faith. Though I shall be looking at fifteen separate cases, I shall also be looking for commonalities in the small sample. If some commonalities can be found in attitudes and if these men are in any sense typical, I shall make the leap and say that such commonalities *probably* exist for a significant number of their peers. I shall also boldly point out how theories that have been empirically tested elsewhere apply to this small sample.

A second way to answer this question requires no such logical leap of faith. I shall look for relationships between experiences and attitudes. If such relationships are universally valid, they should hold true for even a small sample such as this. Moreover, one can argue that this study is exploratory in that relationships will be sought that others may empirically test in larger samples for the purpose of statistical generalization.

A third answer to the question of the significance of this study is to turn the question around. The initial question posed the problem of the validity of applying the attitudes of fifteen workers to some larger population. Taking the entire population and the environment surrounding it, the political and social systems of our society, one might ask what significance the larger system has for one small group of men. In treating this small sample as a dependent rather than an independent variable, one may in effect test the quality of our political and social system. One way of approaching difficult normative questions concerning the quality of the society in which we live is to take an in-depth look at the quality of people's lives. The statistical quality of life studies that compare objective figures for literacy rates, crime rates, incomes, percentage having indoor plumbing, health statistics and the like are often criticized on the grounds that they ignore everything that cannot be counted. Intangibles such as a sense of safety and belongingness and connection with one's family, friends, and neighbors, often turn out to be the most important predictive measures of life satisfaction in the opinion of some critics.[1]

An ever-growing body of important research approaches the study of our society through the eyes of individuals rather than through significance tests. In a classic study of race relations in the South, *Caste and Class in a Southern Town*, John Dollard used the conversational interview method. Because he did not have a tape recorder at his disposal in the 1930s, he had to record the discussions from memory.[2] After spending half a lifetime living with and coming to "know," as opposed to "studying," many of the poor people who live in the South, Robert Coles portrays their lives through their own words. He argues that becoming familiar with the lives of people reveals many more truths than can be learned from using simplistic socioeconomic categories and theories that explain behavior of people.

> Lives, as opposed to problems, may puzzle the fixed notions of theorists, while at the same time adding confirmation to what has been revealed by such keenly sensitive ("if methodologically untrained") observers such as Dostoevski or Zola, Orwell or Agee, who have managed, regardless of time and place to set something down both comprehensive and enduring about human beings the rest of us have pigeonholed. . . . American southern writers like William Faulkner and Flannery O'Connor and James Agee almost drove themselves and their readers crazy trying to say there are many truths—so many that no one mind or viewpoint or discipline or profession can possibly encompass and comprehend them all, nor do justice to them in words, even intricate and specialized ones, or "neutral" ones.[3]

The sort of knowledge that Coles is talking about is often called "phenomenological" knowledge, "fusion" knowledge, "interpersonal" knowledge, "I-thou," or "caring" knowledge.[4] The conversational-interactive method that was used to gather the seventy-five hours of discussion upon which this study is based captures an advantage of phenomenological knowledge. We become much closer to the subject than we possibly could in a survey approach. If this closeness and interaction does help us to get closer to that elusive state of knowledge called "truth," then what is lost in ability to generalize is indeed a bargain.

I am particularly indebted to two studies that also used the conversational small group approach in examining political attitudes. Karl Lamb's 1970 study of twelve middle-class families in the Los Angeles suburbs offers a good reference for comparisons across class and regional lines.[5] Robert Lane's study set in the 1950s of fifteen working-class men in New England had an even greater impact on this project; I borrowed many of the questions he asked as well as some of his methods and theoretical questions.[6]

Before introducing the main questions of this project and the characters who helped "write" it by sharing their lives and feelings with an unknown audience via tape recorder, I should note that all names of places, people, and organizations in this book are fictitious. Some of the unimportant details in the lives of these men, such as the number and sex of their children, have been altered. Though several said anonymity was not important to them, I promised as much as possible to minimize an invasion into the privacy of their personal lives. That promise shall be kept. Nonetheless, I hope that when reading this book they will be able to recognize themselves. For I have tried to draw their portraits to resemble the complex and multidimensional people that they are. Inevitably, something of their personalities will be lost and distortions will be made in the effort to capture them on tape and transform the recordings into written words. For that inevitable injustice, an apology is due both to them and to the reader.

Acknowledgments

I have learned that even though a single name may appear as the author of a book, it is the product of the efforts of more than one person. The very existence and many of the merits of this work are largely due to others, though I am solely responsible for any shortcomings. I owe a great debt to George Rabinowitz for both his professional advice and his personal encouragement. For their constructive criticisms of an early draft I owe thanks to Merle Black and Jim Prothro. Frank Munger merits special thanks for encouraging me to pursue publication as well as for raising interesting questions and suggesting issues to pursue. I must also thank the University of North Carolina Press and my editor Malcolm Call for help, encouragement, useful suggestions, and the freedom to present the material as I wished. Trudie Calvert edited the final draft and made many helpful suggestions on style. My wife, Carol Sears Botsch, suffered with me through the entire project from helping me improve my interviewing style to editing the many drafts that were written and revised. I hope that my son, David William, who was born in the midst of the project, will someday understand why I encouraged him to sleep late and take long naps.

We Shall Not Overcome

CHAPTER ONE

Introduction

> *Life, not statistics, teaches a man how to vote. And for all but a few Southerners, life wasn't good. This was the simple formula for the chemistry to Populism. Populists did not fondle the romantic images of the past. They wanted meat on the table. The only way to get it they said, was for the people to regain control of the institutions which affected them. Theirs was the language of reform, economics, and self-interest. . . . The politics which prevailed, however, was not the politics of restoration, but of racism.* [H. Brandt Ayres, "You Can't Eat Magnolias," p. 8.]

On 2 November 1976, Jimmy Carter was elected president of the United States. One of the many keys to his success was his almost solid victory in the South, with the sole exception of Virginia. Carter won 55.5 percent of the popular vote in North Carolina, where 63 percent of the registered voters cast ballots.

In the small town of Furntex, located in the rolling hills of the Piedmont section of North Carolina, turnout was unusually high. Over 70 percent of those on the registration books voted. No doubt this interest was partly generated by a hotly contested congressional race, but local enthusiasm for Jimmy Carter also had an impact. In the thirteen precincts in and immediately surrounding Furntex, Carter commanded 58.6 percent of the vote.

On the night of the election, Jim, a thirty-one-year-old furniture worker, was talking about his feelings toward Carter.

JIM: *I told my wife when I heard Jimmy Carter at the national convention and heard him speak [on television], I said that is the only real politician that I can honestly say I would work for and support with no doubts.* [He expressed some dismay that in fact he had done nothing for Carter other than vote. He was then asked about the 1972 election and how he felt about George Wallace.] *I guess if Wallace would have run in '72 I would have voted for him cause he said a lot more I was satisfied with. I was really impressed with him, and I really felt like we needed the change. But he was shot. . . . I didn't care for McGovern at all. . . . I voted for Nixon out of the necessity of putting an "X" in a box. [Paper ballots are still used in Furntex.] This is the only election [1976] that I voted in as far as I'm concerned that I felt like I really had a choice. When I left the voting booth here today I told my wife I really feel good cause I had voted my conviction and I know I had a choice. . . . This year I really paid attention to what they had to say cause I really feel like the election this year, the one we voted on today, is going to be very, very important in the future of the United States. I really feel like that. I guess the reason I voted for [Carter] is because of what I heard him say, the way he talked, the way he presented hisself. And another thing, me being a southerner, I was pleased to see someone from the South finally get a chance at the White House.*

QUESTION: *Suppose Wallace would have run as a third-party candidate in 1976. Is there any chance you might have voted for him today?*

JIM: *No. [He mentioned that "some things" have come out between Wallace and his wife—Jim is highly concerned with personal morality.] To me, Carter was saying the things this year that Wallace was saying in earlier elections. The only reason why I thought Wallace was a bunch of bunk while Carter knew what he was talking about was because of Carter's background. The guy was raised on a farm, and he was the first one in his family to get a college education. I can kind of relate to that a bit. I guess that's the reason why I would have still supported Carter. I feel like he meant what he said. You know, he'd been the road.*

What follows is a description of the lives and beliefs of ten white and five black furniture workers who have lived in or on the outskirts of the town of Furntex for most of their lives. Jim is unusual in this group of fifteen men in that he was extremely vocal and articulate in his enthusiasm for Carter. He is also unusual in that he voted. But he was not alone in his support for Carter. Nor is he the only member of the group who had previously felt warmly toward Wallace and now favored Carter over Ford.

The Question of a
Populistic Coalition in the South

Several sets of questions shall be addressed in this in-depth study of a microsample of fifteen southern workingmen. The election of Jimmy Carter and the dialogue quoted above serve to introduce the first set of questions. These questions concern the nature of the coalition in the South that supported and elected Carter. Following the election, there has been ample evidence that Carter was able to put together the old New Deal coalition of blacks, working-class whites, and enough farmers to bring him victory. A more important and difficult question is whether this coalition was held together by more than Carter's appealing personality and southernness. Jim and some of the others in the group were aware of Carter's personal and regional appeal. But they were also aware that Carter sounded a little bit like Wallace on a number of issues. For the most part, these are not racial issues. Rather, they are issues that raise questions about the fairness of the distribution of wealth and services and the integrity of those who control this distribution both privately and publicly. In short, these are the issues of populism. The question, then, is whether the issues of populism are more potent than racial hatred.

The status quo of the mid-1970s in North Carolina and in the South indicates little evidence that blacks and poor whites have been able to join forces in any meaningful way. Populist-oriented political candidates have had only limited success. At the time of the study, North Carolina had the second lowest level of unionization and the lowest industrial wages of any state in the nation.[1] Most other southern states were not much further ahead. Are wages low and unions weak because workers are conservative and content? Or do barriers such as racism stand in the way of effectively organizing worker discontent? The failure of populism in the 1890s demonstrates that racism can disrupt a black/white political coalition.[2] Political scientists have been debating the future possibility and fate of populist-oriented movements.

Chandler Davidson argues that a black/white political alliance for the purpose of economic reform is possible in the South because working-class racism has been exaggerated. Using precinct data on selected elections, he shows that in many cases racism in terms of voting choice is supported more by the upper class than by the working classes.[3] V. O. Key argues that once the peculiar institutions that separated the South from the rest of the nation (disenfranchisement, the one-party system, malapportionment, and Jim Crow laws) were out of the way, workers and rural farmers would once again have a strong liberalizing influence on southern politics.[4]

On the other side of the issue, Numan D. Bartley and Hugh D. Graham, using precinct data in an analysis of southern political history from 1944 to 1974, conclude that "the Republican sweep of the South in 1972 may well have reflected a quite traditional southern triumph, under a new partisan label, of her more dominant social conservatism over her game but historically outweighed populism."[5]

This important issue cannot be resolved by studying a microsample of fifteen southern workers (ten of whom are white) because their degree of prejudice certainly cannot be generalized to the South as a whole or even to the other employees of factories in which they work. Some light can be shed on the issue, however, by exploring the relationship of their prejudices to their attitudes on economic and political issues. All of these men are relatively young. The eldest is thirty-three and the youngest is eighteen. Most can remember the segregated South. But to most of them the old southern battlecry of "never" is something out of history that their fathers may have said. Most attended integrated schools for at least some portion of their lives or have children who attend integrated schools. All of them, unlike many of the middle- and upper-class residents of Furntex, must deal across racial lines on a daily basis, for they work together. But they do not live together, nor do they worship together, nor do they belong to the same secondary organizations (few belong to any organization other than church). They have experienced some of both worlds: the South under siege by civil rights laws and the accompanying white backlash, and the South of today, where the races seem to get along even if they do not love each other. Their attitudes on race relations will be explored to determine whether they are more oriented toward the past or toward the future.

The exact nature of the racism and prejudice that they display will also be explored. Students of prejudice often distinguish between two different types of prejudice that have important behavioral implications. Functional prejudice emanates from the ego and personality of the subject and serves important psychological needs. Folkways prejudice is an etiquette system rooted in learning acceptable speech and behavior patterns from one's peers.[6]

The importance of this distinction lies in its implications for social change. Richard Hamilton makes a clear statement of this significance: "If racism were 'personal,' that is, if it were a case of widespread, open, aware and committed intolerance, the problem of social change would be a formidable one. It would involve going against the will of a sizable and committed majority. If the majority were tolerant, the possibilities for change would be much greater."[7] If it can be established that the prejudice of the microsample is more of a folkways than a functional type, then it is likely that working-class problems cutting across racial lines may be more salient. This would at least be a necessary prerequisite if class politics is ever to replace race politics in the South.

If prejudice emanating from folkways can be distinguished from that which is functional and we find that most of these attitudes are not deeply held by these young workers and that they *do* hold economically liberal views, the important thesis offered by V. O. Key would tend to be supported. As mentioned earlier, Key views the political conservatism of the South more as a result of differential rates of political participation among occupational groups than of the overall distribution of public opinion.[8] This point is especially important in view of recent proposals for voting without prior registration. If such proposals are ever enacted into law, those people who presently do not vote may determine the outcomes of future elections. It is well known that nonvoters tend to be poorer, to be less well educated, and to hold less skilled jobs than do voters. In short, many of the characteristics of nonvoters are the characteristics of this small group of workers, most of whom did not and have never voted.

This possible change in registration laws suggests several questions that might be explored. It is easy enough to say that a biracial coalition is possible in terms of common issue interests. But can people who have common interests be politically mobilized to the point of voting? Would automatic voter registration get them to the polls on election day? Are any institutions available that could serve the educative function of linking their economic condition to their vote? This last question is especially important in the South, where labor unions, which often serve this function, are weak. At the time of the study, none of the factories operating in Furntex were unionized.

All of these issues will be addressed in my examination of this small group of workers. If these workers can perceive the existence of group economic interests and not be distracted by racial issues, and if they can be mobilized to vote and understand the linkage between their vote and their personal situation, they might be attracted to populist-style political candidates.

The Setting

Furntex is located in the rolling hills of the Piedmont of North Carolina, a red clay section of the state that lies between the hazy ridges of the Appalachian Mountains and the sandy soil of the Atlantic coastal plain. This town of about twenty thousand also lies between the two geographically opposite sections of the state in a political sense. The mountains of North Carolina have long been a stronghold for the Republican party in the state, while the eastern coastal plain has been dominated by the Democratic party. In most statewide elections, the East and the industrial cities of the Piedmont have been able to carry the state for the Democratic party.

Duane County, of which Furntex is the county seat, is a mixture of the influences of East and West. The outlying areas of the county are populated by small dirt farmers who often farm only part time and whose main source of income is working in the factories and mills of Furntex or other cities of the area. They inherited their Republican identification from their forefathers, who had little in common with the more prosperous slaveholding landowners of the East.

The population of Furntex is only 16 percent black, a significantly lower proportion than in most small towns in the deeper South. One might ask whether this demographic fact means that conditions and attitudes in Furntex are likely to differ from those in other southern towns. It is well known that prejudice varies directly with minority density—that one is most likely to find discrimination and prejudice in areas with higher proportions of minorities.[9] Certainly great caution must be used in suggesting any generalizations. It can be argued, however, that if black and white workers are to transcend prejudice and join together in pursuit of common interests, such a union is most likely in a setting like Furntex. If the workers of Furntex cannot accomplish this feat, it would seem even less possible for their kin in the deep South. Therefore, I would caution the reader to limit the generalization of any positive findings as merely suggestive and hopeful. On the other hand, negative findings can probably be generalized as becoming even more negative as one moves further South.

The city of Furntex is a Democratic stronghold, as is generally most of the South. But the Democrats of the town are numerically outnumbered by the Republicans in the county, and, as a result, the county as a whole goes Republican in most elections. In fact, the county has not gone Democratic in a presidential election since 1944. The closest the Democratic presidential nominee has come to carrying the county since then was in 1976, when Carter polled 48.3 percent of the popular vote. The Republican domination of the county and the Democratic strength in the county seat (the largest city of the county) leads to open and often bitter contests over countywide offices such as sheriff. Because the outcomes of these contests are often close, both political parties are unusually active compared to party organizations elsewhere in the South. A result of this party activity and competitiveness is that voting turnout is generally higher in both the city and county than in the rest of the state or in the South.

Does this mean that the political situation in Furntex is so atypical that nothing can be learned from the political lives and personalities of a small group of its citizens that can be applied to the rest of the South? Though, ultimately, the reader shall have to be the judge, it can be argued that the answer is no. My interest in this study is in some of the citizens of Furntex and its immediate vicinity rather than residents from far out in the county. Except for the condition of higher turnout, Furntex and its immediate vicinity seem to vote much like the state as a whole. This higher level of party activity and turnout means that the partisan pressures on the average citizen to register and vote should be greater than is typical elsewhere in the South. I am particularly interested in the segment of the population that is least likely to vote. This group of almost 30 percent who did not vote is overrepresented in my small sample of fifteen workers. Ten of them did not vote in 1976. Partisan competition and competitive elections failed to motivate many of these people to vote. Therefore, since these two key variables of political science have already been accounted for, one may ask what additional changes must take place to mobilize this group of nonvoters. Alexander Heard, a student of V. O. Key, argued that the reemergence of two-party politics would greatly improve the prospects for liberalism in the South.[10] In this book, I will examine this proposition in terms of the effect of party competition and close elections on the political cognitions and actions of a few of those southerners who must become politically active if liberalism is ever to become the dominant political force in the South.

Furntex is atypical in another respect in that the city owns and operates all of the major utilities in the town, including water, electricity, and natural gas. For the average citizen of Furntex, this has meant that utility bills and local tax rates (since profits go into the general budget) have been lower than in most other places in the South. These city-provided services could have an impact on the salience of local government for the citizens of Furntex as well as on their perceptions of the proper role of government. The town is like its inhabitants, a complex mixture where simple labels are misleading. It is liberal—even socialist—in terms of some services it provides, while it ignores other areas that would concern a consistent liberal, such as public transit. Its liberalism has a definite bias since the provided services benefit high energy users (the middle and upper classes) while ignoring those without private transportation (the lower classes).

Though local government is a major business in Furntex, the economic life of the city is dominated by two types of industries—furniture and textiles. A number of apparel-related industries are also located there. The large industries most recently established near the town are two chemical companies. As the interviews will reveal, both of these companies have a significant impact on labor conditions in the town.

Furniture and textiles became established in Furntex in the 1880s and 1890s, which was a period of industrialization all over the South. The pattern of growth and development in Furntex was typical of the rest of the South. The industries began as small, locally run and owned enterprises that grew as wealthy citizens of the town invested in them and plowed profits back into growth. A spirit of business-oriented progressivism prevailed, and social and civic organizations made it their chief aim to boost the growth of industry in the town.[11] A board of trade was established in Furntex just after the turn of the century, and by 1925 the town boasted around forty manufacturing industries. Many of the streets, schools, and recreational facilities today bear the names of the founders of these industries. Mills with outside ownership did not appear until after the turn of the century.

The tradition of local control was accompanied by a heavy flavor of paternalism. The combination of these two forces resulted in an atmosphere where, even though wages were low and workers may have been exploited for high profits in good times, owners felt some personal responsibility to the workers in poor times. Following the rapid growth of all these industries from 1900 to the 1920s, when profits were high and poor dirt farmers and their families were flocking to the mills to escape subsistence-level farm wages, the textile industry went into a decline when the industries of Europe rebuilt after World War I.[12] All the rest of the industries in Furntex suffered as the Great Depression deepened. A local history of Furntex states with great pride that nearly all the owners of local mills and factories kept their employees at work during the Depression even though this caused them a significant financial sacrifice. Industrial wages in Furntex were said to be a minimum of 19¢ per hour in 1932 while for the South as a whole a minimum of 10¢ per hour was not uncommon. Thus paternalism, local control, and personally felt responsibility for one's employees were not without benefit for the working class of Furntex.

The organization of industry in Furntex today is a curious mixture of the old and the new. Furniture, textiles, and related industries still dominate the town, but total ownership and control of these industries by local families is no more. Just as the large corporation has come to dominate the economy of the country as a whole, the large corporation now owns most of the industries in Furntex. The computer-printed bonus has almost completely replaced the turkey, food basket, and handshake. The old elites still retain some power, however. A number of the older and smaller family-run furniture and textile plants have been bought out and merged under single corporate entities. It is not unusual for the former owners to retain management responsibilities, though their power has been diluted by the standard organizational procedures of the corporation. The hierarchy of these plants is a mixture of corporation men brought in from the outside and old family owners and their cronies. As we shall see, the workers are aware of these changes and have been influenced by them in the way they relate to the organizations for which they work.

All of the men in my small sample are furniture workers. Though in number of workers, the furniture industry is the third largest in the state, in Furntex it is of about equal importance to textiles. In North Carolina in 1976, average hourly wages in furniture were virtually the same as in textiles, $3.57.[13]

All of the workers in this sample work for one of two furniture companies in Furntex. One company, Multicorp, is a branch of a large corporation that has only recently moved into the furniture business; its principal operations are and continue to be in textiles. Significantly, the industrial balance of Furntex was altered by conversion of Multicorp's large textiles plant to a furniture plant. The corporation also bought out several family-owned and run furniture companies in Furntex and in surrounding towns (though the previous owners still are largely responsible for management) and united them all under a newly created furniture division of Multicorp. Multicorp now operates five furniture plants in Furntex with a total of over two thousand employees. Each plant manufactures its own lines of furniture, though a significant number of common parts and operations are centrally produced and carried out in several of the plants. Personnel, shipping, and sales are all under centralized management located in Furntex.

The other company, Johnson's Cabinet Company, is much smaller than any of the Multicorp plants and has only one location in Furntex. Johnson's has slightly over one hundred employees. Despite its small size, however, this company is also part of the corporate system. A sister plant is located in the North, and both are under the corporate entity of a large food corporation. Johnson's, which is well known for its high-quality furniture, retains only the name of the founding family. The plant supervisor is brought in from the outside by the parent corporation.

Management systems in both companies are hierarchical, with the lowest level of supervision being foremen and assistant foremen, who report to department supervisors, who are in turn responsible to the plant manager. As we shall see, the supervisory positions in the plants are considered by the workers to be high-pressure jobs and are not always eagerly sought. Turnover in these positions seems to be high.

Sample Selection and Recruitment

The ideal method of selecting a small sample of furniture workers who were native to the town, were under thirty-five years of age, and were in a variety of work roles would have been random selection from the personnel records of the companies involved. This was the approach I intended to use when the study was begun. But, as so often happens in the world outside the laboratory, the ideal was not possible.

I approached the management of Multicorp and Rebel Furniture Company, the two largest furniture manufacturers in Furntex, and asked them to cooperate in the project. I explained that complete confidentiality would be maintained and that the names of employees would be used for no other purpose than this project. I offered to pay for secretarial costs of compiling the list from records and promised not to duplicate and to return the master list after the sample was drawn and contacted.

Unhappily, I received a polite but firm "no" from both companies. In their refusal letter, Multicorp cited conflicts with company policy and legal complications, though they stated that they "desire to support worthwhile educational pursuits whenever possible." The personnel manager of Rebel Furniture Company informed me by phone that though the company had no set policy on such matters, he had been given a negative response when he raised the issue with those in upper management. When I had met with him about a week earlier, he had stated that he believed that cooperation was unlikely because the company was "a little peculiar" about such things. His own distrust of those associated with formal educational institutions surfaced in our conversations. He stated that educators at local high schools make his job more difficult because they attempt to discourage students from going to work in furniture plants. They use furniture factory work as an example of the miserable employment options available to those who drop out of school. He felt that such examples were unjustified and gave the industry a bad image.

The overall impression gained from both these rejections was that the dangers resulting from publicizing poor working conditions and dissatisfied workers outweighed any benefits they might obtain in learning how their workers adjust or fail to adjust to their work roles. One expressed concern was that workers might learn of the company's part in the project and that for some reason they would object. The overriding impression was one of fear—fear that any outsider talking to workers about their jobs might somehow lead to that disease of which southern manufacturing interests live in fear—unions. This impression could have been mostly in my imagination. But, as we shall see, nearly all of the employees I eventually interviewed shared the same impression.

Despite lack of cooperation by management, I was able to select a sample of nine Multicorp workers, though the procedure was less than ideal. It so happened that while negotiations with company management were taking place, I was teaching a course in the evenings at a community college located just outside of Furntex. One of my students worked as a local truck driver for Multicorp. I explained the recruitment problem to him. He was very friendly, personable, outgoing, and enthusiastic about helping to recruit subjects for the project. I gave him a letter with a University of North Carolina letterhead explaining that he was helping to locate some typical workers who had lived in Furntex most of their lives whom I wished to interview for a book I was writing about the town. He was instructed to approach workers in a variety of production jobs and to include black workers. All were to be between the ages of eighteen and thirty-five. In a period of about two weeks, during the normal course of his work, he was able to cover most of the departments in several of the Multicorp plant locations. He returned with a list of fourteen names and addresses written by the workers themselves on the back of the letter. All fourteen were screened, and nine had the characteristics I was seeking. The other five were either too old, had not lived in Furntex long enough, or lived too far out in the county. Of these nine, I was successful in obtaining seven interviews. Two additional Multicorp workers were selected and referred by another student who worked in a department not visited by the first contact.

The other six men, who were employed at Johnson's Cabinet Company, were located from the personnel files of the company. In this case, the management was very cooperative and expressed interest in aiding the project.

Several factors seemed to account for the difference in managerial attitude. First, Johnson's is smaller, and the responsibility for making a decision rested entirely with two men, the personnel manager and the plant superintendent. When power and responsibility are less fragmented, the safe decision becomes less salient. They did not have to worry about objections from others in the hierarchy. Another factor was the genuine intellectual curiosity displayed by the personnel manager at Johnson's, a quality that was less apparent in the more businesslike personnel managers of the other two companies. Johnson's personnel manager was interested in the work adjustment process and in attracting more highly motivated workers, especially blacks, into the industry. He had attended seminars on these subjects and cited a study that showed a vast reservoir of untapped black talent of which the furniture industry should be taking better advantage. The other factor that seemed significantly different was that Johnson's plant manager, who gave final approval, was from the North rather than native to Furntex. Perhaps he was more accustomed to dealing with outsiders and did not perceive the prospect of having an outside agent talking to his employees as threatening or as out of the ordinary. Northern industries are more accustomed to the norm of having agents outside of management, such as union officials, deal with their workers. Nor was he a product of the southern culture that tends to distrust social research. Of course, one cannot say with any certainty which or what combination, if any, of these factors enabled me to gain the cooperation of the Johnson's management. But they did seem to find the decision easier in that they made it on the spot without the need to consult others, and their intellectual interest outweighed any fears they may have had.

The six Johnson's workers included in my sample were on a list of eighteen workers supplied by the personnel manager. According to the manager, these were the only workers at Johnson's Cabinet who were male and under thirty-five years of age. Eight were eliminated from consideration because they lived too far out in the county. The other ten were sent letters of introduction in the mail, explaining that the University of North Carolina was sponsoring a study of the lives and opinions of working people in and around Furntex and that they had been selected by chance. This was a slight deception because it was their company, rather than they, that had been chosen by chance. Each of these ten was visited at his home within a week of his receipt of the letter. Seven of these ten fit the demographic characteristics I was seeking. One was older than the personnel manager had thought, and the other two had moved to Furntex in their teen years or later. Of these seven, I was able to obtain six interviews. Thus the subsample of the six Johnson's workers represents almost everyone at that plant with the desired demographic characteristics and is not a random sample.

The reader might ask whether the manner in which the sample was selected biases the data so that there is no justification in making the logical leap from this small group to other young southern workers. In other words, is this group of workers so atypical in some systematic way that what we learn from it cannot be generalized in even a nonstatistical sense?

One can feel fairly confident that this fear is not true of the six Johnson's workers because there should be no bias in their selection. They represent all of the production workers at that plant who are under thirty-five and who have been long-term residents of Furntex and its immediate vicinity, with the single exception of one who refused to participate. Proceeding logically back in time, however, a bias might exist in questioning whether the way these workers were recruited for their jobs results in their being systematically different from the workers in other small furniture factories.

I cannot give a definitive answer to this question, although some light can be shed on the issue by comparing worker recruitment patterns and procedures of Johnson's with those of Multicorp. The personnel managers at both companies were asked how they recruited workers. Even though Multicorp is about twenty times larger than Johnson's, the procedures are similar. Both rely primarily on what is best described as an informal contact method. That is, some worker in the plant may have a friend or relative who is seeking a job. The personnel manager hears of this either directly or indirectly through supervisors, and the potential worker is contacted and recruited. The importance of this recruitment method was verified in that several of the workers in my small group reported that this is how they obtained their jobs. Both personnel managers also maintain informal contacts in the community through which they locate potential workers. This "friends and neighbors" web of communications aided one of those in my small group in finding employment. The importance of this method was further verified by one perceptive and articulate black worker. He felt that this process made it more difficult for blacks to obtain the more attractive jobs since the informal communications network tended to exclude black contacts. Both personnel managers reported that they recruit a few workers through industrial and vocational courses at the local high school. One worker in the group did obtain employment in this way. The other major method of recruitment is that the applicant walks in seeking employment. The managers reported that they have to rely on this source to a significant degree, but both indicated that their best workers tend to be recruited through the more informal methods.

Given that both personnel managers are middle-class, long-term residents of Furntex, they probably move in the same social circles and have a number of common contacts. Since both companies have comparable pay and benefit schedules, they have probably been recruiting from the same pool of workers.

Some light may also be shed on this issue by looking at the employment patterns of the small sample. The most striking single factor was a high degree of horizontal mobility and instability. Four of the men have worked at both Johnson's and Multicorp at one time or another. Nine out of the fifteen have worked for two or more furniture companies in Furntex. Of the remaining six, two have just begun working, one has worked in a variety of jobs outside of furniture and has been in and out of furniture work, and only the last three can be said to have established a relatively stable career in furniture work at one particular company. In fact, one of the workers at Johnson's quit his job between the time of initial referral and the interview. Another Johnson's worker, who declined to participate, also quit his job during the short period of time between referral and personal contact. Both personnel managers reported that turnover is generally high, even in times when there is a surplus of labor as was true when the fieldwork for this study was being done. Eddie, the most stable of the workers in the sample, said there was a 130 percent turnover over a one-year period in one department at Multicorp several years ago, when business was good and labor was short.

The nine Multicorp workers in the group pose a greater problem of potential selection bias. Since they were recruited by two of their fellow workers who were simply told to approach those who appeared to fit the characteristics desired, in all probability a certain degree of self-selection took place. No doubt the recruiters approached those who appeared to be the most friendly, and no doubt they were able to obtain signatures from those who were the most outgoing, secure, and least suspicious. The two recruiters reported that several workers would not give them any information because they thought something was being sold to them. Thus some of the group may be atypical in that they are likely to be more trusting and to feel more secure in strange situations.

This psychological bias in selection may have an impact on the subsample's demographic characteristics. A slight difference existed in the educational levels of the two subsamples. The Multicorp workers' average number of years of school completed was 11.3, whereas the six Johnson's workers were a little more than half a year behind, with an average of 10.6 school years completed. Hourly salaries were also different for the two groups. The Multicorp workers had an average salary of $3.96 per hour; the six Johnson's workers had an average salary of $3.39 per hour. The explanation for this significant difference does not lie in the skill levels of the jobs in the two subgroups because each had only about 30 percent in higher skill levels. The difference is explained by the average length of time in the job: Johnson's seven months and Multicorp, four years, four months. For some reason which I can only guess, my recruiters selected three Multicorp workers with unusual seniority: seventeen years, seven years, and five years. The seniority of the rest was comparable to that of the Johnson's workers.

The two subsamples were also slightly different in terms of verbal communication. Two Johnson's workers and one Multicorp worker were subjectively judged to be extremely inarticulate. At the other extreme, four Multicorp workers and two Johnson's workers exhibited high verbal skills. This difference in articulation levels is probably directly related to the self-selection of subjects in the Multicorp sample.

Each of the men approached for an interview was offered the modest sum of ten dollars as an inducement to participate and complete the interview. Given that the interview was designed to last about three hours, this fee was approximately equivalent to the wages most of them make. I felt that such an inducement would be necessary to obtain a sample that included anything other than intellectually curious workers, those who would be flattered by being asked to be in a book, or those who would be motivated to participate because of expressive needs. Once the offer was made and accepted, it was not mentioned again until the interview was concluded. I now feel that the payment had little impact on what was said in the course of the discussions. One worker refused payment, saying that he did not want to take money for something as simple as what he had done. He would offer no further explanation. Several others claimed to have forgotten about the promised payment when given the money. A few, however, openly admitted that the only reason they agreed to participate was for the money. This suggests that the money had the positive impact of reducing the refusal rate.[14]

The refusals lend insight into an interesting behavior pattern that most of these men seem to share. In the course of preliminary work and sample screenings, I visited approximately forty workers in their homes. All but two seemed willing to cooperate and help in any way asked. Given that the usual refusal rate is around 25 percent, the degree of cooperation was unusually high. This might have been attributed to the monetary inducement. The effective refusal rate turned out to be much closer to 25 percent, however, because four of those who promised to cooperate failed to do so—they were not at home at the arranged meeting time. In each case, excuses were offered and a second meeting time was arranged and, once again they failed to show. Apparently, these people were psychologically incapable of directly refusing to cooperate. They refused without the psychological discomfort of a direct confrontation. No doubt this pattern of behavior applies to other situations. The reputation these blue-collar workers have for being unreliable is probably built upon this behavior pattern. Unreliability—"you can't seem to get good help these days"—was the chief complaint of all the personnel managers to whom I talked. An inability to refuse someone directly also gives these people the reputation of being prime prey of encyclopedia, Bible, magazine, insurance, and all other varieties of door-to-door salesmen.

The Discussions

Once the men had been selected and recruited, meeting times were arranged at their convenience. The conversations that comprised the interviews usually took place on weekday evenings, though several of the sessions were held on weekends.

The process began when I met each man at his house at the appointed hour. This method afforded me a second opportunity to observe their homes (the first being when they were contacted following selection) and to meet their families. We then drove to a private home in a middle-class neighborhood where I had borrowed a room in which to conduct the interviews. The drive lasted at least five minutes, allowing time to break the ice. Not surprisingly, the most frequent initial topic of conversation was the weather—the fieldwork was done in the harshest part of an unusually cold winter. The drive back to their homes afforded the opportunity to ask them how they felt about the discussion we had just completed. The experience seemed to have a cathartic effect for several of the men. They said they felt extremely tired and at the same time very relaxed and glad they had decided to participate.

There were several reasons for conducting the interviews outside of the workers' homes. Perhaps the most important was simply not wanting to be disturbed. Many of these men lived in households that included several children and had very few rooms. Since several subject areas concerned family relations, the presence of a wife or child doubtless would have inhibited open and honest expression. Since these conversations were being recorded (with the knowledge and consent of all participants), it was also necessary to control the layout and environment.

The environment was kept as relaxed as possible. We sat in stuffed chairs at right angles to each other so that eye contact could be made or broken without discomfort. Between us on an end table lay a cassette tape recorder that could be ignored but was readily accessible for changing tapes. In front of us was a small table from which coffee was served.

A critical determinant of the success of the conversations was my ability to establish and maintain good rapport with these men. A different rapport-building technique was used for the whites than for the blacks. With the whites, the emphasis was on my being one of them, on being a resident of the same state, who was a product of the same culture as they. Because I had lived in the same general region since the age of six, my accent did not betray nonnativeness. While driving to the place of the interview, I mentioned having worked in a furniture plant and told them that I was interested in learning how things had changed. Sports was another frequent topic of conversation. I made a point to mention high schools that might have been common football opponents. I generally posed as one who would understand their inside jokes and not be critical. With blacks, more emphasis was placed on my presently being an outsider—one who had once lived in the region but had no remaining ties. I explained to them that one of my central concerns was to learn how things had changed since I left, but with them I candidly explained that this concern was to be focused on changes in race relations. I took this approach because I felt that the blacks would be more open with an outsider than with someone who had obvious ties with whites of the region. In retrospect, I feel that both of these techniques along with casual dress and a relaxed atmosphere succeeded in establishing good rapport.

The questionnaire that served to stimulate our conversations had been designed so that the interview would last about three hours. I felt that this was about the maximum amount of time that could be expended before fatigue would begin to take its toll. My budget was also such that I could not afford to pay for a second session. In practice, the actual conversations averaged almost exactly five hours each. The most inarticulate members of the group, Melvin, an eighteen-year-old in the shipping department, and Roy, a twenty-seven-year-old spray-gun operator, took less than three hours each. Jim, a thirty-one-year-old, articulate and bitter furniture packer, talked for almost six hours. He and Eddie, a utility man in the finishing room, who was a bit more long-winded than articulate, both willingly returned for a second session. Eddie talked for over six hours. All the rest of the interviews were completed in single sessions, usually lasting between four and four and a half hours. All totaled, there were seventy-five hours of recorded conversations in which we talked about everything from their first sexual experience to the future of democracy in America.

The transcripts of these conversations, which are a mixture of paraphrases and verbatim quotations, filled more than 1,600 double-spaced typed pages. The shortest was 68 pages, the longest was 166 pages. Thus this book is in reality the synthesis and explanation of fifteen books.

Profile of the Group

Before you meet these fifteen men, let me note some of the vital statistics of their demographic profile. These facts, of course, apply to the men's statuses at the time they were interviewed.

1. All of them are male blue-collar workers who are employed in the furniture industry, with a single exception. Rick quit his job between the time he was recruited and the time of the interview. He was then unemployed.

2. Ten are white and five are black.

3. They range in age from eighteen to thirty-three, with a mean and median age of twenty-six.

4. All but three are married. Ten of the twelve married men are fathers, though one of them, John, has fathered only illegitimate children outside his marriage. Of the three who are unmarried, one, Rick, is divorced. Brent has never been married but has an illegitimate child. The last, Mark, is one of the two youngest members of the group and is just beginning to think about marriage.

5. All of the men have lived the vast majority of their lives in Furntex. The parents of all but three lived in or near Furntex at the time these men were born. Lewis's parents moved to Furntex when he was six, and Roy's parents moved there when he was nine; both of their parents were from southern families. The single member of the group with nonsouthern roots in his immediate family is Paul, who moved with his family from Philadelphia when he was eight years of age. Paul's mother is from Alabama, but his father is a Connecticut Yankee.

6. All but one of these men come from a working-class background. Most are preceded by a generation of furniture or textile workers and several by two or more generations in factory work. Several can trace their roots back to farming in no more than two or three generations, though

some are ignorant of their family background. Paul is again the single notable exception. He is an interesting case of downward mobility because both his parents are college-educated.

7. The mean hourly income of this group of workers is $3.75 per hour; the median is $3.55 per hour. John, who holds a relatively highly skilled job in which he has seven years of longevity, reported that he makes $5.18 per hour. At the other extreme, Melvin and Mark, the two youngest, who are in much lower-level jobs, reported wages of $2.70 per hour. Family income has an even wider range, from $3,600 to about $20,000. Some of the men did not have a working wife (though most did), and several were unemployed for some significant period of the previous year. Judging from their hourly salaries, several of them seem to have significantly inflated their family incomes. Eddie, for example, reported that he made about $12,000 the previous year and that his wife contributed another $8,000 to the family income. This total of $20,000 was the highest for the group. Given that Eddie makes $4.68 per hour, however, his family income is probably inflated by about $2,000. If he had worked every weekday of the year, he would have made about $9,850. He reported no other source of income and was not able to get much overtime in the past year because business was not very good. In order to have made an extra $2,000, he would have had to work thirty-six days overtime at time-and-a-half pay. This case of exaggerated reporting of income was not atypical.

8. The religious backgrounds of these men reflect the strength of the Baptist denomination in the South. Seven of them come from families that were Baptist. Only three of these seven, Mark, Jim, and Junior, are active churchgoers. Of these three, only Mark, a nineteen-year-old worker who lives with his parents and whose father has been going to night school to become a lay minister, is extremely fundamentalist in his beliefs. Jim, the thirty-one-year-old packer and utility man who is angry about many political issues, and who claims to be a reformed alcoholic, is moderately strong in his fundamentalism. Junior, who attends church regularly with his wife and frequently goes to revivals, is moderately fundamentalist in that he believes the Bible to be literally true. He says, however, that he is not "saved" and perhaps never can be because he does not wish to be a hypocrite, which is how he views many of those who claim to be saved. No others in the group are at all active in any church or hold fundamentalist beliefs. Of the remaining eight workers, three come from Methodist backgrounds and one each from Lutheran, Episcopal, Holiness, and Jehovah's Witness backgrounds. One does not know his family's religious affiliation.

9. The median number of school years completed for the sample is eleven. The three who had dropped out of school and later achieved high school equivalency degrees were counted as having twelve years of schooling. Two of the workers, Jim and Terry, were taking courses at the local community college and were counted as having completed thirteen years of schooling. Paul, the downwardly mobile worker, had completed a year of college before he dropped out to drive a forklift for Multicorp.

Roy, who only completed the eighth grade, is the least educated member of the group.

10. Six members of the group rent the dwelling in which they live. Four own modest homes, one of which was built by the worker himself on land given him by his family and is not yet completely finished on the outside. Three of the younger workers live in trailers in mobile home parks on the outskirts of Furntex. Buying a mobile home seems to be the most viable route to new "home" ownership for young people in these salary ranges. The other two, Mark and Melvin, live with their parents. Melvin hopes to be able to buy a trailer and move to one of the small parks within the next six months so that he can move his bride of two months and their one-month-old baby out of a badly overcrowded household.

CHAPTER TWO
Fifteen Workers

The life of a community or of a people is, of course, made up of the life of individuals. [W. T. Couch in the Preface to Federal Writers' Project, *These Are Our Lives*, p. x.]

Before addressing the main questions of this study to see what can be learned from conversations with these fifteen blue-collar workers, I will describe each of them in detail. They are listed alphabetically to provide a convenient reference for the reader. The introductions present a brief factual description of their physical living conditions, demographic characteristics, family relations and family backgrounds, political activities and preferences, career patterns, and personality traits that were obvious to my untrained eye. I shall shy away from any detailed analysis or explanation at this point, except for an occasional brief comment concerning obvious or important relationships. To give the reader a more personal sense of the flavor of the conversations and acquaintance with these men, I quote them liberally. I also comment on the atmosphere and surrounding circumstances of the meetings if there was anything unusual to note.

Albert: The Athlete

Albert, a twenty-six-year-old black worker, rents a four-room brick-veneer house in the largest black neighborhood of Furntex. The street is paved but has no curbing, and his small yard has little or no grass. The neighborhood is a mixture of rentals and small homes owned by their working-class occupants. One block away is one of the few middle-class black neighborhoods in Furntex, where grass grows on well-kept lawns and the houses double and triple in size. The interior of Albert's home is neatly kept and modestly furnished. When first contacted on a Sunday afternoon, he was watching basketball on his black and white television. He has been married for about four years and has a well-mannered little girl of about the same age. The family owns one car, a thirteen-year-old sedan.

Though he has never voted and says he only occasionally talks politics, Albert identifies himself as a weak Democrat. He likes Carter and was glad that a southerner won the 1976 election. He remembers that his parents were Democrats who liked and talked about John Kennedy.

Albert and his family are able to maintain what he feels to be a reasonable but not luxurious standard of living, although both he and his wife must work to maintain the status quo. He confesses that he wishes she could stay home. They both work at Multicorp. She has worked in the sanding room there for three years. Albert, who makes $3.55 per hour driving a forklift loading lumber from trucks onto platforms where the first cutting is done (this area of the plant is called the "rough end"), has worked for Multicorp for five years. This places him third in the group in longevity in his present job. Albert estimates that he and his wife together make between $15,000 and $17,000 a year. Judging from his hourly salary and their life-style, this estimate seems a bit inflated.

Before coming to work for Multicorp, Albert worked in the shipping department of Johnson's Cabinet Company for about six months. He says he left Johnson's because "I just didn't fit in with it." He was unable to offer any further explanation. Before that, he worked for one of the recently established chemical companies near Furntex. Though jobs there generally pay better and fringe benefits are better than in the furniture factories, the chemical companies require employees to work on a swing shift. Albert and several other workers in the group preferred to trade these benefits for regular hours so they could spend more time with their families. Though Albert has some complaints about low pay and not enough vacation or paid holidays, he is generally satisfied with his work and feels he is "cut out" for furniture work. (One week, that of the Fourth of July, is the standard vacation for all furniture and most textile plants in Furntex.) He summarizes his feelings toward his work in saying, with a shrug of his shoulders, "I do good enough to get by."

Albert's grandparents on both sides of his family were farmers. His father was a farm laborer when young, but did construction work for a concrete contractor after Albert was born. He died about ten years ago. Albert fondly remembers his father taking him along to work, teaching him to drive the tractor, and playing ball with him. These pleasant memories seem to outweigh the criticism that "he didn't try to be a good provider for us." Albert's mother did and still does domestic labor and also worked as a cook in the public schools. She performed the provider role, and her eldest son credits her for this. "See, we was poor, you know, and I think the good point about her was that she tried harder than my dad did. She tried harder to provide for us, to get the things we needed. She really went out on a limb doing things for us."

Because he did not do well in school and, as a result, did not enjoy going, Albert dropped out in the tenth grade when he turned sixteen and went to work in a grocery store. Albert saw his main problem then and now as simply not having the ability to understand and achieve as others do. "The reason I didn't go back to school was that I wasn't a real smart kid in school. I didn't think I could learn like everybody else, you know. . . . I still don't learn fast, you know. But I manage to get by."

Albert's source of pride is that he does "manage to get by" despite his self-acknowledged limitations. "After I quit school, I worried about how I would make it after that. I think that's about the only thing I did worry about. I didn't worry about it, I thought about it a lot. I worried about how I would make it after I got old. What would I do. . . . You know, all the people that talk about it, you know, say that if you don't have an education you would be digging ditches. I thought about that, and it bothered me a lot. You know, I found out, you guess, no matter how much education you got in life, it depends on what you want to be. If you can survive, I guess it's all the same thing. If you got a four-year education or whatever it takes to have a high-paying job with a future in it, that's cool. But if you can survive with no education and get by, uh, I think you can make it if you get by." Albert is saying that he is doing all right because he is achieving the limited goals he has set for himself.

In extending this lesson of life to his judgment of others, he is ambivalent. He feels that others should try harder to make things better for themselves so that they, too, can "get by." But he feels that some people cannot get by even as well as he does no matter how hard they try, and that some people have more than they deserve. This conflict will be discussed in greater depth in the examination of attitudes toward the justice of the reward system in our society.

Albert stands over six feet in height and is a very muscular and athletic 180 pounds. Whatever his perceived intellectual deficiencies, he does not think of himself as flawed in physical prowess. He plays in a very rough city basketball league and is active in other sports. He probably underestimates his mental abilities, for he was thoughtful yet quick in his answers to most questions. There were only a few times when he drew a complete blank. When he did have thoughts on a subject, he seemed to have little trouble expressing himself. Whatever he lacked in verbal ability, he more than compensated for by being very open and friendly.

Brent: The Disappointed Dreamer

Brent, who is black and thirty-two, is one of the most articulate members of the group. He is also in one of the worst personal and financial situations. He lives alone in a small, tin-roofed, three-room house near one of Multicorp's plants in a neighborhood of old houses built by the company for its workers that once formed a small village around the plant. When ownership of the plant changed, the houses were sold to other landlords. The rest of the town has now grown around this village, and it has become a black laboring-class enclave. The interior of this structure, which he rents for $56 a month, was neat and clean but equipped with old and well-worn furniture. He tried to achieve the effect of a bachelor pad by painting the walls in bright colors and covering one wall with do-it-yourself mirror tile. He does not own a car and has to depend on others for his transportation.

Brent is unusually sophisticated in his political opinions in that he is self-consciously ideological. He considers himself a liberal because liberals want to spend money on social programs that may help the poor to escape poverty. He sees conservatives as having the attitude: "I have mine so let them take care of themselves." This ideological conflict is based on class conflict that he believes is central to all conflict in society. He is sophisticated enough to realize that the rich pay external costs in order to maintain exploitation of the poor: "The poor steal and rob and then the rich have to pay in this way." His party identification is Democratic, and he has voted for the Democratic presidential candidates in 1968, 1972, and 1976 because the Democrats are the more liberal party. This is clearly ideological thinking.

Brent's work history is long and varied. He says he does not like to work and has always had trouble keeping a job. Because he wanted to have "nice clothes" he began his working career as a shoeshine boy when he was eleven or twelve down on Main Street in Furntex. Since then he has worked as a grocery bag boy, a kitchen hand, a roofer, on the railroad, for a machinery company sanding floors for a private contractor, served two years in the army, and finally went to work for Multicorp after a very difficult period of adjustment following military service. He has now been at Multicorp for three years working as a furniture packer. He is learning to do minor repairs on furniture before it is packed for shipment. His salary is $3.38 per hour, and he claims to have made between $5,500 and $6,000 in the previous year, which is probably a reasonable estimate. With the exception of a job he held for six years (he claims he stayed that long just to show his critical friends and family that he could hold down a job), his present job appears to be the most working stability he has ever had.

The immediate cause of instability in his life is excessive use of alcohol. He characterizes his drinking as more excessive than mere social drinking. He has not let it interfere with his present job because he has been able to restrict his heavy drinking to weekends.

Drinking seems to be a refuge from the rest of his life, for he is a very disappointed man. He was born illegitimately and lived in a very rough neighborhood. Despite these handicaps, his mother worked hard as a dishwasher in a local restaurant, kept the family together and off welfare, and encouraged him and his brother to dream and to finish school. He feels that graduating from high school was the most important event in his life because it was so important to his mother. He dreamed of solving problems and accomplishing things so that everyone would be proud of him. He also dreamed of marrying the girl who lived down the street from him. His success ended when he finished high school. The girl turned him down, he began drinking, he fathered an illegitimate son, and he found that the high school diploma guarantee of success was a sham. He is bitter now, partially blaming others for building his expectations too high. But he also holds himself to blame. In talking about the faults of Furntex, he says that too many people blame the town for what are really shortcomings of the people themselves. He seems to be talking about himself. He says that he is constantly searching for a marital partner and worries even to the point of lying awake at night. He is no longer very close to anyone in his family. He finds himself pleasing to no one, including himself.

Twice during our conversations he spoke of a dream or a strange feeling he often has: "I have something that is boiling inside of me saying that one day you're going to do this, you know." Earlier in our discussion, he talked about the feeling that something exciting was going to happen to him. He harbors doubts about the feeling: "But it might just be a fantasy I am living. I worry about this, you know. You've heard the slogan: 'I think I missed my calling,' you know. In other words, I've always felt that I could do better than I am doing, and the thing that worries me is why I don't apply myself to do this, you know. I'm wondering, if and when it does happen, will I say I'm too old or waited too long." Because Brent is unable to plan or determine how he should achieve his ambitions, he lives from week to week and grows older in a job he finds tolerable at best. He finds some escape through drinking on weekends. He waits and worries about something that *might* happen to change his life.

The disappointments Brent feels and expresses seem to be taking their toll on him physically and emotionally. Though he is one of the most likable people in the group in that he is sensitive, introspective, and very responsive, he is also one of the most outwardly nervous. He fidgeted and chain smoked throughout our conversation and never was able to relax as were most of the others.

Dave: The Danger Seeker

Dave is twenty-one years old, white, and works as a lathe operator for Multicorp Furniture. His wife of a year also works for Multicorp in the cabinet room at the same plant as Dave. They live in a nicely furnished trailer in a small mobile home park on the outskirts of Furntex. They have no children and have no immediate plans to have children because they are struggling to pay their bills.

Dave barely ranks as even a political spectator; he only occasionally discusses politics or issues with friends. He claims to have registered to vote, but never has voted. He does not ally himself with either of the major parties, claiming to be an independent. His nonpartisanship seems to have been inherited from his parents, whose party sympathies he does not know. Nor did he have any clear preference in the 1976 presidential election. He leaned toward Ford because Carter was an unknown quantity: "Everybody in the United States knows what Ford will do cause he's already been in office . . . but like I said I wouldn't have voted for neither one of them." Dave does have one strong feeling about politics, an attitude he shares with his parents. He and they both like the Kennedys. He thinks John was a good president who "really tried to help the United States." He says he definitely would have voted if Teddy Kennedy, "the man I wanted in office," had run. There seemed to be little obvious substantive content to this preference beyond simple affect.

Dave comes from three generations of mill and factory workers. Both of his grandmothers were textile workers, and one of his grandfathers works as a night watchman. He does not know the occupation of his other grandfather. Both of Dave's parents also work for Multicorp, his father in the same department as Dave.

Dave and his father have jobs running two of the more dangerous machines in furniture, which, according to Dave, is why they get higher wages than most other workers. A comparison of Dave's hourly wages with others in the group tends to bear this out. Though he has been with Multicorp for only six months, Dave earns $4.50 per hour. Only two other men in the group exceeded this hourly rate of pay. Dave's father, who runs a molding machine, reportedly operates the *most* dangerous machine in the industry. He has lost several fingers in the course of his work. Dave, his wife, and parents all worry about the dangers of the work, but he seems to feel that his wages compensate for the danger. In a macabre sort of way, Dave describes his work as a daily contest between him and the machine, with the payoff being survival. "It's just that it's challenging. It's just if I think I can do that eight hours a day and get by without getting hurt, I think I've got the best of the machine. It's just one of them things. But it's something that you gotta watch, I mean. You don't ever think you've mastered the machine cause that's when something will hurt you bad, when you think you've got it beat."

Other than being able to boast about the danger of his job, most of Dave's pleasures are external to his work. He lives for weekends when he can hunt or fish or go bowling with his wife. He is more caught up in a consumption-oriented style of life than anyone in the group. His biggest current problem is paying the bills he and his wife have accumulated in buying things on credit (the trailer, cars, stereo, color television, nice furniture, citizen's band radio for both cars, and a base station for home). He acknowledges that he has overextended himself and worries about it. But, unlike Brent, he and his wife have a plan of action to alleviate their problem. She is taking night courses to become a legal secretary and thereby increase their family income. Dave plans to keep his present job because he claims to enjoy it and feels that he is well compensated. The next want he plans to fill is ownership of a Siberian husky—a dog that he says costs over $400.

Eddie: The Unambitious Do-It-Yourselfer

Eddie, white and thirty-two, is one of the older men in the small group. He has been in his present job in the finishing department of one of Multicorp's plants the longest of anyone in the group, nearly seventeen years. He remembers two short breaks in his work record when he quit in anger, but these periods were not long enough to affect his seniority. He also talked the longest of anyone in the sample, over six hours in two sessions.

He and his wife, who works third shift in a textile mill in Furntex, and their two children, aged eight and ten, live in a modest yet attractive three-bedroom frame house that Eddie built himself. The house is not quite finished on the outside, and grass has not yet been planted. When we were arranging a meeting time and Eddie was giving directions to his house, he apologetically explained that he could not afford to live elsewhere once the house was habitable. He has to do the work himself, and "it takes a long time that way." We talked a good deal about building houses. He told of many things he has learned from his experience and of his future plans for completing the house and making additions. He also related, with pride, how he refinished all the furniture in the house. In fact, the furniture did appear to be the work of an expert craftsman. Several of the men build or refinish their own furniture because they cannot afford to buy the products of their labor.

It was obvious that Eddie was proud of his craftsmanship and ability to be independent of others in building and repairing. He was also proud of his knowledge of cars and auto repair which he learned from his father, who is a professional mechanic. He recently did the body work on a relative's car that had been in an accident and modestly described himself as a "pretty fair shade tree mechanic."

Eddie identified himself as a weak Republican and said he is not very interested in politics and does not discuss political issues very often with his friends. His parents and grandparents were all strong Republicans who lived and farmed (at least part time) in Republican Duane County. Of his father, Eddie said, "If his best friends had been runnin' on the Democrat ticket, he would vote Republican." He identified himself as a conservative, saying that "a conservative is looking out but he don't want to go too far ahead . . . saves things for the future," and he feels that the Republicans *used to* be conservative. But he feels that this is no longer true, that both parties want only to win elections at all costs. As a result, he feels he cannot be a strong Republican.

Though Eddie has no strong party allegiance, he does feel a strong allegiance to one political figure who has played an important role in presidential politics—George Wallace. The only time Eddie remembers voting was in 1968 when Wallace ran and received Eddie's vote. Though he expressed some doubts about Wallace's stands on "racial problems," Eddie believes "he could get more done in a direct way," and he strongly supports Wallace's stand against "forced busin'." He said that had Wallace run again in 1972 or in 1976, he would have voted for him.

In choosing between Ford and Carter in 1976, Eddie preferred Carter and gave two reasons. "Seems like he's more of a southerner. It's been awhile since there's been one up there. . . . I believe that he could have stopped part of this busin' in the South, and in the North, too, really. I'd like to see him try it anyhow, if there's anything that comes up on forced busin'. At one time it seemed like he wasn't whole hog for it."

Though Eddie's job as a utility man in the finishing department does not have a high rate of base pay, he has been able to build up his hourly rate via seniority to where he is the second highest paid member of the group at $4.68 per hour. As noted in Chapter 1, Eddie may have slightly exaggerated his yearly income. An underlying motive for many of Eddie's statements was to build up a low sense of self-esteem. This slight exaggeration may be another example.

Despite his record of job stability and his relatively high wages, Eddie has had some problems in his career at Multicorp. He was promoted to foreman and held that position for fourteen months. This job proved to be too great a strain on him. He did not like the pressure of meeting production quotas and had difficulty asserting his authority over subordinates. "Well, to me it got to be too much of a headache to handle. It seemed like I couldn't get the work out of my assistant that it seemed to me that he should be doin'. And I had two lead men workin' under him, and he couldn't commune with the lead men. It seemed like everything was just workin' against each other. It was just a friction there that wasn't nothin' comin' out right. . . . And I just threw up my hands one day and said, 'I've had it!' And I got dropped back then." Now, because of his experience, Eddie can handle any job in the finishing room. He also trains new workers and does special work on sample furniture. Thus he achieves variation, control, and autonomy over his work without the pressures from superiors for production or the unpleasant confrontations he suffered when he had to make demands on workers. He takes pride in the assertion that he was very good in the human relations part of being foreman. He was friendly to all the workers and tried to show them he appreciated their work. He was good at being friendly, but not at making demands.

This failure activated fears that he had felt since youth—fears of not belonging, not fitting in, and not being able to "hold up my end." When he was foreman, he found it difficult to maintain comfortable social relations with other foremen. He used this discomfort as an example of how hard it is to move from one class to another. The impression one gets is that he compensates for this perceived inadequacy by trying to be extremely friendly and sociable with his fellow workers and neighbors. Much of his self-image seems to be built on this quality.

Eddie's house is located on a piece of land a few miles out of Furntex given to him by his mother. His house is surrounded by the houses of relatives because the farm land of his grandparents has been divided and subdivided among succeeding generations. The division has meant that few of Eddie's generation can make a living through farming. Their ties are now closer to Furntex than to the land. But Eddie is only one generation removed from the farm, and he still occasionally helps his paternal grandfather farm the land he retains. His views of politics, economics, and social relationships are colored by traditional southern rural values: a sense of frontier-style individualism and belief in its code of honor, distaste for government regulation, a strong sense of family and kinship ties, and a code of neighborly obligations.

Alcohol has played havoc in the lives of several of the people in the group. It had an adverse impact on the kinship ties in Eddie's family. Eddie's mother and father divorced because of his father's abuse of alcohol. Eddie recalls that his father had many of the characteristics of an alcoholic, such as D.T.s. The heritage of his father's problem has some positive aspects. Because Eddie and his brother suffered physical abuse from whippings given by a drunken father that would sometimes "draw blood," Eddie is very concerned about and sensitive to the problem of child abuse with respect to disciplining his own children. Because Eddie's father "didn't care as much as I thought he should at that time about having food there or something to eat all the time," Eddie places much emphasis on the material well-being of his family. He has just obligated himself to over $1,200 for braces for his ten-year-old daughter. As we shall see, this expense has an impact on some of Eddie's political opinions.

Jim: The Enthusiastic Carter Supporter

Jim, a white thirty-one-year-old, lives in a comfortable three-bedroom frame house in a working-class neighborhood. He has recently fallen on hard times. He bought the house a few years ago when circumstances were better. He was also able to buy a late-model Ford sedan during that period. At that time he worked in the plastic shop at Multicorp making the molds used to cast the plastic trim that was used on much of their furniture. He liked that job because it was clean, quiet, varied, and creative. The energy crisis touched him personally. As the price of petroleum-based products increased, Multicorp found that it could make many of these trim pieces more economically from wood. The plastic mold shop reduced its workload, and Jim was without a job. He was transferred to the packing department, where he stands at the end of a moving line and places pieces of furniture in boxes as they come off the line. He says that he "hated this job from the first day," and he still does.

Jim did make an effort to escape the factory work he despises. He went into a small business partnership with his father-in-law finishing the seams on plasterboard walls in houses. The work and the relationship were pleasant, but they were unable to find enough work to keep the business going. Once again, changes in the nation's economy had adversely affected him. Having failed at this, he agonized for a month and then went back to work at Multicorp at the job he hates. During this same period, his wife quit her job as a secretary and gave birth to their first child. As a result, his hourly salary of $3.77, which is slightly above the mean for the group, is not enough for him to maintain his family at their previous standard of living.

Jim is making another effort to escape factory work. He has enrolled to take evening courses at a nearby community college and hopes eventually to get a two-year degree in criminology. This venture has the side benefit of bolstering his family income because he is a veteran and collects G.I. Bill educational benefits.

Jim comes from two generations of textile workers. The family settled in Furntex because they lost their jobs elsewhere and heard that work was available there. The family included twelve children, and Jim recalls that, although times were often difficult, they did get by. The family's difficulties were partly caused by the stubbornness of Jim's father, who seems often to have been insensitive to the physical and emotional needs of his family. Jim remembers two painful instances when his father delayed taking him and his brother to the hospital for appendicitis attacks. The delay nearly caused death on each occasion. Jim feels little affection for his father and rarely sees him.

On the other hand, he described his mother as being almost angelic. "It may sound unrealistic to say, but I can't say my mother had any bad points. She was always fair and compassionate and understanding when we did something or wanted something. She would sacrifice something she wanted to have just so we could have something. Many times she would give up dresses or going somewhere. . . . She was an ideal, perfect mother." Jim said he wanted to repay his mother for all she had given him. "I would buy my mother things that she wanted and take care of her for the rest of her life. But, . . . that never happened." He cannot, for she died a few years ago. Jim spoke about the things he wants to give his wife and child. He seems determined to give them what he could not give his mother.

When he was younger, Jim had wanted to go to college, but couldn't because of family conditions. Not only was his family unable to support his ambitions financially, they also frustrated his dreams by forcing him to lower his expectations to those more appropriate for the working class. He feels he did well in high school but could have done much better. "My main problem was that I knew I could not go to college, so I guess I figured, what was the reason to put so much into it. Now I could kick myself. I always heard from my older brothers: why take hard subjects like chemistry and other things when I knew I was not going to college."

Jim makes a direct connection between his material difficulties and the political forces that control Furntex. He has some radical courses of action in mind. "I've had a visualization of being the leader of bringing the South to where you get the wages you deserve to get paid and don't get cheated every week. Get people to tell the 'man' that you don't have to, and won't work for these wages, and get everybody to quit and go home. I don't know about unions, but I would join just for better pay." He is also concerned because only poor housing and health care are available to many poor and working-class people. He has the ability to empathize.

Jim is religious and is active in the Baptist church to which he belongs. He is a deacon and a Sunday School teacher and sings in the choir. His strong religious beliefs stem partially from his very religious mother. He was also influenced by his wife, who helped him solve a drinking problem by leading him to a solution based on religion when he felt he was on the verge of becoming an alcoholic. His beliefs are fundamentalist and rigid to the point of being authoritarian with respect to pornography and the use of alcohol. His tolerance and ability to empathize do not include those who use alcohol, who peddle pornography, or who are atheistic, though he is generally tolerant of other religions. He is less fundamentalist regarding interpretation of the Bible and gambling.

This combination of economic liberalism and religious conservatism along with a strong regional identity fits with Jim's enthusiasm for Jimmy Carter. He voted for Carter and wishes he had done more than merely vote. Had Wallace been less "bigoted" about race, he might have been able to support him in earlier elections, because "Carter was saying a lot of the things that Wallace had said in the past." Jim's enthusiasm for Carter, perhaps the greatest of anyone in the group, even moved him toward claiming the Democratic party identification of his parents. He talked about changing his registration from Independent to Democratic. Jim's ardor for voting and for Carter seems best explained by his unusually clear perception of the links between his lifelong struggle for upward mobility and political activity. He recognizes that there is a link between politics and the justice of the reward system in our society. Only a few others in the group were able to perceive this connection.

John: The Quiet Black Homeowner

John, who is thirty-three years old, owns his own home in the same neighborhood as Albert's rented house. The two-bedroom white frame structure has a fenced-in yard and noticeably more grass, trees, and shrubs than the rental units located on the same street. Parked in the driveway beside the house was a late-model sedan John shares with his wife. The furnishings were not new, but appeared more numerous and in better condition than was average for the men in the group. Since John's hourly wage of $5.18 was the highest among the fifteen, and since his wife also works (in textiles), and they have no children of their own, one might expect them to be relatively even better off materially. John's income is drained, however, by child support payments for the two children he fathered out of wedlock. This obligation has an impact on many of John's political and social views. He feels it is unfair that he gets no greater deduction on his taxes for these payments than all of those "sorry people that don't half take care of their kids."

John identifies himself as an independent and does not lean toward either of the major political parties. He claims to have voted in the past, but did not vote in any presidential election that he can recall. He feels that his vote would not make any difference and that a lot of votes "get lost" before reaching Washington. He is one of the more politically cynical members of the group. He has a little more faith in local elections, feeling that here his vote does count and makes some difference. But here, too, he is cynical. "Before an election they don't lock nobody up for being drunk. But after the election they will lock you up and keep you in jail for just being drunk." When specifically asked, John had no preference between Ford and Carter, but at one point in the discussion he volunteered that he was happy about the election in 1976, indicating that he probably did slightly lean toward Carter.

John is among the three workers in the group with a high degree of job stability. He has worked setting up lathes and molders in the rough end in one of Multicorp's plants for about seven years. His primary job is to fashion the knives that cut the wood on the machines to obtain the desired shapes. He then sets the knives into the machine and adjusts the unit for operation. He does very little in the way of actual machine operation. "Machine tenders," who are considered to be in a lower skilled job level, do most of the actual operation. Since being discharged from the military in about 1969, he has worked for only one other company besides Multicorp, one of the relatively new chemical plants located outside of Furntex. Like several others in the group, he did not like the swing shift he was required to work. Unlike the others, he did not have to take a pay cut when he came to work at Multicorp, where he could work days.

A foreman position was offered to John a few years ago, but he turned it down. Asked why, he explained: "In this town everybody knows everybody. And everybody wants the easy jobs. But all of the jobs got to be done and somebody has to do the hard jobs. You see, it's hard when you have to tell people to do things." Like Eddie, John is very uncomfortable when he has to assert authority and make demands on people.

Considering his background, John has achieved some measure of material success and upward mobility. Not surprisingly, he is critical of those whom he sees as not trying very hard to work to support themselves. He was born out of wedlock and cared for by an aunt and uncle, for whom he does not have fond memories. He remembers his uncle as being overprotective and spoiling him. He feels that as a result of this treatment he did not know how to "hustle things up" for himself and thus was at a competitive disadvantage later in life. He also partially blames this overprotectiveness for keeping him from ever developing an interest in sports. But because his uncle did seem to care about him, he is able to feel forgiveness.

He cannot forgive his aunt because he feels that she exploited him and is the root cause of many of his problems. She forced him to do housework, "women's work," and he feels that she was trying to make him effeminate, "like a girl." He is certain this is another important reason why he never participated in sports and even today does not even enjoy watching them. His uncle died when John was sixteen. John left home shortly thereafter following an incident where he was involved in a fight at school and expelled. He somehow manages to blame this, too, on his aunt because she did not encourage education and only wanted him to work and give her the money. He then went to live with his natural mother and says that he enjoyed living there. He may have been more comfortable there partly because several girls lived in the house, and he was no longer asked to do "women's work." He never returned to school after leaving the eleventh grade.

John's doubts about his masculinity (he ranked third highest on a sexual tension scale) result in his being extremely shy and nonassertive. If pushed or threatened, however, he will fight. He bears a jagged scar across his face as the result of one such fight. His small physical stature (he stands only about five and a half feet and weighs about 130 pounds) and lack of interest in sports serve to reinforce his doubts.

The interview with John was one of the most difficult of the group. I was lucky even to get it. When I arrived to pick him up at the appointed time, he was eating dinner and had forgotten all about the meeting. He was surprised and seemed undecided whether to participate. He looked at his watch and asked how long it would take. I told him about three hours. He responded, "Okay, let's do it, I guess."

The interview took about four hours, but the tape contained less than two hours of conversation because he talked very, very slowly with extremely long pauses after questions that were often followed by little more than "I don't know." Getting any answer was like pulling teeth. He spoke so softly that transcribing the conversation was an extremely difficult and frustrating task.

The reason why a physical description of the interview is noteworthy is that it led to the impression that rapport was never really established and that the discomfort I felt during and after the conversation was shared by John. If so, the entire conversation may have had little value in its substantive content. Immediately after the interview, however, John stated that he had really enjoyed the experience and did not mind at all having taken an extra hour because time passed quickly and he felt very "relaxed from it." One should be careful not to project one's own feelings onto interview subjects.

Junior: The Angry Ambitious Worker

Junior, a thirty-year-old white worker, is another of the few in the group who owns his own home, a small, white frame house just inside the city limits. Junior is adept in the skills of carpentry and has added a small den onto the two-bedroom house and built all of his own furniture. The house and yard are kept in immaculate condition. He and his wife have just added a new child to their family (their first child is hers by a previous marriage), so he now feels the house is too small and is trying to "trade" for a larger dwelling.

Although he has never voted and says that he seldom discusses politics, Junior did express a clear preference for Carter over Ford in the 1976 election. His preference is probably not related to inherited party identification because all he knows about his mother's political views is that she "liked Ike." He described himself as a weak Republican two years ago, but now feels that he is a weak Democrat. He was unable to explain this change in his feelings. He explained his preference for Carter in terms of trust and regional identification. "Well, I would have voted for Jimmy Carter because he just seemed like a good ole country boy that wasn't trying to pull the wool over our eyes like the rest of 'em's tried. He said 'I'm going to try to do all this.' Now, he didn't say, 'I'm gonna do it.' . . . So he didn't tell us a lie to start with." Though he did not vote, Junior did care about the election. He bet $5 that Carter would win.

With an hourly wage of $4.50, Junior is tied for third highest of the fifteen and is the highest paid of the Johnson's workers. Because his wife works for a wholesale distributor of women's apparel, his family is probably one of the relatively affluent in the group.

He is also one of the most obviously dissatisfied. Junior wants more money and material things and has spent his life pursuing both. As a result, his is one of the most unstable career patterns in the group. Instability seems also to be the defining characteristic of other areas of his life.

Junior has worked for three months as a door hanger for Johnson's Cabinet. His pay is fairly high because his job is considered to be relatively highly skilled, but also because Junior is an industrious and competent worker. Since coming to Johnson's he has earned a 50¢ per hour raise—a large raise for a furniture worker. He must have impressed his superiors. Junior expects that before too much longer he will be offered a foreman's job and then will be able to move up to being plant superintendent. This expectation is more than an idle thought. "If I can't get the chance of getting it, I'm not gonna stay there and waste a year or so. I've done been too many places to know. If you can't get halfway what you want, or they ain't kinda helping you, you just ain't got a chance. You can go in every day for nothin' and the same old job and I'd just rather have something knowin' that I'm going to have some future there."

Junior firmly believes that hard work ought to be rewarded. Yet he feels that at nearly every job he has worked hard and been treated unjustly. Once he reaches this conclusion, he soon leaves. He has worked at nearly every furniture plant in Furntex, including three different plants run by Rebel Furniture Corporation. He worked for Multicorp for three months, with the same result. "If I don't get the money I ask for I'll just go quit and start somewhere else and start all over again—build back up and maybe they won't tell me a lie. I went to work for Multicorp for three months and they lied to me. They said, 'You've been here too long and you're too good a worker and you ain't gonna quit.' And I said, 'I ain't quitting, I just gonna get me another job and I ain't coming back. . . .' They didn't believe that I would quit. They promised me a raise and they didn't give it to me. They come up with some junk that I was reclassified. That's why I didn't get my raise and I tole them that was an awful excuse and quit. And I went to work at Johnson's for less money. . . ." He has also worked at several jobs outside the furniture industry, including being a cook. His most stable job was at another, even smaller, furniture company, where he and one other man ran a department that had previously required seven workers. He stayed there five years "off and on." When the owner refused his request for a raise and offered him stock instead, he left, feeling that he had no real future there.

His experience in the Air Force resulted in another perceived injustice. He enlisted for the air police and instead was assigned to be a cook even though he scored well on the qualification tests. "I know when I went in I had the idea that it'd make a man out of you. After I's in three months I seen right then. I mean I put in for air police, and I made high grades and passed the test awful high for just a tenth grade graduate, but I put in for air police, and I got listed as a cook, and I didn't like it one bit. And I burnt everything I could trying to get out: potatoes, eggs, pies—I done everything wrong I could do. Still didn't do any good. So they told me I was going to cook for four years like it or not. I told 'em there wan't no way I'd cook for four years. I said I put in for air police and made eighty-nine on the test. I said they told me I'd get it, and I'm going to find out why I didn't get it. Well, I never did get a good answer." Later in his military experience he suffered another injustice when he had to spend thirty days in the brig for going AWOL to see his dying grandmother. He was not allowed emergency leave except for a death in the immediate family.

He says that he left the military a changed man with a less than honorable discharge after only four months. "After I got out my momma said I'd changed so much she could tell it: ill, hateful, just irritable, really. I can tell that it has made me nervous from being in the service—awful bad temper. . . . They made me meaner and more hateful." His self-acknowledged hostility has made life difficult for him. He says he has few friends because of his temper. He does not trust potential friends, expecting that inevitably all will take advantage of him. He spoke of former friends who attempted to seduce his wife.

He is now in his second marriage. Both marriages are characterized by a significant element of physical violence, though he feels his present marriage is much better than the first, when he married a fifteen-year-old who later "ran around" on him (another injustice). He is not close to anyone in his family other than his mother. He is openly unhappy and dissatisfied with his life and feels that making more money will give him happiness and improve his temperament.

He is further embittered over his first marriage because his wife caused him to miss the only real opportunity he has had for upward mobility. At that time, he had worked his way from stock boy to assistant manager of a chain store in Furntex and was offered the opportunity to go to another state and manage a new store. But his wife did not want to leave the area or her family, so he stayed and went into furniture work. He has never had such an opportunity again and is openly disappointed. His wife overextended their credit, and Junior blames her for his having had to declare bankruptcy. He is still trying to reestablish credit and pay old debts.

Junior does not know anything about his father because his mother was divorced and moved to Furntex when Junior was quite young. She worked most of her life in textile mills to support Junior and his two older brothers. For the past ten or twelve years, she has only been able to work part time because she has been afflicted with arthritis and bursitis and has had two cancer-related operations. Yet she still works part time at a local rest home and cares for Junior's young baby while he and his wife are working.

Health problems play a significant role in Junior's life. One of his most traumatic memories was his grandmother's death. "She just laid so much till bed sores just got to the point where it was just a pussy mess. That's just what it amounted to. I think she died from laying there more than anything else." When young, Junior suffered a severe rupture that was misdiagnosed and went untreated for several months. He remembers that the only way he could stop the pain was to stand on his head. He also periodically suffers from severe migraine headaches. At the time of the interview, he had just recovered from the flu, and both his wife and young child were suffering from the illness. Missing work, drug costs, and doctor bills were placing a severe financial strain on him. These experiences had a direct impact on his feelings about political issues related to health care.

Junior is ambivalent about religion. He attends church regularly with his wife and wants to believe and be "saved" but does not trust his own motives. He worries that he might be declaring salvation publicly in order to rid himself of the pain of his migraines. He takes pride in the fact that he is not a hypocrite and will not be saved until he is sure that he is ready to change his life completely. "The day I sit down and read the Bible and say that I'm saved I want everybody to know it. I want to change, no cussin'. I want to live right and not put on an act. But I know you back-slide . . . I've seen it done . . . I've seen too much of it."

During our four-hour interview, Junior put more words on tape than Jim did in six hours. He talked extremely fast and frequently responded to questions with a discussion of his personal problems that was often irrelevant. He and Brent were the most outwardly nervous men in the group. Junior drank several cups of coffee, chewed his nails, and avoided eye contact during our discussion. He exhibited little shyness, speaking freely as the interview began. Despite this openness, however, it often seemed as though he was not aware of my presence and was talking to no one in particular.

Kevin: The Self-Confident Optimist

Kevin, who is twenty years old and white, expressed few bitter feelings and is one of the more optimistic members of the group. He, his wife, and their young child own a trailer in one of the larger mobile home parks on the outskirts of Furntex. The trailer is furnished in the "elegant-cheap" style that usually comes with a furnished trailer. Kevin is proud of his large collie and of a late-model sedan that announces its arrival with the bang and pop of loud mufflers. Having a sleek, fast car is important to Kevin. So are the other material things that money can buy. He would rather have a house than a trailer and feels that this is what he misses most because his present income does not permit him to buy a house. He is one of the few in the group who thinks the rich are happier than those with average incomes. (Not surprisingly, Junior also took this position.)

Kevin, who presently makes $3.86 per hour setting up and operating automatic sanding machines for Multicorp, is consumption-oriented, ambitious, confident, and optimistic. "I like to shoot for a goal. I've never shot for anything like ten years or nothing, but I'm shooting for a supervisor. When I get that I'm not going to be satisfied. Like I told you, I'm never satisfied. After I hit that goal I hope to be assistant superintendent. Then I'll probably go to plant manager or whatever comes next." In fact, his goals extend well beyond ten years.

Though Kevin said he does not often discuss politics, he did vote in 1976 and was one of the more enthusiastic Carter supporters in the group. Carter's strong Christian background and credibility seem to be significant explanatory factors. Kevin's mother also exerted a strong influence on his preference. "My mother told me to watch [Carter] because he is a good Christian man, in his church and all. To me, you know, all of them is going to tell you what they're going to do. They might be lying. You don't know. But to me, I think the man's honest." Kevin identified himself as a weak Democrat. He knows that both his parents are Democrats, but also that his mother "really did like President Eisenhower."

Though Kevin gave a religious justification for his support of Carter, he himself does not go to church and has few fundamentalist beliefs. His mother, who has a good deal of influence on him, is very religious and is a member of a fundamentalist church. Kevin expressed some feelings of guilt about not going to church and vows that his child will go and will be brought up religiously. His mother has exerted some pressure here. Thus Kevin's religious rationale for supporting Carter is probably more the result of his guilt and his mother's influence than of his own strong belief in any religious norms.

Kevin and his wife both work at the same Multicorp plant. She temporarily left her job about ten weeks before the time of the interview when their first child was due to be born. Her job also involved sanding, but it was in a different department. She plans to go back to work as soon as she is able, even though Kevin would prefer that she stay at home. This is not a strong preference, however; they need the money, and she enjoys working.

Kevin is presently in the third job he has held at Multicorp. He began working in the rough end through the industrial education program of the local high school. He tired of this job and decided to try textile work but found that he was bothered by the lint in the air and by having to work with so many women. He returned to Multicorp, only to leave again to work for his brother in an auto body shop. But the business failed, and he was out of work. After being unemployed for a while and then briefly working at a low-paying job in another textile mill, he was finally able to go back to Multicorp via the informal contact route, rather than because of his job skills. Kevin's brother, who works for Multicorp, played on the plant softball team. He told his supervisor that the team desperately needed a good shortstop and that Kevin was a good ballplayer. Kevin is very confident of his athletic abilities. Kevin got the job, and he is proud of this accomplishment. "I was the first person hired back during the recession in all the plants. It made me feel really good."

Regardless of how Kevin secured his job, he shows unusual enthusiasm for furniture work, Multicorp, and his future opportunities there. His only significant dissatisfaction is his present rate of pay, but he sees personal salvation via promotion.

Kevin knows little about his grandparents except that on his mother's side they did some farming. His parents settled in a mill village adjacent to Furntex when he was about five years old and spent most of their lives working for the large textile mill located there. Within the last three or four years they both left the mill, went to work for one of the chemical firms near Furntex, and moved from the old mill village into a newer home in Furntex. Thus Kevin is a second-generation factory worker. Of the other four children in his family, two are blue-collar factory workers.

His sister married up economically and is now a housewife, and his other brother moved into a white-collar job with a local insurance agency.

Kevin's life, like those of several other men in the group, has been affected by alcohol abuse. Kevin says his father was almost an alcoholic at one time, which created financial and emotional strains, but apparently the strength of his mother held the family together. Kevin reports that his father is about to overcome this problem through the support given by the close-knit family. The only obvious impact of his father's weakness on Kevin is that his mother is the single most significant, dominant, and influential figure in his life. He is luckier than some of the others.

Despite Kevin's materialistic orientation, he is not without compassion. He has volunteered to sponsor a convict who is an alcoholic and is on work release at Multicorp. He was asked about the importance of friends in a person's life. "One person can change your life. This man I was telling you about I was sponsoring. He's been coming over to my house, eating supper, [I have been] taking him shopping, helping him. One person, you know. He has become my friend . . . and I liked him a whole lot. In fact, I say I could trust that man. [This is a significant statement, for Kevin did not trust many people and had a high score on a misanthropy scale.] He's been in prison . . . but I've been around him to think, you know, I could trust him. But he changed my life. By working with him every day and knowing him as a friend, working toward a goal of getting him out. You know, getting him out two or three times a week, shopping—me and him getting out together and me trying to help him. Now that he's out I take him to see his kids every once in awhile . . . Seeing how he's changed my life and all, and me bein' with him and bein' my friend, you know— somebody that I never knew!"

Lewis: The Black Conservative

Thirty-year-old Lewis is the only black in the small group who lives in a significantly integrated neighborhood. In fact, the house he rents is only about three blocks from the white middle-class home in which the interviews were held. The neighborhood immediately surrounding his dwelling might be described as transitional. Most of the original upper-working-class white owners have left or sold, and now the majority of homes are rental units. A small enclave of five or six black families live on Lewis's block. Lewis told me that the neighborhood became integrated when a white "girl" rented one of the houses and moved in with her black husband.

All of the houses in the neighborhood, whether rented by blacks or whites, have deteriorated in the last few years. The house that Lewis, his pregnant wife, and two small children rent is no exception. It is a two-bedroom white frame house that badly needs repainting. There are boards missing from the front porch, and an old, broken-down kitchen range sits on the back porch enclosed only by battered remnants of screening. Fifteen feet of bare ground separate his front porch from the street. He talked about planting grass and fixing up the house, but fears that if he were to do so, the landlord would raise his $60 monthly rent.

The inside of the house is in no better condition. The furniture is old and in poor condition. When I arrived for the first visit, he was listening to old forty-five rpm records on what appeared to be a fifteen-year-old portable phonograph. Lewis complained about the condition of his house. "When I moved in—I know you probably think I'm exaggerating—but when I moved in my house, the toilet was sitting halfway under the house. You could stand in the bathroom and look down through the floor. In fact, one day I got up to go to work—when I got up, it was a rat sitting down by the bed, I don't know how long he had been there, but when I woke up he was there. He had gotten through the hole in the floor in the bathroom. I chased him out and blocked the hole up, but it didn't do much good. I mean he didn't get back in but the hole was still there, you know." Several months later, when the whole floor fell through, the landlord put in a new floor. Lewis blames these conditions on the landlord but feels there is nothing he can do about it.

Beside the house rested Lewis's car. It was not in running condition and had not been for several months. When I came to meet him for the interview, he was replacing a flat tire with an inflated tire (that lacked tread) so he could push the car to a shop to have its problems diagnosed. Lewis had overextended his credit a few years earlier and was just now getting out of debt. He did not have the cash or the credit to get his car fixed or replaced.

Lewis only occasionally discusses or talks politics with anyone and has never voted. He said he would register as a Democrat if he were ever to vote "because most of the Democrats that I've heard speak, uh, they go along with what I think." Though he is knowledgeable about many things, he was not knowledgeable about where many presidential candidates stood on key issues in 1976. Lewis said that he preferred Carter to Ronald Reagan because Reagan wanted to stop making weapons in the false hope that the Russians would follow suit. He offered this as an example of how Republicans differ from Democrats. Thus his sympathy toward the Democratic party is probably not the result of what he has heard candidates say. His parents were both apolitical, so they probably had little influence. More likely, his beliefs reflect what he has heard from black peers about the two parties. He was proud and pleased that the black vote was one important reason why Carter won in 1976. His analysis of the impact of the black vote was quite astute and factually correct—a sharp contrast with his knowledge of Reagan's position on defense.

Lewis makes $3.40 per hour as a veneer press loader and unloader at Multicorp's centralized veneer-making facility. His job is one of the most repetitive and machine-controlled of any in the sample. He must repeat a simple operation approximately every minute—loading sheets of wood that someone else has covered with glue into the press and, after a fixed time, taking the heated and compressed product out of the machine. The work area is extremely hot, and the air is fouled with the smell of vaporized glue. Though he complains about these unpleasant conditions, he seems to accept them as a fact of life that he must bear in order to survive and support his family.

Lewis has held this job for about a year and a half. Before that he worked second shift for one of the chemical companies near Furntex. He quit that job just before his second child was born because he did not want his wife to be home alone at night. Prior to that he worked at Rebel Furniture Company. Should he find an opportunity elsewhere, it seems likely that he would leave his present job.

Lewis's most important goal is to provide for his family. The work he endures and the fact that he has had to walk over four miles back and forth to work every day for the last several months (since his car has been broken) lends credibility to this claim. But his desires and goals reach well beyond mere survival. After talking about an older fellow employee who has worked hard all his life with little to show for it, Lewis spoke of his own dreams. "When I get to be sixty years old, I don't want to be payin' for a house. And he drives a little '64 Nova—looks like it's going to fall apart. I mean, that might be his second car. But when I get in my late fifties, even my second car, I don't want it to look like that, if we still be drivin' cars then, you know. When I get in my late forties or my late fifties, I want to be able to work at a part-time job and still have everything I need because I will have laid the foundation today. I want to get me between a twenty and thirty thousand dollar home and get it paid off. I want to get me a pretty nice luxury car, you know, and then have a second car. And I want to put all my kids through school. And if they want to go to college they can go . . ." Lewis mentioned these plans several other times in our conversation. They are not idle daydreams. Yet he has planned no course of action that will give him the higher salary he needs to achieve these objectives. His present employment situation probably never can bring him any of this because he reports that the highest salaried worker in the veneer plant makes only $3.63 per hour. He sees his chances for promotion at Multicorp as nonexistent. He will have to be very lucky to find a significantly better job with only a high school education. He feels that further education is the key to success and also that a little extra education can compensate for the discrimination blacks suffer in employment. But he has no plans for further education. When pressed on this matter, he described an electronics course he would like to take by correspondence but cannot afford. The only significant steps he seems to be taking to realize some of his dreams are getting himself out of debt, restoring his credit rating, and saving a little money, but these accomplishments require him to suffer severe deprivations. His wife has been enrolled in an electronics course under a federally sponsored program. Although this offers some hope for improving the family's financial picture, she has had to drop out of the course temporarily because their third child is due. Another addition to a family that is already struggling to get by does not portend well for the future.

Lewis does not have middle-class income or status and seems unlikely ever to achieve either unless some radical change occurs, but he has many of the values of someone who has achieved middle-class status and wants to protect it. Even though he feels himself to be the victim of discrimination and obviously needs material aid (his family is enrolled in the food stamp program), he was socially one of the more conservative and economically the *most* conservative member of the group. He does not feel that any further government action is necessary to help blacks overcome discrimination because they can overcome this obstacle with a little extra effort and a little extra education (though he does not disapprove of past government actions). He is opposed to national health care and expansion of welfare or food stamp programs because government is already too big and too many undeserving people are already obtaining benefits. He is also more opposed to unions than are most others in the group.

This curious combination of aspirations and values might be explained by his background. Lewis comes from a highly evangelical and authoritarian family (though not fundamentalist in the sense of being opposed to gambling or alcohol). His parents, who both work in other furniture plants, moved to Furntex for religious reasons when Lewis was about five years old. Lewis's father was and is a lay minister in a Jehovah's Witness church (which notably is about the only significantly integrated church in Furntex). Dress, behavior codes, and discipline were extremely strict in Lewis's family. He resented many of the restrictions placed on him, such as being forbidden to play sports in school and to wear stylish clothes. This resentment along with his father's severe temper led to a falling out between Lewis and his parents. He left home when he was sixteen and has been on his own since then. Though he no longer goes to church and still maintains a strong sense of independence from his parents, Lewis has had a rapprochement with them and does not categorically reject their religious beliefs. He expresses respect for his father for doing what he thought was right. Even though he does not go to church, he feels religious and approves of the strict behavior codes of his church. His clothing and hair style are notably conservative. Thus Lewis's political values may reflect the authoritarian values of his religious background and upbringing. He had the second highest score in the sample on an authoritarianism scale. It would have been the highest if he had not disagreed with the statement that strict discipline is the most important part of bringing up children, explaining that he interpreted strict discipline as child abuse, of which he disapproves. He may well have had some personal experience here.

Though he acted friendly toward me, Lewis harbors a great deal of hostility. He has a hot temper, has been in a number of fights, and views people as not very trustworthy. His is one of the three highest scores in the group on a misanthropy scale. Lewis feels the most important lesson of life is "not depend on someone else to do for you." He found that none of the people he thought were his friends could be counted on to give him a ride to work when his car broke down. He said his so-called friends drive past him as he walks to work. Lewis has acquaintances, but few friends, if any.

Lewis is insecure about his masculinity. Several times during the interview he volunteered his strong dislike for homosexuals when the subject seemed out of context. He is also troubled by changes in sex roles. The women's liberation movement threatens him. "I don't see why they want to be us. I can't understand why a woman wants to be a man. And I don't care how a woman might dilute it or water it down or change it around. When I examine it I come around to the same thing, that all they want to do is take over what we have. They just want to be us. And when they say they just want to be equal to us, I don't believe that. I think they want TO BE US! And see, uh, that's what bothers me a lot." Lewis permits his wife to work only because it is necessary and stipulates that she not do any "man's work," like in a furniture factory. He had one of the higher scores in the group on a sexual tension scale.

Mark: The Evangelical Christianized Pseudo-Marxist

White and nineteen years of age, Mark is the second youngest member of the group. He is ummarried and lives with his parents in what is by far the most attractive and expensive house of the fifteen, a three-bedroom brick-veneer home with a large den, carport, and a large yard. The house is filled with attractive furnishings that could well be the products of local furniture plants. It is located in a middle-class neighborhood of modern homes built just over Furntex's city line. Mark's family moved here from a smaller house in a working-class neighborhood in Furntex about five years ago. They own a well-cared-for ten-year-old sedan, and Mark drives a late-model Ford compact. The family's relative affluence is probably due to the fact that both of Mark's parents have worked for the same furniture plant (in a small town near Furntex) for many years, building up seniority and promotions. Mark's father moved into a semi-white-collar job as an inspector several years ago. The fact that Mark is their only child helped make their financial burden easier.

On his father's side of the family, Mark is a second-generation factory worker. His father's parents were and still are farming near Furntex. His mother's parents were factory workers. Mark hopes to be able to move up and out of factory life. He dreams of becoming an artist and did art-related work when he lived for a period in a nearby city. Mark made a poor beginning in realizing his dreams, however, when he dropped out of school in the eleventh grade and went to work in a grocery store.

Since then he has had a series of jobs, including working for the furniture plant where his father is employed. After a falling out with his family, he left home and worked as an engraver for about a year. He returned home, made a reconciliation with his parents this past summer, and obtained the job he now has with Johnson's Cabinet through a relative, who is a neighbor of the personnel manager at Johnson's.

Mark is tied for the lowest hourly pay of anyone in the group at $2.70. He described his job as a combination of hand carrying damaged furniture from the line to where it is repaired, working on repairs, and returning it to the line where damages he has repaired and sanded are finished. Since returning home he has obtained his high school equivalency degree and plans to work at Johnson's only until he saves enough money to enroll in a drafting program at the local community college. Given that he has strong parental support and is obviously intelligent and capable, it seems likely that he may succeed in moving from blue-collar production work to a somewhat more creative job. He is much more realistic in his goals and plan of action than are some of the others in the group (such as Lewis).

Mark's most striking characteristic is his extreme opinions and issue positions that are rigid, conservative, and authoritarian in some areas and yet radically permissive and egalitarian in others. At times he spoke like a socially sensitive radical and at other times like a demagogic authoritarian.

QUESTION: *What are some of your dad's bad points?*

MARK: *Well, uh, like I say he's ignorant in some of his convictions, as far as liberal-minded. He's still old-fashioned. [For example?] I have a friend that's gay. I don't put him down because he's gay. He's a good guy as far as, you know, spiritually and mentally he's all right. But he [dad] don't see anything in that. He's not liberal-minded at all.*

QUESTION: *What kinds of things should government do?*

MARK: *Well, like I said, they should illegalize a lot of alcohol, and, well, things like pornographic material and stuff like that. They should put military rules over things like that. But still I know that's contradicting what I just said that people should put out their own point of view. A lot of this is not coming out as art, you know, like pornographic materials. It's not coming out as art. It's coming out as lust and sex. Nastiness, that's all it is. I've seen some books that do show the art form. That's what it is, art form, but not, you know, the lust.*

QUESTION: *You can tell the difference?*

MARK: *Yeah.*

The tension in Mark between acceptance of homosexuality and rejection of pornography shows up in the sexual tension scale, where he has the highest score of anyone in the group. He has a political value conflict between liberty and repression. He has other conflicts as well. Much of this conflict in values is a reflection of the conflict in his own life that he is only now beginning to work out. In this sense, he is less stable and mature than the others in the group.

When Mark left home, he rejected a very fundamentalist, authoritarian religion along with his parents. For several years, his father has been studying at night to become a minister. Mark rushed to embrace the other extreme. While living in the other city, he became involved with a left-wing radical antiwar group and with the drug scene that accompanied it. From this group he acquired some Marxian rhetoric and radical ideas about a totally equal distribution of wealth in the country. No other member of the group supported total income equality. It was also here that he became friends with a homosexual and became a libertarian with respect to sexual preference. At some point, perhaps when the group began to plan violent actions, he was overcome with guilt and remorsefully returned home. He accepted most of the moral norms of his parents, with a few notable exceptions such as views on homosexuality and racial relations, and became very active in the church. He blamed all of his unacceptable behavior and ideas of the recent past on the evil influence of alcohol and drugs.

This young man is remarkable not for his idiosyncrasy but rather his similarity to many of the others once we account for his radical rhetoric and fundamental religious rigidity in a few selected areas. For example, despite some radical rhetoric about equal income for all, he ranked in the middle of the group on an economic liberalism scale.

His political preferences have been strongly influenced by his father. Though he does not like Wallace because he is "too much against blacks," he nevertheless identifies with the American Independent party of George Wallace. His father is registered as an American Independent. Given the turmoil that he has recently experienced in his life, it is not surprising that he failed to register or vote in 1976. Nor did he have any clear preference between Carter and Ford. His curious combination of moral and economic values did not translate into any clear choice. Of all the candidates running for the presidency, he slightly preferred Ronald Reagan. This preference seems best explained by the issues of credibility and tax reduction.

Melvin: The Young Racist

At the age of eighteen, Melvin, who is white, is the youngest member of the group. He and his bride of two months and their one-month-old baby live with his divorced mother and his two brothers, one older and one younger, in a dilapidated old three-bedroom frame house they rent in a lower-working-class neighborhood. The house contains old and well-worn furniture and is heated by an oil-burning stove. When I arrived to meet Melvin for the interview, his mother was trying to provide some additional warmth in the house on that particularly cold winter's day by adding extra kindling to the old wood-burning stove in the kitchen. They had closed off the front room to reduce heating needs and had tacked cardboard around the wide cracks in the back door of the house. Both of Melvin's brothers were in the back yard working on a twelve-year-old automobile that appeared to have suffered much abuse from other back-yard mechanics. Melvin's old car, which was in equally bad shape but was at least roadworthy, was also resting in the middle of the near barren back yard. Melvin brought the Pepsi he was drinking as the sum total of his evening meal to the interview.

Melvin was old enough to have voted in the last election, but he did not vote and expressed little interest in politics. He did identify himself as a Republican and preferred Ford in the 1976 election mainly because he does not like Carter or the Democrats. His reasons are racial.

QUESTION: *Has there been anything in the news recently that made you mad?*

MELVIN: *The only thing I can think of that really made me angry what's in the news on TV when Carter won. Yeah, when he beat out Ford. I just don't think Carter's the man for the job. I just think Ford's doin' better. Well, they say that Carter's for the niggers. I don't care nothin' about the niggers myself. But I have known some that be all right but most of 'em ain't. Most niggers just smart.* [By "smart" he means something like "wise guy."]

Showing little differentiation and much open hostility, Melvin is the most racially prejudiced member of the group. He is also relatively farther to the right on economic issues and on the issue of social control. Contrary to the image that is usually associated with long hair (Melvin has shoulder-length hair), he is strongly opposed to the use of drugs and supports severe penalties for drug law violations. Most of his friends reside in the country, where his grandparents live. He has little use for people of his own age who live in Furntex because they are into drugs and, like blacks, they are "smart."

Like some of the others in the group, Melvin is a second-generation factory worker. His mother has worked in textiles most of her life, but also in furniture plants. His father, from whom Melvin's mother is divorced because of a bad drinking problem, worked all his life for Rebel Furniture Company, but is now unemployed. Melvin's grandparents on his maternal side were farmers.

Melvin, unlike any of the others in the group, remembers nothing about his early religious training. He recalls going to a church when very young, but has no idea what denomination. Probably he has the least religious background of anyone in this small sample.

Melvin's pay at Johnson's Cabinet is tied with that of Mark as the lowest hourly wage, $2.70. He works in the packing and shipping department, where his function is to take packed cartons of furniture off the end of the line and hand carry them to the small warehouse area in the building. He also puts together orders from the storage area that are to be shipped out. This is the only job Melvin has had since dropping out of school in the tenth grade at the age of seventeen. He has been on the job for about a year and a half.

Melvin's greatest concern is money. He left school because he wanted money and did not like school. "That's one thing about school. You don't make any money. Like when I quit I got me a job where I'm working now. You're not supposed to do that. I told them I was eighteen and got away with it. I'm eighteen now. I was just seventeen. I've been working there since." His main complaint about his job is that he does not make enough money to get the things he wants—a trailer out in the country into which to move his family and a new car. Now that he is eighteen, he may find it easier to locate a slightly better paying job elsewhere and to make credible raise demands on his present employers. If he can bring his wage up to the average of the group and if his wife finds work again after the baby grows a little older, he may be able to achieve his two immediate desires—barring such unforeseen events as more children.

The interview with Melvin was one of the more difficult. He was very withdrawn and spoke softly, slowly, and with much hesitation. He was totally unresponsive on many questions, and a good deal of effort was required to draw answers from him. Because of this, many of his answers and expressed positions may be of very low intensity. He seemed somewhat suspicious and distrusting, and good rapport was never established. This seems an accurate observation because he scored very high, equal to Lewis, on a misanthropy scale. Only twice did he speak with passion or feeling. He expressed intense dislike for blacks and for drug-using hippies. After the interview, he disclosed a creative ambition with noticeable feeling. He talked about wanting to go into business doing body work on cars. The monetary incentive was important, but in addition he expressed his joy in taking something "that doesn't look good and making it into something that looks good again."

Paul: The College Dropout

White, twenty-three-year-old Paul is the unique member of the sample in several ways. Born in Pennsylvania, he is the only worker in the group who was born outside the South. He is also the only one with a parent who is not of southern origin. His father is from New England. His mother, however, is from the deep South. Both his parents are college-educated, and his father works as head salesman for an industrial equipment manufacturer in Furntex. Paul is the only member of the group to have experienced downward social mobility. He completed a year of college at a four-year school in the state university system before he dropped out to take a factory job. Despite these differences in background, I did not reject him in choosing the group because he satisfied other requirements and was an interesting case of downward mobility. He moved to Furntex when he was seven years of age and works in a blue-collar job as a forklift driver in Multicorp's warehouse.

Since dropping out of school, Paul has had several jobs. He worked in the metal shop of another furniture company and then was employed at another metal shop making awnings. He enjoyed that job, but resigned to take a more monotonous job running a saw because it paid an additional 30¢ per hour. He needed the money because he was planning to be married. He left that job when he was able to secure a job driving a forklift for Rebel Furniture for 10¢ per hour more. Then he went to Multicorp because he thought working conditions and pay would be better. He stayed six months and then worked installing burglar alarms, but left after he had several conflicts with the boss. His next job was an effort to move back into the white-collar work that was more characteristic of his family background. But Paul failed to succeed as a car salesman and went back to work as a forklift driver for Multicorp. He had been back for one month when we met.

QUESTION: *Does your job ever seem like a never-ending process?*
PAUL: *Well, the first time I worked there it seemed like a never-ending process. Then I got a taste of other types of work and now it doesn't really seem like a never-ending process. Like when I was selling cars, I hated that with such a passion—sitting in a place for eleven hours and then getting chewed out cause you're not doing anything. Because he's under pressure, the boss is under pressure cause you're not sellin' 'em. And that's eleven hours of sitting like this. You can imagine how boring that is. So actually it was a pleasure getting back to doing this. It's not that bad!*

Like most of the others in the group, Paul has strong complaints about his work and does not aspire to remain with Multicorp the rest of his life. He now plays in a band part time and hopes to become a full-time musician in a few years.

Paul and his wife live comfortably in a rented two-bedroom brick-veneer house in an upper-working-class neighborhood. His wage of $3.38 per hour is supplemented by his wife's income as a nurse in a nearby hospital. They own two cars, one of which is about twelve years old, but in good working order; the other is a late-model compact. The house is comfortably though not lavishly furnished and equipped with a black and white television and an expensive component stereo system.

Paul is among the five men in the group who reported having voted in the 1976 election. Paul claimed also to have voted in 1972. He is articulate and among the most knowledgeable about current events and politics, even though he said he is not very interested in politics and only occasionally discusses issues with friends. His articulation and factual knowledge are not surprising considering his education and family background. In 1976, he voted for Jimmy Carter over Gerald Ford despite the fact that he considered himself a strong Republican and previously had always supported the Republican candidate. The campaign caused him to move away from the Republican party, the party of his father and family, and now he declares himself an independent. Carter succeeded in appealing to him as a worker. "I switched over to Carter about a month and half before the election. A lot of things started clicking in my mind. Like I know that, you know, Ford had done good. And I know that Carter was talking good. It was a hard decision. . . . Something in the back of my mind just kept saying, 'Is Ford and the Republican party just giving us the illusion of well-being until the election to get their man in for another four years and then swing big business all that much more?' And that really kept annoying me. And I finally said, 'I can't vote for him and feel confident.' So I voted for Jimmy Carter." Among other things, Paul, as many other Americans, voted his pocketbook and his achieved economic class in 1976.

In one sense, Paul's background is similar to that of several others in the group. His family life was disrupted by his parents' abuse of alcohol. Paul feels that his father's heavy drinking led to his mother's heavy drinking and this in turn led to the bitter fights and disagreements that drove him and his older brother and sister from home. The end result is that though his parents seem to have solved their problem, the family is not at all close.

Though Paul is not a native southerner, he feels the strong regional allegiance of a passionate convert. In fact, his affection for the region and the state is stronger than that of most others in the group. He revealed a belief that the South is discriminated against in rates of pay relative to the rest of the nation. He also loves the land itself.

QUESTION: *Would you say North Carolina is the best state in the union?*

PAUL: *I would say it is the most beautiful. I've seen pictures of other places. I know the Grand Canyon is beautiful. But I went to college [in the North Carolina mountains] and I lived in the mountains there for a year. I'd just go out on weekends sometimes and drive through the Piedmont, and all around me I'd just see how beautiful it is. I guess that's the way John Denver feels about Colorado. That's the way I feel about this area.*

Rick: The Black Political Activist

Rick, who is black and thirty-one years old, lives alone in a two-bedroom apartment on the edge of the exclusive country club section of Furntex. His apartment and the four others attached to it are all occupied by blacks and set off from other dwellings by their location in a small valley surrounded on all sides by woods. These are the only black-occupied dwellings in the area. The units themselves are brick veneered and not totally incompatible in design and appearance with the less expensive white-owned homes that also border the housing of the elite of Furntex.

Rick's apartment is neat and clean but has little in the way of lavish furnishings. The sofa and old stuffed chair in his living room are covered by old bedspreads, and his kitchen has a bare appearance that indicates little cooking or eating within its confines. The only apparent luxury item is a console stereo and a few record albums.

Times are not good for Rick right now. Between the initial contact and the interview, he resigned his job as a packer for Johnson's Cabinet where he had made $3.00 per hour. He estimated this past year's income at $3,600, the lowest in the group. He does not own a car. Thus, it is particularly difficult for him to follow up job openings. He reported having just missed a promising job as a handyman for a rest home the day before. It took him a day to arrange to borrow a car to go see the owner of the home. By the time he arrived, someone else had already been hired. Rick is also trying to gain admission to the local community college and pursue a degree in electronic communications. Lack of transportation has made it difficult for him to visit counselors at the school or to see veterans administration officials about receiving educational benefits. Furntex has no public transportation. Lack of a car will make transportation to school a problem if he does enroll and will create transportation problems to whatever job he is able to find. He had a hard time getting to Johnson's while he was working there. The personnel manager had indicated that Rick did not have a good work record. No doubt lack of a car was a contributing factor. Rick will be unable to purchase an auto anytime soon because he has no money for even a down payment. He is presently two months behind on his rent.

Rick's high level of political interest and participation place him near the top of the group in that category. Not only has he consistently voted, but he has been a member of a group that was organized solely to intervene in local politics. He described this organization as a group of young black men who came together to attempt to get more local revenue allocated for recreation, housing, and community development. The group's activities did not extend beyond attending a few city council meetings and asking some questions. After getting what Rick described as a "bureaucratic run-around," they became frustrated and disbanded. Rick's involvement in this activity resulted from friendships and acquaintances made while he was involved in a summer jobs program organized by the local Community Action Agency.

Rick identifies himself as a strong Democrat. Like Brent, he is unusual in that he explained this identification in ideological terms. Also like Brent, he is one of the more articulate men in the group. He explained that he is a liberal and that the Democrats are more liberal because they favor faster social and economic change that will create greater opportunity for the average man. Rick remembered that his parents were strong Democrats who always voted and frequently talked about politics. Rick insisted, however, that his Democratic allegiance is a result of his own thinking and preferences rather than merely inherited.

Though Rick ideologically explained his party choice, he explained his preference for Jimmy Carter in the 1976 election in other terms. Rick is glad to see a southerner become president because he was getting tired of "listening to all of these slick Yankees who think they know everything and have all the answers, yet they don't." He said that he feels more comfortable with a southerner because a southerner is easier to understand and trust, even though his issue positions might not be those Rick prefers.

Rick does not know anything about his grandparents. His mother worked in the apparel industry and as a cook most of her life. Today she has a much better job at one of the new chemical plants near Furntex. Rick's father was a migrant farm laborer from eastern North Carolina before he came to Furntex and met and married Rick's mother. As Rick remembers, life was a struggle for his family when he was young because his father lacked skills and because it was more difficult then for any black man to secure a factory job. "Believe it or not, but they demanded more, it seemed like to me, out of a black man on the job, as far as quality goes, back then than they do today! Why he had to be able to read and write. If a guy wanted to get a job tending a saw then, he would dang near have to finish twelve years of school. Just to run a saw! That's the way it was. And, ah, hell, my father, listening to what he had to say about it, he started out running a saw, cuttin' wood. You understand he used to go out and come back and be pissed off because they said he didn't have no experience, or he lacked a certain amount of education for this or that. He came back pissed off at everybody—pissed off at the whole world. These days the slightest little thing that you would say would offend him, aggravate him, and he'd be ready to swing. Him and my mother, you know, they was always arguing."

Fighting over money problems eventually led to the breakup of Rick's parents' marriage. A few years later, the death of his father, who had continued to give some aid to the family, made survival as a family unit particularly difficult for Rick, his four sisters, and his mother. But his mother was strong and kept the family together. Rick has deep feelings of affection for his mother that are revealed in his description of her efforts. "She was all on her own. And she didn't desert us. I remember one time people came out and believe it or not they tried to send us off to an orphan's home, cause they didn't want to give her welfare. My father was dead, and she was only making $30 or $35 a week then. Rent was $6 or $8. God! She kept us there! No, she wasn't going to let us go. She kept us there!"

Rick has had a wider range of experiences than most of the men in the sample. He is very perceptive and sensitive and readily makes connections between these experiences and his present attitudes.

He dropped out of high school in the twelfth grade to begin what he thought would be a military career. After his first tour of duty, he decided he would rather pursue a formal education than remain in the military. He was unsuccessful in adjusting to and supporting himself in school and returned to the military, where at least "I know where the money is coming from and have a cot." This time he was sent to Vietnam, where he was wounded and soon became disillusioned with the war, the government, and the hypocrisy he saw in "democracy" in the country. He became aware of the civil rights movement and was disturbed that he was bleeding for other men's freedom but was not free in his own home town. He told of being baited into a fight by some "drunk rednecks" while home on convalescent leave. After leaving the military, he married and moved to New York City, where he felt there were more opportunities for blacks. Two of his sisters already lived there. He secured a job with the telephone company and was trained as a repairman. He was fired from this job for a poor work record, which he attributed to marital difficulties. He and his wife would fight, she would return to Furntex, he would follow her, and the cycle would repeat. Eventually, he lost both his job and his wife. After losing another job as a communications worker for the New York police as a result of an economy move by the financially troubled city, he returned to Furntex. Unable to find another job, he went to work as a packer for Rebel Furniture. He left after six months to take a similar job at Johnson's, where he was promised more money and better promotional opportunities. He feels he was misled because he received neither.

Roy: The Family-Burdened Ex-Con

Twenty-seven-year-old Roy endures the poorest living conditions of any of the ten white men in the sample. The small two-bedroom house he rents, which is located in a tiny lower-working-class neighborhood sandwiched between two middle-class areas, is bursting at the seams with occupants. Roy and his wife have only one child of their own, but each of them has two children by a former marriage. All live with them, and all are under seven years of age.

When I called on Roy to recruit him and when I met him for the interview, my first impression was that these children were starved for attention. While the older ones danced and jumped, frantically attempting to gain recognition, the younger ones tried to climb onto my lap—practically before any introductions had been made. Pity the poor salesman who enters this home with a briefcase filled with attractive display items!

On the Sunday morning I arrived to take Roy to the interview site, two of his older brothers were visiting. One was on pass from the local prison farm. All of them were sitting in a small living room viewing a religious revival on a color television, the single symbol of affluence in Roy's life. He has little else. Like several others in the sample, he has no private means of transportation and must depend on others to get to work or to the store. He did have a motorcycle but it "broke down" last summer. He would like to buy another because riding gave him a feeling of freedom.

In addition to being too small, the house he rents is in poor condition. It is badly in need of paint and is missing floor boards on the porch. His strongest want, besides a motorcycle and a car, is to own a better house for his family. He realistically assessed his chances of getting a better house as not very good because of his low level of income, $3.20 per hour. Though his wife once worked, at present she remains home and cares for the children. No doubt the cost of day care for five young children would consume most of any wages she could earn.

Roy is one of the more inarticulate members of the group. He had some difficulty understanding the nature of the project or what was being asked of him. Similar problems made the interview itself difficult, though he was open and friendly and made an earnest effort. Had his wife not been so interested and enthusiastic about the project, he probably would not have participated. He seemed somewhat intimidated. She acted as an intermediary in the explanation process. Her enthusiasm may have ensured his presence at the appointed meeting time.

Roy has a low level of interest and participation in politics. He only occasionally talks politics and has never voted. He identified himself as a weak Republican and feels that Ford would have made a better president than Carter because he "had more experience and he was already in there." He knows nothing about his parents' political preferences or partisan identifications. Roy's strongest political preference was for George Wallace. He was unable to explain why he liked Wallace other than "the way he talked I liked him better." Given that Roy is one of the least racially prejudiced members of the group on both objective and subjective measures, his positive affect for Wallace must be explained in other than racial terms.

For the last six years, except for a nine-month period last year when he worked for Rebel Furniture and a year and a half in the army, he has worked for Johnson's Cabinet as a sprayer in the finishing department. He met his wife at Johnson's, where she was working after having left her home and a bad marriage in the North. Roy obtained his job at Johnson's through his father, who also works as a spray-gun operator in the finishing room. Roy's supervisor is his second cousin. In view of these close family ties to his job, Roy's relative job stability is not surprising. As he had shown the year before, however, the promise of a small raise is enough to make him change jobs and then come back again.

Roy's grandparents on both sides were small farmers. His father has always been in furniture work. He worked in furniture in a town west of Furntex before moving his family to Furntex when Roy was nine years old. Roy also said his father made moonshine on the side and had a bit of a drinking problem that caused many arguments with his mother. Unpleasant memories of these arguments have caused Roy to resolve to avoid arguing with his wife. My brief encounter with the couple gave the impression that relations between them were warm and pleasant. Roy's mother, who has been dead for several years, bore eleven children. Roy was the ninth of the eleven, but he was the baby of the family because both of those who came after him died when they were quite young. One of the older children later died. Not surprisingly, survival was the dominant problem for Roy's parents and their family. Because he "didn't like it," and because the family needed any extra money they could obtain, Roy dropped out of school in the eighth grade to go to work. All of his brothers and sisters also dropped out of school at an early age for similar reasons.

Survival remains the dominant problem for Roy's generation. After an unsuccessful marriage that left him with two children to care for when his wife abandoned the family, Roy remarried and gained a loving wife, but doubled his financial burden because she had two children of her own. He joined the army in 1973, but was given a hardship discharge because his wife and family could not survive on the income he was able to send home.

Earlier, in 1970, he served a three-month sentence for theft at the local prison farm. He explained that he learned his most important lesson in life from this: "not to take things that don't belong to me." Today, Roy seems to have adjusted his wants so that his desires do not go beyond survival, and therefore theft is not at present a necessary means to his goals. "Well, a lot of people, money makes them happy. But it wouldn't really make me happy. Just having a family, though, and someone that cares about you, you know." This ego-defensive rationalization seems more than a superficial self-justification. Roy, who does have some modest material wants, seems to reap a significant measure of satisfaction from his personal family life.

Terry: The Gun Fancier

Terry, a thirty-one-year-old white worker, is another member of the group who has achieved the middle-class status symbol of homeownership via the short-cut method of purchasing a mobile home and renting a small strip of land for it in one of the small trailer parks that lie on the edge of Furntex. The mobile home he owns is unusual in its furnishings and size. It is a three-bedroom model with two baths and a living room that extends from the side of the trailer. The furnishings were plush, as was the shag carpet, and both appeared to be of higher quality than the usual mobile home offerings. Terry, his wife, and their two small children, one of whom was born a month before our meeting, also own a number of other material possessions, including two late-model cars, a stereo, and a color television.

Terry has been able to make these purchases through his and his wife's joint incomes, through credit, and from a windfall inheritance his wife received as beneficiary of a life insurance policy on her deceased mother. But Terry is not yet satisfied. He talked about wanting a boat for fishing (he is an avid hunter and fisherman) and a "brick home." Acquisition of these is important to him.

Terry has worked for a month as a case fitter for Johnson's Cabinet. (A case fitter fits drawers into cabinets, called cases, a tedious process of sanding drawers until they fit evenly and slide smoothly.) This is considered to be one of the more skilled jobs in furniture and as such pays a higher wage than do many jobs. Terry's hourly wage is $4.25.

Prior to coming to Johnson's, Terry worked for Multicorp as a case fitter and made $3.77 per hour. His job change was not caused by wages alone. He was discontent with working conditions at Multicorp, especially with management attitudes and policies. Terry's complaints concerned the great pressure for production and insensitivity toward the individual worker that he felt existed at Multicorp. At Johnson's, he has more control over the work process and feels they appreciate and care more about him.

Since leaving school in the ninth grade because he was "bored," Terry has worked in several furniture plants as well as in textiles for short periods of time and spent four years in the service. While in the navy, he divorced his first wife and met and married his present wife. After leaving the service in 1970, he came back to Furntex, went to work for Multicorp, and completed high school at the local community college. He has been taking courses there ever since. He openly admits that he is more interested in collecting G.I. Bill benefits than in any program goals. He does hope, however, that the courses he completes will help him secure a position with the state as a prison guard because pay and benefits would be better. So he does have some modest educational goals.

Terry does not discuss political issues with his friends. He is a member of an organized interest group, the National Rifle Association, and is aware of and openly embraces their political aims. He reads their literature and expresses regret that he has not written to public officials as the NRA has requested from time to time. Terry declared that he is a political independent because "I vote for the man and not for the party." But Terry has never registered or voted. He does not know his parents' partisan preferences. In 1976, Terry favored Carter over Ford for two reasons. First, he just did not like Ford. Second, "I liked Carter. I thought he would be a better president. I can't recall a president being from the South, and I guess that is really why I favored him." Terry is not the first in the group to be influenced by regional identification.

Terry is a third-generation Furntex blue-collar worker. His maternal grandfather was a truck driver; his paternal grandfather was a diesel mechanic. Terry's father, following in his father's footsteps, is also a diesel mechanic. Terry's mother works for Multicorp in the sanding department. His family's financial status was a little better than that of most of the men in the group because both parents worked, his father is in a highly skilled job, and because there were only two children in the family.

Terry harbors some resentment toward his father for not teaching him more about mechanics: "Most of the time when your grandfather and father are mechanics, then the son is also a mechanic." He says he wishes he knew more so he could repair his own cars. Instead, he has to depend on his father. When he was a child and tried to help his father, he was chased away. He rationalizes his father's behavior, saying that it resulted from fear of injury to the child. As a result, today Terry feels much closer to his mother than to his father and gains significant psychic satisfaction in talking about how he now makes more money than does his father.

CHAPTER THREE
Economic Liberalism

Populism started with the rhetorical assumption that there could be no progress until there was a consciousness of class interests. A people must know what it is reasonable to want, and then seek to achieve it through concentrated political effort. Yet, the great majority of Populists, black and white, had their aspirations shaped by a society that placed great confidence in a program of self-help. Reared on this tradition it is not surprising that the movement was largely a refurbishing of the Protestant ethic. [Gerald H. Gaither, Blacks and the Populist Revolt, p. 131.]

Many political observers have argued that the working class in the South is much more liberal on economic matters than are the politicians who represent them. Using 1956 public opinion data, V. O. Key examined five issues that involve the question of economic liberalism: government responsibility that everyone can find a job; government control of the influence of corporations; government control of the influence of unions; government involvement in supplying power and housing; and government responsibility that all get low-cost medical care. Compared with the rest of the nation, he found that "the South takes positions in mass politics remarkably similar to those of the nation." In fact, on the issues of the government guaranteeing a job to all who want to work and guaranteeing low-cost medical care, the South was significantly more liberal than the rest of the nation. Key concluded that "the similarity in opinions between the South and the rest of the country [can] be reconciled with the conservative outlook of many southern Senators and Representatives [in part by] the marked differentials in the levels of political participation among occupational groups in the South, as compared to the North. . . . In the South the classes that tend to be conservative approach in their levels of political participation comparable groups outside the South. On the other hand, southern blue-collar workers (both white and black) are far less active in politics than nonsouthern blue-collar workers."[1]

In his study of social class in the United States, Richard Hamilton drew a similar conclusion from 1964 public opinion data. He found that the South is as liberal as the rest of the country, or more so, on the issues of medical care, guaranteed standards of living, and aid to education.[2]

Using 1968 data, James R. Clotfelter and William R. Hamilton found that support in the South for more spending on health, jobs, and education was comparable to support in these areas in the rest of the nation. They noted that black support for the economically liberal position was extremely high.[3]

The theme of southern working-class economic liberalism was challenged, however, by Numan V. Bartley and Hugh D. Graham in an extensive analysis of precinct voting data from 1944 to 1972. Studying issue positions across class and racial lines in the South, they concluded that blacks and lower-class whites have grown further apart on both social and economic issues. Looking specifically at the issue of a government guarantee of a job for everyone who wants work, they found that in 1956 the views of lower-class whites were closer to those of blacks than of upper-class whites. But, since 1956, lower-class and upper-class whites have come closer together, both decreasing their support for a government guarantee of jobs, while blacks maintained a relatively stable high level of support. They concluded: "The vast and generally growing difference between blacks and lower-status whites over such matters as partisan identification, the federal government's role in minority rights, and New Deal-type welfare measures seemed to offer little foundation for the resurrection of the alliance of have-nots across color lines."[4]

Bartley and Graham explained this divergence as a reaction to federal intervention in the South following the civil rights decisions of the courts and laws passed by Congress. They argued that southern political leaders waved the red flag of racism and interpreted economic issues in ways that threatened the status of working-class whites so as to maintain their control of southern politics and protect themselves from the insurgence of new black voters.

> The racial turmoil and unrest of the 1960s were making a shambles of the Democratic New Deal Coalition, and one-party politics was coming to an end throughout the South. To survive this onslaught, the Southern Democrats were to devise a new tactic, or more precisely, to resurrect an old one, namely, the race baiting that had so successfully destroyed the Populists and blunted Republican fusion in the 1890s. The combined efforts of the Southern Regional Council's Voter Education Project and the voting rights act of 1965 had prompted a surge of voter registration throughout the South that during the 1960s added an estimated 6 million new names to the rolls, of which roughly 30 percent belonged to blacks and 70 percent to whites, and the majorities of both races continued to identify themselves as Democrats. Southern politicians were not unmindful of this arithmetic, and in response to it the threatened Democrats counterattacked with the newly enfranchised army of poor whites.[5]

The appeal of racist slogans will be examined in chapter 4. The focus of the present chapter is on these men's positions on several important economic issues around which a biracial coalition could conceivably be constructed.

These men were ranked on an economic liberalism index according to their reactions to four statements made to each of them during the course of our discussions. The four statements were:

1. The government in Washington ought to see to it that everyone who wants to work can find a job.

2. The government in Washington ought to help all people get doctors and hospital care at low cost.

3. If cities and towns around the country need to build more schools or water treatment facilities, the government in Washington ought to give them the money that they need.

4. The government should leave things like energy and housing for private businessmen to handle.

In examining the scores of these fifteen men, the most striking point is that all but one of them fall to the liberal side (calling for greater government involvement) of what might be seen as the neutral point. (See Appendix A, Table 1.) Only Lewis, the black conservative member of the group, is on the conservative side (calling for generally less government involvement in these matters). The only item on which he called for more government involvement was the last one, when he explained that government should have a "little something" to do with energy and housing—"just a part, not completely dominate."

Another observation is that race seems to have little bearing on their opinions. The five blacks are fairly evenly scattered among the whites in their positions on these issues. (See Appendix A, Table 1.) What Bartley and Graham found to be true for lower-class whites in the 1960s is obviously not true for this small sample of working-class whites in the late 1970s. They are very close to their black coworkers in whether they think the government should be involved in helping to locate jobs, provide housing, build schools, assure medical care, and control energy supplies.

A number of other variables that might be expected to have an impact on their opinions were also examined. Most of these variables were found to have no obvious relationship to economic liberalism. (See Appendix A, Table 1.) Their hourly salaries seem to have little relation to their feelings on these economic matters. Nor did education have any obvious impact despite the fact that Paul, the college dropout who had the highest level of education, was the most economically liberal of the group. Two of the three men at the lower end of the index had completed high school, and Junior, the angry, ambitious worker, who was second only to Paul in economic liberalism, had completed only the tenth grade.

Some relationships, however, are significant to the eye if not to the calculator. Four of the five most economically liberal voted in the 1976 election. Only one other member of the entire group voted. Though this suggests a possible causal relationship, one must be very cautious in moving beyond mere suggestion because there are a number of possibly confounding factors. For example, those with a higher sense of personal confidence and efficacy may be more likely to hold and express strong opinions on any subject (including economic liberalism) as well as being more likely to vote. Such confidence is unusual among these men; there is a strong flavor of resignation and fatalism in their political beliefs. Most of them are much like the citizen in what Gabriel Almond and Sidney Verba call the "subject" political culture: "The subject is aware of specialized government authority; he is affectively oriented to it, perhaps taking pride in it, perhaps disliking it; and he evaluates it either as legitimate or not. But the relationship is toward the system on the general level, and toward the output, administrative, or 'downward flow' side of the political system; it is essentially a passive relationship."[6] Comparing the economic liberalism scores of these men with their scores on a personal control index that was administered during the conversations indicates a slight positive relationship. (See Appendix A, Table 1.) Those who are economically most liberal seem to be more likely to express a relatively greater sense of control over their own lives.

The other noteworthy feature also bears on voting—on voting choice. Of the five most economically liberal, all were either moderate or strong Carter supporters. Of the five least economically liberal, two were strong Carter supporters (one of these two voted), one was a very weak Carter supporter, and the other two were moderate and strong Ford supporters. This suggests a positive relationship between economic liberalism and support for Carter. The key question is whether these men consciously translate economically liberal issue positions to support for Carter and whether this strong preference is sufficient to explain a decision to vote. To answer these questions, let us turn to a detailed examination of these workers' attitudes, paying particular attention to the linkages they make between the cognitive and behavioral elements.

The Government and Jobs—
Are Jobs a Basic Right?

Each of the men in the small group was asked an open-ended question early in the interview that was similar in content to one of the close-ended statements used to determine the economic liberalism index. "Do you think that the government should provide jobs for those who can't find work and who want to work?" This question was followed by: "Do you mind having some of your tax money spent on this kind of thing?" Their answers to these questions as well as some of their comments on other questions reveal how they feel about whether or not a job is a right that should be guaranteed by the government. The opinions of the ten white men cover a fairly wide range.

Terry, the gun fancier, would not consider the question as stated. "Well, I'm not going to say cause I've always been a firm believer that if anybody really wanted to work they could find a job. I believe they could. Some people say that if they are in, say, a field of an executive, that's all they would want is an executive. They wouldn't get out and work in a furniture plant like I would. I feel if they really want a job they can find a job. . . . Everybody that's ever wanted to work has always got a job—or I have." When pressed, Terry stated that if a person really could not find a job, then the government should help.

In the abstract, Terry fully supports government guaranteeing everyone a job, but in practice his view is much more limited. It is limited in two ways. First, the goverment is not responsible for providing or guaranteeing high-status jobs. People should be willing to take any available job. Second, the government is only the provider of last recourse. As long as jobs are available, people should take them before turning to the government.

Terry's opinions are based on his life experience. He has always been able to find work, so why can't everybody else? This view is quite close to the conservative mental set of "I made it, so why can't you?" A strong hint of resentment permeates Terry's words. If he is willing to take a low-status, menial job, why should someone else merit a better job that is partially paid for out of his tax money? Thus a job may be a right, but a good job must be earned on merit. Terry, who partially bases his self-esteem on the fact that he is willing to work hard at a low-status job and on his sense of independence and self-reliance, does not feel that others who are unwilling to bear similar burdens merit any better job than he does.

The theme of abstract acceptance of the concept but partial rejection of the actuality of government aid in the face of practical realities surfaces in the statements of other white workers in the group. These practical realities involve both a claimed personal knowledge of the availability of some kind of work and a statement of their own sense of self-worth and merit. Eddie, the unambitious do-it-yourselfer, and Dave, the danger-seeking worker, serve as particularly good examples.

EDDIE: I would rather see 'em provide jobs for the ones that want to work and can't find it than I would to pay the ones that don't have a job and don't care to find one.

DAVE: Yes, if they really want to work. But I would have to go back and say that I have never seen the time that a person could not find a job somewhere.

QUESTION: So you don't really think it is necessary the way things are now?

DAVE: Well, not the way it is now because—well, back last year when they had all these plants was laid off—Multicorp and everywhere, and everybody claimed they were out of work. We worked down at Master Molding Company sixteen hours a day—first and second shifts and needed help all the time and we very seldom had people come in and ask for a job. A person is not really going to want a job as long as he can sign up and make a living doing it. [Unemployment.] As long as he can do it and have enough money to live off of. I wouldn't if I could do it. I'll be honest with you! I'll be honest with you! I wouldn't go to work if I could do it, if I could live off of it.

QUESTION: Do you think you could get enough off of it?

DAVE: *Nope. But I wouldn't be working today if I could. Today is the last day of duck hunting season. I would have been duck hunting!*

Several others echoed this theme that jobs are a right only for those who merit them—for those who really want them. Jim, the enthusiastic Carter supporter, thinks that it would be "nice if the government could provide jobs for everyone," but he fears that there simply are not enough resources available to the government to do this. Right now, he says, "there are jobs available to those who really want to work" even though they are not good jobs. He, too, pointed to his own job as one that is not very desirable but one he is willing to accept in the absence of other available employment. He expects other people to be willing to do the same. He went a bit beyond this position, however, because he is particularly dissatisfied with his work. He speculated on the possibility that the government could secure high-quality jobs for Americans in other countries that have labor shortages, such as Australia, since resources are too scarce here to provide good jobs for everybody. After considering the quality of currently available work, he called for the government to take action, saying, "There needs to be something done in the national government in order to secure people good jobs—good paying jobs." Most of his compassion is for the working poor with whom he can better identify.

Paul, the college dropout who scored highest on the economic liberalism scale, also touched this now familiar theme of individually earned merit. He directly translates his position on the issue of jobs to his support of Jimmy Carter.

PAUL: *So far as providing jobs, I would have to think on that cause I don't know what that would involve. Now, certainly, if a man wants to work they should help him find one. Now, that's something I must say helped me to decide to vote for Mr. Carter. He says that people that don't have jobs—we're gonna find 'em a job and train 'em for it. Then if they don't want 'em, we're gonna kick 'em off welfare and we're gonna kick 'em off all the money they got comin' in. And I agree with that 100 percent. If a man wants to work, let him work. If a man don't want to work, cut off the money you're giving him cause I don't believe in anybody taking a free ride.*

The two least articulate members of the white subsample, Melvin, the young racist, and Roy, the family-burdened ex-con, both said it would be okay if the government found people jobs with the understanding that the tax burden would not increase. Both men feel very little intensity on the issue unless it were to involve higher taxes, in which case they would probably oppose government action.

Mark, the evangelical Christian pseudo-Marxist, is highly concerned about promoting the economy and feels considerable empathy for the unemployed. He believes that government-provided jobs would further stimulate the economy and help people: "Tax money should be spent on

[this]—more employment." He has no fear of increased taxes for these programs and is aware that the government is presently engaged in this endeavor. On the next question in the interview, the subject of unemployment again rose, and Mark talked about individual merit. It seems that he does not in fact want the government simply to provide jobs, but rather to *force* people into jobs. Why? Because such experience will teach people the value of hard work—it makes them virtuous.

MARK: *It would be good if we could go back to the old times and teach people how to work for a living.*
QUESTION: *Do you think some people are sorry and just don't want to work for a living?*
MARK: *Right.*
QUESTION: *Is that a cause of poverty?*
MARK: *No. That contributes to the unemployment rate which makes the economy worse. And you know as far as paying out taxes and welfare, I don't believe in welfare—if a person can't get out and work and the only people that should get welfare is the disabled. That's the only people I think should have welfare.*
QUESTION: *You don't like giving welfare to those who don't want to work?*
MARK: *Right. There's blacks and whites out there, and they collect welfare, and, uh, they could work, they could work. They collect that welfare because they just too dang sorry. If I wanted to I could go out here and find some shack and just, you know. I don't know anybody. I'm off to myself. I need welfare. And they'll pay it!*

Kevin, the optimistic, self-confident employee who is generally one of the least economically liberal, is also quite interested in the impact that government-provided jobs could have on the economy. Though he remarked that he has always been able to find a job, even during the recession, he did show some empathy beyond his own personal condition and decided that some people probably are looking for work who can't find any jobs and that the government should help them. Nor would he mind having his tax money spent on this because "if there are more people working, the economy would be going better. And the whole thing is the economy. That's the whole thing about living is the economy." He added that his realization of the need for more jobs in the future resulted partly from his wondering what would be needed when he saw several newborn babies at the time his wife was in the hospital having their first child.

Junior, the angry, ambitious member of the group, defined the issue in terms of self-interest and is aware of some of the external costs of unemployment.

JUNIOR: *I think they tryin' to do that now. I think they tryin' about as good as they can do. They's just so many things that take in consideration for that, it's hard to say. The government, they—I don't guess anybody, unless they in it, knows what they talking about cause I'd say I* couldn't. They probably trying to get 'em jobs. They could probably, uh, well, the people that want jobs and can't sign or something like this, they got to do somethin'. That's the ones out here robbin' and stealin' right now is the ones that can't get anything. Part of it is just sorryness and a lot of it is just because they can't really find anything.

QUESTION: Would you mind having some of your tax money spent for that kind of thing?

JUNIOR: It'd be better than worrying about them breaking into your house and they shoot you for $20 and steal your car so they can get $200 out of it or something like this.

One of the black men in the sample also analyzed the need for government-provided jobs in terms of self-interest. Brent, the disappointed dreamer, wouldn't mind having some of his taxes spent on this because "it is better to pay some taxes on this sort of thing than to be afraid to come out of your job with your check and be afraid of having your money being robbed or taken."

Two of the five blacks in the subsample raise the familiar theme of individual merit in conjunction with the government providing jobs. John, the black homeowner who is about the highest paid member of the group, unambivalently resents his tax burden. Albert, the athlete, feels a great deal of empathy for those less fortunate than he, but he is ambivalent on the issue.

ALBERT: If people have no place to turn they should have help from somebody.

QUESTION: Would you mind having some of your tax money spent on this kind of thing?

ALBERT: Well, it's going on now. I mean the people on welfare. That's coming out of my tax money. So I think it would be a good thing to do. Well—I kinda think it do and I kinda think it don't. It's kind of hard to answer. But to a certain extent I guess there is no other way. If a person had no other way to turn I guess he would need help from somebody.

We get a clue to the feeling underlying Albert's ambivalence and limiting his sympathy for those who have nowhere else to turn in his answer to an earlier question about major problems facing the country. He said the major problem is people's attitudes, and again his ambivalence is evident.

ALBERT: I guess you could say that people don't care whether you're making it if they are making it. If you got more than enough, and if you could share with people and try to make them have just a little more, then the world would be a better place. I mean you can't just go around giving people this just because you got it, I mean. But I don't think people have enough love for one another.

QUESTION: Do you think there is anything government can do to get people to share better with one another?

ALBERT: I don't really think the government can do much. I think they

*can do things, but, uh, I guess everytime you turn around that's who
they's blaming, saying that the government ought to do this and the government ought to do that for you. I think maybe they [the government]
could do a little more than what they do. I think people can do more for
themselves than what they do. I don't think things is always as bad as
people make it seem. But I do think that maybe the government can do a
little more.*

John's support for government aid in providing jobs goes beyond the
abstract idea only as far as his pocketbook. He at first responded "sure" to
the idea of government providing jobs for those who want to work. But
when asked whether he minds having his tax money spent for this sort of
thing, he quickly began to back away. He noted that the government is
already spending too much of his tax money for federal salaries and pay
raises. The little of his tax money left from this would not go far to help
people get jobs, and he can afford no additional taxes. He wound up getting himself thoroughly confused, and after a long silence simply said, "I
don't know." The topic of unemployment was again broached later in our
conversation. This time he took a clearer position that defines the question in terms of individual merit.

JOHN: *According to what I heard, right now there is 1.5 million people
unemployed in the U.S. Suppose fifty-two jobs might open up in Furntex
tomorrow. You'd be lucky if you could get fifteen willing to work on the
job very long. . . . They drafted me from a job when other guys I know,
too sorry to work, was on the streets. I went in and came out, and they
was still on the streets. They was too sorry to even work in a pie factory—just eatin' pies!*

Lewis, the black conservative, who had the lowest score on the economic liberalism scale, answered the question of government involvement in a manner that seems consistent with his conservative score.

LEWIS: *I don't think so. I think some means should be made available
for people who can't find jobs to find work, but I don't think government
should have a hand in it.*

Rick, the black political activist, who was unemployed at the time of
the interview and has been unemployed many times in the past, took the
strongest position of anyone in the entire group in favor of the government providing jobs. As with the others, his position on the issue comes
from his own experience. When he was unemployed while living in New
York City, he was able to obtain a position as a radio operator with the
police force through a Comprehensive Employment and Training Act
(CETA) program. He candidly and openly stated that such programs
might help him, and this is why he favors them. He also feels that job discrimination in Furntex prevents blacks from competing on equal footing

with whites. This may be why he strongly favors government development of high-quality jobs rather than merely menial public service jobs. He argued that in the long run society will benefit because government intervention will result in more and better services and greater wealth for all. Rick and, to a much lesser extent, Jim, are the only members of the group to emphasize a government responsibility to provide employment opportunities that are competitive with those in the private sector.

The simple fact that fourteen out of the fifteen men in this group stated that to some extent they favor the government providing jobs for those who want to work and cannot find work could easily lead to an incorrect conclusion unless we listen to their explanations and qualifications. A summary of their opinions on this issue would be close to the following proposition: The government should provide jobs if (1) merit is proved by the potential employee's willingness to take jobs like those that these men have been willing to accept in their lives; (2) jobs such as these are not available (most of the men believe they are available) and there is nowhere else to turn. A majority of these men, both black and white, also believe that government-provided jobs should not be of higher quality than those they endure. Enthusiasm is notably lacking for increasing taxes to finance the creation of such jobs. Junior, who is more enthusiastic than most about the necessity for government-provided jobs, feels that money for such projects could come out of tax money that is "wasted" on such things as "bringing back pieces of rock from the moon."

What is striking is that this theme of a limited right based on merit is common to both the blacks and whites in the group. There were only four exceptions out of the fifteen. Lewis, the black conservative, is somewhat anomalous in that he disavowed all government responsibility, even though he recognizes that a need exists. He would seem to prefer private and/or individual solutions. He does not see any conflict with his position on this issue and the fact that his wife has been enrolled in a government-financed job training program that, upon completion, will enable her to operate and repair photocopy equipment. In this sense, Lewis's views resemble those of some of the unemployed engineers in southern California in the study by Karl Lamb: "There is evidence that human beings are not so intent upon making their ideas so consistent with each other as some social scientists have presumed them to be. Particularly when a direct personal interest is involved, political actions may not be constrained by an ideology which, if logically pursued, would limit such actions. That is, an engineer may continue to believe that all welfare recipients are bums, while waiting in line for his welfare check, secure in his feeling that he deserves better from the government than others." [7] Because Lewis feels he works very hard, and in fact he does labor at the most miserable job of any in the group, he may think that he and his wife deserve a chance to improve their family income and achieve his dreams of a house and two cars.

The real exceptions on the more liberal side are Brent, Junior, Rick, and perhaps Kevin. Brent and Junior see government-provided jobs as a necessity to protect property. Rick has personally benefited from government job programs. Kevin, who feels some compassion and empathy, is concerned about job opportunities when his child grows up.

Underlying what these men have said about government responsibility for providing jobs are some important commonly shared values and characteristics. The first is a belief in self-reliant individualism. Each man is ultimately held responsible to care for himself and his family and should turn for help only when it becomes a matter of survival. Time and time again they talked about the satisfaction they get from knowing that they earn what they have and from feeling relatively independent of others. Such comments were often offered as an alternative satisfaction to the material possessions they do not have. The comments of Kevin, the optimistic and self-confident employee, are typical.

QUESTION: *How do you feel about being a member of the working class?*
KEVIN: *Well, to me there's only one good thing about it. What I got I work for. Nobody else can't say they gave it to me. I've never wanted anybody to hand me nothing. What I got is mine. I got it. I worked for it. That's the only good thing about it.*

When asked what was the most important lesson he learned in life, Paul, the college dropout, expressed similar sentiments.

PAUL: *The most important[lesson] I ever had to learn was being on my own, providing for me and my wife. . . . I've got a good life. I've got a wife that keeps a very clean house. . . . I've got most of the things now I've wanted for a very long time. I really don't think of a whole lot that I want that I can't afford. I'm not setting my standards so high that I can't really afford 'em. I try to be realistic about things. . . . [What's most important is] being able to get along on your own, not having to depend on others. That's something that's grown very important to me. And, uh, I've been able to live by that, too. I've gotten along very well.*

John, the black homeowner, expressed pride in supporting the children he fathered out of wedlock. He is disgusted with those who do not adequately support their own children, yet get the same tax deductions. Brent, who is ambivalent over whether he or society is to blame for his present life condition, argued that most of the problems people say exist in Furntex are really only excuses for their own individual shortcomings. He was, of course, in part talking about himself. He feels guilt for not being stronger and more independent.

These men express their strong sense of individualism and self-sufficiency in other ways as well. Many expressed a good deal of pride in their ability to make their own furniture and fix their own autos. Eddie, Kevin, Junior, and Melvin believe that they could make a living doing mechanic and body work on automobiles. Confidence in their abilities gives them some feeling of independence from the job insecurities that are characteristic of employment in the furniture industry.

In a very real sense, the frontier-agrarian rugged individualism that W. J. Cash saw as characteristic of the forefathers of these men has been inherited—even across racial barriers. "The farmers and the crackers were in their own way self-sufficient too—as fiercely careful of their preroga- tives of ownership, as jealous of their sway over their puny domains, as the grandest lord. No man felt or acknowledged any primary dependence on his fellows, save perhaps in the matter of human sympathy and entertainment." [8]

JUNIOR: *I run my own life. I don't want anybody, unless I ask for the advice, I don't want any. If I feel like I need it I'll ask somebody that I think will help me. I've been in a couple of jams several times—financial jams that I've had to ask. When I ask, I'd like to have an answer if they've got it. If not, I'll ask somebody else that I know will give me a fair answer. But as far as somebody tellin' me how to do, what to do, when to do, I'd just rather do what I feel is right. And then if it's wrong, my wife can tell me. I don't want my next door neighbor telling me.*

This strong sense of individualism and self-sufficiency gives these men a limited view of society's collective responsibility for providing jobs. Many of them honestly believe that they are independent of the economic forces that control their jobs and wages. A few may actually be indepen- dent of these forces. Some might be able to go into automotive work, and Eddie might be able to return to farming, but the fact is that most would be without any effective recourse should layoffs or "short time" (the four- day or three-day week that often accompanies a decline in furniture sales) depress their family wages. The logic of their expressed independence is self-defeating in an economic sense, even though it is functional in serv- ing their egos. If government is to provide low-quality jobs only to those who are unable to obtain even the most menial and lowest paying factory jobs in Furntex, the employers will have no incentive to improve working conditions or wages. In fact, this was precisely the condition of the job market in Furntex for many years, until new industries not related to tex- tiles or furniture moved into the area. As shall be seen when the question of wages and income distribution is examined, the realities of other pos- sibilities for work and income have modified this one-sided picture of self-serving and self-defeating rugged individualism that has been drawn in considering government-provided jobs.

A second characteristic implicit in these discussions of government- provided jobs is the tendency to tie the question to welfare. This tendency is doubtless also tied to strongly held values of individualism. Anything that one is not able to do for oneself is, almost by definition, welfare. Therefore, government provision of jobs is another form of welfare, es- pecially when those who accept such jobs have already violated the code of individualism by not accepting what jobs are available. Because these men see themselves as upholding the code, they feel they are in a position to make moral judgments involving the familiar distinction between the deserving and the undeserving, or to make a distinction between those who "want to work" and those who are "too sorry to work." Doubtless they find these judgments easier to make when applied to people other than themselves (though this does not seem to bother Lewis). Given the emphasis they place on the phrase "those who want to work," it is doubtful that they could have supported even the abstract principle of government-provided jobs had the requirement of proof of moral worth been excluded. Again it is noteworthy that both blacks and whites tend to link the question to welfare issues. Whether or not whites associate questions of poverty, welfare, and moral blame with perceived racial differences will be considered when racial prejudice is examined. Such association would seriously dampen any hopes that may exist for a black/white coalition supporting more social programs.

A third characteristic of these conversations about unemployment and jobs is a lack of empathy. I define empathy to mean the ability to imagine oneself in another condition than that presently occupied. In this case, we are interested in these men's ability to imagine falling into extremely hard times and finding themselves without jobs or opportunities to work.

If one learns from one's environment, then certainly there is no scarcity of lessons about the possibility of unemployment or short time in Furntex. Nearly all of these men know of someone or some plant that has either been laying off workers or working short time. A fairly typical description of the situation was given by Dave, the danger seeker.

DAVE: *Well, I guess you know that Tally Furniture had their big layoff. That happened this week—four hundred. A box factory down here in Furntex is on five hours a day. Phipps, part of Multicorp Furniture, is on short time now, but they claim it's not because of work. They claim they messed something up up there. Universal has not got to work tomorrow. That's part of Multicorp. They claim something messed up. But it's a funny thing that everything is messing up. Now, last year, Universal and Phipps, when Multicorp Furniture was on short time last year, Universal and Phipps would work three days a week and then the chair plant and Redbird Road Plant would work three days a week, and, you know, would alternate like that. And I myself, I believe we'll be on short time in another two months. But they say we ain't.*

QUESTION: *Do you worry about that kind of thing?*

DAVE: *Oh, yeah, you better bet I do! But, uh, they claim we won't. But I seriously believe we will.*

Despite this knowledge, Dave feels that one can find a job somewhere if one really wants to work. Fear of layoffs has been a life condition for him and his family and parents, and they have always managed to survive. Why should the present be any different?

Jim, the enthusiastic Carter supporter, who experienced a four-month period of unemployment in the past year, explained that this is the normal life condition for the working-class people of Furntex. He told how his parents managed to survive when they were without jobs.

JIM: *As far as problems, the main problem was just living, making it from one week to the next. Cause you know at one time—I was told about it but don't remember it—the mill here, it went on strike. Not on strike, but was without work, for a long time. They didn't know what they were going to do. My dad did all kinds of things. He can lay brick, do electronics, do automotive work. One time a guy came up and asked him if he could lay brick, and he had never laid a brick in his life and he said yes. And the building's still there. And when we grew up it was understood that we would help out the family. . . .*

Jim feels that at present enough jobs are available so that people can survive using the same pluck, determination, and resourcefulness that his father exhibited and the same willingness to endure that he has displayed in going back into furniture work.

In addition to being aware of the fact of job insecurity and knowing that the condition has existed for generations, most of these men, like Dave, worry to some extent about job insecurity. The only exceptions are those who consider themselves particularly resourceful like Junior and those who have a good deal of seniority and experience in relatively skilled jobs like John and Eddie. Even Lewis, who opposes all government efforts to provide jobs, openly admitted "insecure feelings about my job—that I might be terminated at any time."

Thus there would seem to be a very strong experiential foundation for the ability to empathize with a condition of unemployment that is beyond one's control. But there is also a strong experiential foundation for the belief that one should, can, and will endure and survive. Albert, the athlete, expressed this belief and will, which is a central focal point in these men's sense of self-esteem and identity, in two separate passages.

QUESTION: *How secure would you say your job is?*

ALBERT: *Anytime you doing furniture work there is always a chance of being laid off, or, uh, there's always a chance of things happening that could cause your job to go down, and you can be laid off. It's not too secure. I mean you can't really say, "Well, I know I'll have this job five or ten years from now."*

Earlier in our conversation we were talking about education and what he had learned from life.

ALBERT: *If you can survive, I guess all and all it's the same thing. If you got a four-year education or whatever it takes to have a high-paying job with a future in it, you know, that's cool. But if you can survive with no education and get by, I think, uh, I think you can make it if you can get by.*

Only about a third of the fifteen men empathized with the unemployed to the extent of blaming the system rather than the men. Rick, the black political activist, who has experienced unemployment and was unemployed at the time of the interview, blames the elites who control industry as well as racial discrimination. Brent, the dissatisfied dreamer, who is also black and sensitive to the problems of discrimination, lays the fault on the rich, "who do not want people to escape from poverty," and on discrimination. Two or three of the white men in the group seem, to a lesser extent, to find someone other than the unemployed person himself responsible. Paul, who says that some people are "too sorry to work," also thinks unemployment results from "slackness" in the economy. He blames this economic slowdown on Nixon and on Congress for spending so much time pursuing Nixon that they all neglected the economic needs of the country. Kevin thinks economic problems might be the root of the possibility that some who want work may be unable to find it. Roy, the family-burdened ex-con, is difficult to fit in either category. He feels that unemployment is a problem and wants government to do something (he is not sure what—though providing jobs is all right with him), but he does not wish to blame anyone for high unemployment.

Though these men do not generally seem capable of empathy with the unemployed, their attitudes about health care issues and about wages and living conditions for those who are employed indicate that they are not totally lacking in empathetic ability. They are not without compassion, nor are they such total individualists as to be incapable of blaming people other than those who suffer for their misery. The lack of empathy in the area of government-provided jobs is mostly explained by the centrality of the ongoing struggle for survival in their own lives and by their self-images. As long as they are able to manage with some comforts and satisfactions, they have little understanding for those with similar socioeconomic backgrounds who are unable to do so.

Wages

If few of these men have personally experienced the deprivation of unemployment, all of them have at one time or another felt material deprivations. At the time of the interviews, every member of the group save four (John, Eddie, Dave, and Paul) expressed some important material deprivation resulting from their low wages. Thus, wage rates would seem to be a better potential issue on which to base political appeals than unemployment.

Discontent over Wage Rates

Most of these men believe that they work hard and that their hard work is not paying off as well as it should. All the members of the group except John, Eddie, Dave, Terry, and Albert openly expressed dissatisfaction with respect to the fairness of their present salaries. John, Eddie, and Dave receive the three highest hourly wage rates in the group ($5.18, $4.68, and $4.50, respectively). Terry just received a $.48 per hour raise in moving from Multicorp to Johnson's. He is presently happy with his wages, though he remembers being very dissatisfied with his rate of pay at Multicorp. Albert suffers from very low self-confidence and figures that he does about as well as a person without an education should do—he manages "to get by." Paul, who claimed to lack no material possessions that he desires (because his wife adds considerably to the family income with her nurse's salary and because he has consciously lowered his material expectations), nonetheless believes he is underpaid. He expressed deprivation relative to wages earned in the North by unionized workers.

PAUL: *We don't make a whole lot of money. And a lot of us resent that. As a matter of fact, I don't think there is a man that does not work in Furntex that does not resent the fact that there is a guy up North doing something about half as difficult as he's doing making about three to five times as much money doing that.*

The remaining workers regarded their pay as unjust in a variety of ways. Rick, who is extremely bitter and characterized himself as an "angry young man," simply said "it sucks." Melvin, the young racist, who has very little to say on most subjects, offered a clear and relatively lengthy statement (for him) about his wages. His belief is typical of the group.

MELVIN: *I just don't make enough money . . . I've been there a year and a half and I hadn't had but a dime raise since I've been there. You have to stay on them all the time to get a raise. You just about have to demand it.*

Their frustration over the injustice of their pay rates is reflected in the scores of these men on the pay satisfaction factor of a job description index.[9] Possible scores range from zero to twenty-one, with a higher score indicating higher satisfaction. Those who verbally express no dissatisfaction with their pay have the highest scores, indicating the validity of the scale (John, 15; Eddie, 21; Dave, 21; Terry, 17; Albert, 12). The remaining scores fall dramatically, with a single exception, Junior, whose score is sixteen. Of the remaining nine, Brent's score of nine is the highest. All others are six or less. Junior's relatively high score reflects the fact that he has only recently taken his job as a door hanger at Johnson's and has been given a $.50 per hour pay increase in the ninety days he has been working there. Nevertheless, he expressed dissatisfaction with the general pay scale in furniture work. He has worked in nearly every furniture factory in Furntex and eventually left his job at each one because he was not given the raises he thought were due him.

Not only are most of these men dissatisfied with their own wages, they are discontent with the rates of pay received by other workers in Furntex, recognizing that the injustice applies to an entire group, not only to individuals. Four out of the five (all but Dave) who were relatively satisfied with their own rates of pay expressed the belief that other workers in the area are underpaid. The comments of Mark, the evangelical Marxist, sum up the feelings of most of the workers.

MARK: *But they gonna have to look at it as the employee has to have money to make it. Like now to live comfortably, you have to have at least six or seven hundred a month. That is, if you're married and have children you have to have at least six or seven hundred a month.* [Mark is not married and has no children—he shows the capacity for empathy here.]
QUESTION: *Don't most people make that?*
MARK: *No. I don't! I couldn't afford to have a family on what I make now, but there's not—there's no hope right now.*

Jim nearly worked himself into a passionate rage in talking about the injustice of industrial wages in Furntex.

JIM: *But, heck, man, let them live like human beings. There are people whose whole life is fighting from payday to payday. A man shouldn't have to fight to make a living! He should make a fair wage for his work and should be able to enjoy living. I'm not saying make everybody millionaires, but make everybody equal to what they should get paid for the job they're doing!*

Dave was the only member of the group who did not at some point remark that wages around Furntex are lower than they should be, although he did state that wages are low. When asked if people pretty much get what they deserve out of life, Dave replied that "people get out of life what they put into it. They make their own life."

Junior also stands out from the rest of the group in his acknowledgment that pay for furniture workers in Furntex is so low that one cannot get ahead, but at the same time he believes that most get about what they deserve. He objects to the unequal starting conditions that cause one to end up in furniture work and the lack of justice for those few who, like him, are extraordinarily capable and conscientious workers. In short, Junior, who is a lonely, friendless man, feels he is a special case in that his wages are particularly unfair.

QUESTION: *What do you think the phrase "all men are created equal" means?*
JUNIOR: *Well, some just get a better start than other people. Maybe some's got rich grandparents and others don't. They say that everybody has got an equal chance of doing something, but 90 percent of the time if you go somewhere and you ain't got a high school diploma or a college degree and you really can't get it, so you couldn't really say that you was equal. Course, you both had the chance to go. But maybe you didn't have the money that the other guy had to go. There'd be a lot of consideration in that . . . the feller that's got a grandma that dies and leaves*

him a half a million dollars is got a good start on life where's the man whose grandma dies and he's gotta pay for the funeral, he ain't got the start the man's got who has the million.

QUESTION: *Do you think people would work as hard [if incomes were all equal]?*

JUNIOR: *I know they wouldn't. Everywhere I've been to . . . we don't even get many people that even want to work for a living anymore. They just want to [sit] eight hours a day, forty hours a week and pay on Friday. They don't care if they stand at the bathroom for seven hours a day. They still want to be paid.*

QUESTION: *So do you think that most people get pretty much [the income] they deserve?*

JUNIOR: *Well, on the average, most of them get what they deserve. And the other average probably does more work than what they get paid for.*

Of course, Junior was talking about himself as one of those in "the other average." This is consistent with his second lowest score on the coworker rating factor of the job description index. Only Lewis, who had the highest authoritarianism and misanthropy scores of anyone in the group (Junior was a close second to Lewis on authoritarianism but was somewhat lower on misanthropy), gave his coworkers (with whom he fights) a lower score. Junior holds his coworkers in some degree of contempt. He characterized them as boring, stupid, irresponsible, and often lazy and disloyal.

Despite these exceptions, most feel a sense of relative deprivation, a belief that they and many of their peers are being deprived of that to which they are entitled.[10] If the vast majority of these men are dissatisfied with the wages they and their peers receive for their labors, as they seem to be, what is the source of this dissatisfaction? What knowledge have they gained that has raised their expectations?

As we learned in listening to Paul, one relevant standard of comparison is unionized workers in the North. Jim, who, like Paul, identifies strongly with the South, is also aware of regional variation in pay and feels definite pangs of relative deprivation.

JIM: *I can't understand why all the car industries are in the North, you know. I mean, look at how many cars need to be supplied to the world. And these people complain about what they make. They make $7 an hour—forty-three days off a year, and they still sayin', "we ain't got good enough stuff, or benefits."*

Several other members of the group also realize that wages are lower in North Carolina than in other parts of the country. Rick, in talking about the major problems facing North Carolina, angrily noted that pay in the state "is about the lowest in the nation." (Jim and Paul are aware that North Carolina has the lowest industrial wages in the nation.) Lewis knows that salaries are much lower in Furntex than in the North, but he rationalized that differences in the cost of living compensate for wage differences.

QUESTION: *What did your parents worry about?*
LEWIS: *I guess their problems was mostly about money cause there wasn't always enough of it. I remember like one time it got to the point where my father had gone to Pennsylvania with my uncle to find a job, but we were living here. And he would catch the train every Sunday night and go up there and work and come home Friday, cause he figured, you know, that since jobs pay almost twice as much up there he'd go up there and work and bring it back home and then he'd have enough, you know. But after, I think, three or four months of that, he found out that he would do just as good to stay here and tough it out, you know. So he stopped traveling back and forth. So I think most of the problems stem from money.*
QUESTION: *How would you feel about moving away from Furntex?*
LEWIS: *I believe if I moved away from Furntex I wouldn't have it as easy as I have it now. I believe that I might have to live a little faster if I moved out of Furntex. Well, where I'm paying $60 a month rent now, I believe I might have to pay $140 or $150, and where I might get by on $30 a week groceries, I might have to spend $70 a week. And I might not be buying that much more, you know.*

Roy, the family-burdened ex-con, is another who perceives that his wages are low but feels little relative deprivation because he rationalizes that cost of living differences compensate.

QUESTION: *What are some of the bad things about living in Furntex?*
ROY: *. . . working conditions could be a little better. Not enough money for what I do. Like up North they pay a lot of money. But the cost of living is much higher up there, too—like for rent and food and things like that.*
QUESTION: *Do you think it balances out?*
ROY: *I guess it balances out.*

Even Rick, who has lived and worked in the North and who is very angry and bitter about working conditions in the South, believes that relatively lower food and land prices partly compensate for lower wages. But, for Rick, it is a long way from balancing out.

Even more important than the knowledge these men have about pay scales in the North is their awareness that some industries that have recently located in the area pay higher wages than do the furniture factories. Because these industries are local, they cannot rationalize that differences in pay are compensated for by higher costs of living. Of particular importance are two chemical companies just outside of Furntex and a beer brewery in a nearby city. At some point in nearly every interview, one or more of these firms were spontaneously mentioned. Several of the men have worked at one of the chemical plants at some time in the past, and nearly all of them know someone who works in the chemical plants or the brewery. At the time of the interviews, the brewery was unionized but the chemical plants were not. The men had much to say about these places of work. Most are glad these industries are in the area and wish more such industries would locate in Furntex. Many feel that their existence has forced other local firms to increase wages and benefits. Many also feel that local politicians, businessmen, and companies do not want these industries in the area because they do offer higher wages. They believe it was no accident that the chemical firms located outside the city of Furntex rather than within the town. The men offered a variety of explanations as to why they do not work for one of these companies.

QUESTION: *Have you ever thought seriously about some other kind of job—what might make you think about it?*

ALBERT: *If there were short time or if there were somebody I could not get along with, or if I just had to. It would be something either doing carpentry work or something in industry—like [one of the chemical plants]. I worked there before. I think it would be nice.*

QUESTION: *How did you like it there?*

ALBERT: *Oh, I liked it, but I just didn't like the swing shift. It was good pay and good benefits.*

Four of the other men in the group have at some time worked for one of the two chemical firms (John, Lewis, Terry, and Jim). All left because they did not like working a swing shift. All but John took a pay cut to be able to work days so they could spend more time with their families. Thus, they have placed familial values higher than material values. Nevertheless, the better pay rates and benefits of these companies had an impact on the thinking of these men as well as others in the group.

JIM: *The worst things about Furntex is the places that you have to work. . . . I don't like the way the town's run—the same people control all of the things. There would be better pay and businesses in Furntex if certain businessmen would allow it to happen. It's not as though better businesses wouldn't want to come here, but rather they don't want them here. That's why [one of the chemical firms] is located out of town. They don't want them here because they pay better money. We are located in the middle of a lot more prosperous towns and people get paid a lot less [in Furntex]. The attitude is "Why should I pay people $4.50 an hour when they will work for $3.00 and not move away." That's what bugs me. This is like a hole in the wall compared to other places I've seen. Most other towns are very modern compared to this town. We really have nothing!*

EDDIE: *There's a certain group of people that it seems like Furntex swings the way they want it to swing. If it gets out of bounds on one side they kind of hold up a wall over there to kind of hold it in. . . . It seems to me that when an outside business comes in, if they decide, you know,* that this business will be good for the town, that business picks up. If the merchants and I'd say the upper class, upper income anyhow, feel like they don't handle the quality material we want—the quality of furniture or anything they happen to be dealin' in, it don't make no big headway. And even if they stay in business, they're just stayin' enough to make a living for themselves really. . . . I think we have the people in Furntex, to a certain extent, not to really open up and turn loose for new industry, but Furntex could probably handle a few small industries, nothin' really big. Like when [one of the chemical firms] came in. They came in and opened up. It seemed like it was a hit right away for Furntex, and it seemed like for the workingman. A lot of 'em picked up a job—a lot of 'em that I know—a lot of 'em picked up a job, stepped up in pay. Seemed like their way of livin' even picked up. I don't know if it made 'em feel like they fit into the community better or whether they were more financially responsible, but it just seemed like they picked it up and went with it.

QUESTION: Why do you think some of these people would like to keep these new industries out?

EDDIE: Really, I hadn't got any good ideas on that yet. I don't see what the merchants—it seems to me they would welcome a new industry, more money, and eventually it is comin' back to 'em. It's going to pass through their hands sometime or another. If I was going to put it on anything I would have to say it would have to be on the furniture factories right now. Cause [one of the chemical firms] pays fairly good wages, what I'd say particularly for Furntex and surroundings. If they're payin' that good, they can hand pick their employees. If they have any kind of a setup at all where they can work a hand three months they got an evaluation of what that hand can do. . . . And the first thing you know [one of the chemical firms] is going to have the good hands working down there and the furniture is going to be hung with anything they can hire. [Eddie continued, and the flow of his dialogue led him to wonder if it would not be better if new industries would set their wage scales around the same level as those of existing industries. He feels a certain degree of loyalty to his firm and knows how difficult his job in one of Multicorp's finishing departments can be because he has to train new workers and fill in for ones who have left. But he is ambivalent because he, too, has thought about going to work for this chemical firm. He is relatively satisfied with his present rate of pay and company benefits. Later, he spoke about the impact of the unionized brewery on benefits at Multicorp.] I would say, well, furniture has good benefits. If they'd get any better—I don't see how they could. Really, I think that Multicorp has stepped up their benefits to kinda come into line with union benefits so maybe the people wouldn't be inclined to go with the union.

MARK: W. W. Roberts Cigarette Company wanted to come in [to Furntex] a few years back, and the industries around here wouldn't let 'em. That's what it is. They got a, like a Chamber of Commerce to get together and just put those industries out. [They do this] so they can pay

us what they want to pay us! That's exactly what it is. I mean, I'm not
saying that I know it all. But that's what I think it is. This is what they
want to pay us. We can't say, "Well, the hell with you. We'll go somewhere else and get us a job, you know, that pays more and the benefits
are better." Like Johnson's—the benefits are terrible, let me tell you. . . .
[Wages are so low because] it's either that the big man is either trying to
rip everybody off or it's true that we're just not—well, we've done the
most business that we've ever done here in the past couple of months.
That's at least what my boss man's telling me. And when I ask him,
"Well, where's all that money? Where's the raises coming in from that?"
He says, "Well, they got to pay off this and they got to pay off that." But
still they should be able to pay the employee. The employee's putting
the stuff out for 'em! And, uh, what it is, we're just not making enough
and that they're trying to say that we're not suiting them in their, uh,
working ability. We are! We're putting out more than they're expecting
us to do. Like they laid off the rough mill [the part of the plant where the
rough lumber is first cut into smaller sizes] about a month ago. That's
because they already had the wood cut up and everything. They worked
their butts off. They made 'em work hard and get it out. But after they
got through working, getting it out, they laid 'em off! . . . I was thinking
of going down to [one of the chemical firms]. They have good benefits
and good pay, and the way I heard they respect their employees.
They've better promotion standards down there. [Mark has not gone
there because he hopes to stop working entirely in the next six months
and go to school.]

   MELVIN: I'd like to see more places to work so I could get a better job
and more pay.

   QUESTION: Do you think companies around here pay enough money?

   MELVIN: No, they don't. A lot of people around here don't think they
do. The way I heard it Johnson's is the lowest plant in the state. I'd say if
I was down in Florida [Melvin has been to Florida, but not the North, so
he uses it as a standard of comparison; he also said he would like to live
there], I could make more money than I can up here.

   QUESTION: Whose fault is it?

   MELVIN: I don't know. . . . [There's] not a whole lot we can do. . . . As
long as that place has been in business they [Johnson's] haven't been
making no money—they say. Of course, they do people dirty up there at
Johnson's, too. Like some people come in there and they pay 'em a
whole lot more. Some people been there two or three years and they
ain't makin' nothin' and they hire somebody that comes in there two or
three years later and they make a whole lot more than somebody that's
been there for, say, three years. They're gettin' cheated. It happens. It
happened in the last month. They brought in this guy where this girl
works and . . . he don't do any more work and he makes more money. I
don't think it's fair. . . . People quits there all the time on account of they
don't pay enough and they don't give raises often enough.

   PAUL: A guy here worked in a furniture factory most of his life making

$3.75 an hour. His best friend just quit. He'd been with the company
about twenty years making $3.50 and he quit and went [to the union-
ized brewery] and they started 'em out at about $7 an hour.

Kevin, John, Rick, Jim, Eddie, and Dave also mentioned that the workers at the brewery make a good deal more money than do furniture workers. Dave and Eddie discount this fact because they believe union dues
absorb most of the advantage. The others do not rationalize away the difference. It is an important source of their feelings of relative deprivation.
Jim has contemplated applying for work at the brewery, but he is deterred
by religious reasons.

JIM: *[I] hear people complain at work, "What am I doing here? Why*
am I working at this kind of wage when I could go up to [the brewery]
and get paid a lot more?" But that's a moral issue. People can't work
there because they manufacture beer. . . . In Eden, they're going to have
the largest brewery in the world down there. I'm sure the Southern Bap-
tists frown on that. But, man, there's going to be people drinkin'. I don't
believe in drinking myself. I did when I was in service. I drank like a
fish. I don't believe in it now cause of what it did to my body and my
mind. I now have responsibilities now to my wife and my child. . . . But,
I say there's gonna be people drinking. But, if, [he hesitates] the de-
mand's there. Someone's gonna have to make the stuff. . . . I don't
know—see, I'm torn between religious convictions and what I need to
live as a human being. That's the only reason I haven't went to [the
brewery]. Because if I went to [the brewery]—here I'm a deacon at the
church and a Sunday School teacher. What do you think they would do
to me? They'd probably tell me to leave.

In sum, most of these men feel that their personal wages are too low.
Furthermore, even more of them feel that wages are generally too low for
all furniture workers. The standards of comparison they use are wages in
other parts of the country (especially the North, where the stereotype they
have in mind is the $7 per hour auto worker), wages in the two relatively
new chemical firms located near Furntex, and wages at the unionized
brewery located in an urban center near Furntex. Several of them rationalize that cost of living factors compensate for these differences or that dues
absorb the advantages of being unionized, but most still feel a sense of
relative deprivation. Blame for their condition is laid on a variety of
sources. Favorite targets are corporate greed, local businessmen and
elites, the rich, their own companies, or their own bosses.

All but one of the blacks add an additional factor—racial discrimination in jobs. John, the quiet black homeowner, said that when he looks for
a job he tries to learn whether blacks have been given the worst and
lowest paying jobs. He believes that this was the case at a Rebel Furniture
Company plant where he worked at one time. Brent feels that racial discrimination is one reason why wages are so low in North Carolina, but he
also believes that too often blacks use this as an excuse for their own fail-

ings. He is talking about himself because he has failed to achieve most of the goals he has set for himself and holds himself in low esteem. Lewis blames government and specific policies of discrimination that he feels exist, though he thinks blacks can overcome this disadvantage through education.

QUESTION: *Who would you blame unemployment on?*

LEWIS: *I don't know. I feel like, me myself, I feel like whatever the government does or doesn't do is the reason for it. They trying to do something. They trying to pull off something. I feel like it might be the local government's fault, you know, about local unemployment. I feel like they might have a reason for having a certain amount of unemployment at a certain time, you know. I don't know what it would be. Like in the newspaper, I read an article at one time about the National Guard. And they said the National Guard had been all white up to about '71 or '72 or something like that, except, uh, black people that were in it, they had to have white commanding officers. No blacks were allowed to be officers, you know. And now they say they were integrating the Guard. And then in the last paragraph it had that the enlisters for the National Guard had had specific instructions, and this was in the local paper, to hire as many whites as they could—not to turn away any blacks, you know, but to hire as many whites as they could. And, uh, that was just, what, maybe three or four months ago that I read that. So, uh, I feel like maybe it's the local government's fault that unemployment is the way it is.*

QUESTION: *Are you talking about black unemployment or just unemployment?*

LEWIS: *I guess I started talking about all unemployment but I ended up talking about black unemployment. . . . I guess I was going to say that some white people have it pretty hard, too, you know, that they have it pretty hard as some black people do. But I ain't going to say that. Cause since I've grown up I've seen the advantage—I feel like white people have advantage over blacks, you know, since I've grown up. Now I feel like that if a white person is poor and he's not doing any better than he is or that I am, it's his own fault. That's the way I feel now.*

QUESTION: *What does the phrase "all men are created equal" mean to you?*

LEWIS: *To me that means that I should have the same opportunity that the next guy has. That's what I feel like that means.*

QUESTION: *Is it really that way?*

LEWIS: *No. . . . It's the other way around. I feel like I'm not equal to some people. [Job discrimination] is a factor. Cause if I had the education, then I could probably cope with the race part.* [He feels that generally racial problems and discrimination are less significant in Furntex than in other places.]

Rick also feels that racial discrimination is an important factor in explaining low wages for blacks. In a much more sophisticated analysis than that of Lewis, he explained that most discrimination is subtle—it occurs in the ways people hear about jobs that are available. He went on to argue that in the long run, factory owners are only hurting themselves.

RICK: *That's the bad part about here is the jobs. It's the quality of jobs as far as I am concerned. You see, all my life I have always strived for high quality, you know, what I consider high quality, you know. You see, I made a promise to myself when I was a kid that I would never work in a furniture factory—that's what I said. But when I came back [from New York after being laid off from his job there], it was my only source of income. It was either that or I would starve, so I had to do that. The job situation here in the furniture factories is very bad, especially for a lot of the black guys. They have been in the furniture factories for ten or fifteen or twenty-nine years running the saw and they're still behind the saw. I know it could be better. They just don't get promotions. I know some of these guys cause they used to be my friends. I was born and raised with a lot of 'em. I was born in the hospital right with a lot of them. As a matter of fact, a guy [I saw] today, we was born right to-gether. Our birthday is right on the same day. We went on through school together, and one of them started working for Multicorp Indus-tries and the other started working for Rebel. They still there today. They said at the time they was pleased to go to work for the money they was paying. Me, I refused to go to work for the furniture industry. So, what is bad is the quality of the jobs and the variety of the jobs. Now, there probably are some jobs, but if the information was made available concerning how to get these jobs, that would help a lot, too. You may find out about a job through somebody [and he] through somebody [else]. I hate to say it, but that's the way it usually goes, because I think it is really bad. That's the point right there that I dislike about here in comparison to New York—totally, that is the point right there! If the job is there they should make the information available even if you don't accept the job or don't qualify for the job. At least you should get the opportunity.*

QUESTION: *Who would you blame?*

RICK: *Well, I would lay blame on the management and a lot of these people that runs these corporations. I believe that if they put a little more emphasis on trying to get quality people from this area they could. You know, if they wouldn't discriminate. In my opinion, I have learned this, you know. The color of a man don't make the quality, especially if you got a corporation and you're trying to run it, you're trying to get the best people available. I mean you don't have to socialize with the man. But, I mean, if this guy's a mechanic, if this guy's a first-class mechanic, you know, hire him. You want the job done. They still discriminate. In my opinion, they defeat their whole purpose. They really miss a lot of good people that way. A lot of good people leave this area and go some-where else, and they make it! Now I'm just using myself as a parable because I, well, I've had the experience. Now, I probably never would have gotten that opportunity to work for the telephone company if I had stayed here in Furntex. Up there [in New York] ITT and ATT were both* running a program to try and recruit black people, and it was all competitive. We all had to go down and take tests. We all had to go through physical examinations. I don't mind that at all. I don't mind that at all!

Albert is the only black in the group who does not feel that racial discrimination plays any significant role in worker recruitment or in promotional considerations in Furntex.

ALBERT: I don't see [job discrimination] as a considerable problem. I see that as something people can use to blame. Like if you and I went to a place to get a job and I didn't [get it]. I can use that to blame, say, "Well, you white. They gave you the job because I'm black." Like I said, you can find somebody to blame if you want to. I don't think there is really a racial problem in Furntex today. I think people treat it pretty equal. I don't think there is really a great problem in the racial department.

None of the white workers mentioned racial discrimination as a reason why black wages are low in Furntex, though several believe that discrimination adversely affects blacks in the town. As shall be seen when racial prejudice is examined, many of the whites in the group believe that another kind of discrimination is of danger to them—reverse discrimination.

Equality in Wages and Movement toward Equality

Having established that these men feel that wages are not fairly distributed in Furntex, the next question is how they feel wages should be determined ideally. One possibility would be to allot everyone equal wages—absolute equality, regardless of what tasks the worker performs. Adoption of such a view is one element of what Frank Parkin calls a "radical" value system, a set of beliefs that "affirms the dignity of labor and accords the worker a position of honour in the hierarchy of esteem." [11] Presumably, this belief is accompanied by the belief that all workers deserve equal pay as tribute to their equal honor. If these men do indeed believe that they are entitled to equal pay, then they are certainly ripe fruit for a populist harvest. But their views on the desirability of an egalitarian wage structure are far from radical, although they may lean in that direction sufficiently for redistribution to be used as a potent coalition-building issue.

In the course of the interviews, each man was asked how he would feel about everyone receiving equal wages regardless of the job held. The reader is reminded that we were considering only those who do in fact work because of their views on the moral worth of those who do not work. Their answers may be simply summarized as a resounding chorus of disapproval, with almost a third of the group (Mark, Eddie, Albert, and John) toying with the idea.

BRENT: *I would feel that that was very undemocratic. . . . You would have a breakdown in everything, because human nature wouldn't—say, "Hey, well, I'm going to get the same pay whether I do this, do ten of this or one of 'em." And another thing in every society you gotta have some chiefs and some Indians, and you can't have too many of either one. . . . Now, like I said before, democracy means that everyone is free. Everyone has the same opportunities. . . . Now, simply because they have the opportunity doesn't mean that these opportunities will be realized, you know. I think that's where that part about the American Dream came about. Simply because you lay down and dream a sweet or pleasant dream doesn't mean when you wake up that dream is gonna come true.*

When asked how much movement toward equality he would like to see, Brent heartily endorsed some movement because "I stand on the low end" and because so many are paid so little that they can barely survive. He also endorsed completely the idea of equal pay for equal work without regard to race or sex.

RICK: *I think that [equal pay] would be bad. I don't think that's what democracy is all about. . . . Heck, no, people wouldn't work as hard. Do you think I would be working hard now if I could be sitting and doing what you are doing now?*
QUESTION: *Would you like to move any closer to equality in pay or do you think people get pretty much what they deserve as it is?*
RICK: *No, I don't think people get what they deserve. I think people deserve more than they are getting. Of course, that depends on the quality of the job. But overall, I think that the base pay in this country should be better than it is.*
LEWIS: *I think that would be unfair, because, if you take a man [who] works with heavy construction, say, with a steel company puttin' up girders and everything for a skyscraper, and then you get those painters that are four hundred feet up in the air rustproofing those girders, or like that, and welding them all together and all. I think he should get more for risking his life than the milkman gets for driving around in the morning delivering milk. So if everybody got paid the same I wouldn't feel like it was fair.*
QUESTION: *Do you think people would work as hard?*
LEWIS: *Naw!*
QUESTION: *Would you like to move any closer to equality in pay or do you think people pretty much get what they deserve?*
LEWIS: *I'd like to see it move a little bit closer to the other—a little. But, uh, I'd like to see it move a little closer together so I could afford a few more things than I can now. Not so I could be just like him.* [Lewis is a bit more concerned solely with his own position than are Brent or Rick. He is much less enthusiastic about redistributive movements.]

Jim had said earlier that he wanted to see everybody made "equal to what they should get paid for the job they're doing." It turns out that, like Brent, he meant equal pay for equal work with some minimal level so that people are "able to enjoy living."

JIM: *I wouldn't like that [equal incomes]. I don't think there would be the same amount of initiative. Cause they would think, "Hey, I'm going to get the same amount he's getting, whether I do a good job or a bad job," you know. Plus, I think when people. . . , when a man acquires an education and works and studies, and when he goes to school. I don't think it would be fair for him to receive the same wages as a man who never went to school receives, that never tried to better hisself. Then what would be the reason for going to school? What would be the reason for being a doctor, when you could be making the same amount working as a ditch digger, you know.*

Paul hinted early in the interview, in talking about the major problems facing America, that he would like to see wealth in the country more evenly distributed. Later, when asked specifically about equal wages for all, he took a position similar to those discussed above, calling for some redistribution but not perfect equality.

PAUL: *I feel that, uh, people have gotten too carried away with the kinds of profits they have been making. . . . Then, like I said while ago, you look, here's the oil companies and General Motors making huge profits, more than they have ever made. It is going somewhere, but it is sure not going to the people. We need to get that straightened out. . . . But the major thing I think we have to face is kinda dividing the money a little more evenly than it is now. I think right now it's big industry versus everybody else.*

QUESTION: *How would you feel about the same incomes for all jobs?*

PAUL: *Well, I don't think that would be too cool, because it would take away from any desire for ambition. It would, uh, it would ruin just what America stands for, you know, the chance to advance. I mean, certainly poor people need to make more. Some of the rich might not need to make so much. But still, there needs to be something that gives people the desire to do better . . . it would take away from dreams and ambition. Like, why work your tail off to be a doctor if you can make as much just doing nothin' more than driving a forklift [this is Paul's job at Multicorp] or even digging a ditch. . . . But like some people who make $100,000 a year earn it. Like, if a man comes up with some ingenious invention or somethin' or some guy is running a corporation and he is able to get them through for the least cost and just get everything, you know, perfect as can be, he's earning every cent of his money. And a guy's goofin' off doesn't need to make as much.*

ROY: *If I do a better job than someone else does I don't think they should make as much as I do. Just like the opposite, if they done more than I do, I wouldn't expect to get as much pay as they do. [Roy also favors a moderate redistribution movement. He called for the government to give tax rebates to the poor rather than to the rich and to make sure corporations all pay taxes.]*

MELVIN: *That [equal incomes] would not be very good. Someone might have a harder job. [He feels that people might not work as hard and favors some movement toward equality, though his short answer revealed a notable lack of enthusiasm.]*

KEVIN: *I don't think that would be very good because some jobs are harder than others. Some jobs are harder than others and you just deserve more pay and that is all there is to it. . . . I don't think people would work as hard. I don't think I would. If a man comes over there and learns my job and makes a lot less than I do, then I don't think that would be fair. I mean, I work hard and put in [for] the man a good day's work. I get paid pretty fair. But I think I deserve more. [Kevin is unable to understand what is meant by a movement toward greater equality in wages. He insisted that everything would be okay if prices were lower than they are now. He feels that people in jobs like his deserve more pay—that workers are generally underpaid—indicating some support for redistribution.]*

JUNIOR: *I wouldn't feel it was fair. Cause a person that's really working ought to get more than a person that's just there eight hours a day standing there and looking at you just to get a paycheck. I think the person who works and shows the company he wants to do something for 'em and at least help himself out to get his own self a raise ought to get more money than the man that's standing down there doing a nothing job and getting the same pay. I know I wouldn't like it.*

As we learned earlier, Junior is very contemptuous of the lack of industriousness of his fellow workers and feels that most are paid about what they deserve. The only redistribution he favors is of opportunities and of rewards for those few like himself who are conscientious and competent workers.

Terry, the gun fancier, like Junior, is disturbed by inequalities created by inherited wealth and opportunities. Unlike Junior, he is enthusiastic about redistributing wealth. He came close to accepting the idea of equal pay for all, but rejected it as unfair when he confronted the question directly.

QUESTION: *What does the phrase "all men are created equal" mean to you?*

TERRY: *I guess it means that all men are created equal but that some of them are created with silver spoons in their mouths and they are more well off than others. I feel like, you know, if everybody was about equal in pay and stuff like that, you know, I feel it would be a whole lot better. Course, if they did, if it was like that, I don't reckon people would have too many places to work at, you know. People that owned the fac-*

tories, who have all the money. If they had the same pay as the middle class, they couldn't own 'em. So I don't know. [He laughed.]

QUESTION: How would you feel if everyone did receive the same income no matter what their job was?

TERRY: I figure that wouldn't be right, cause, I mean, a person that just swept the floors shouldn't make $50,000 a year just like a big executive, I guess. It wouldn't be right. Why should a person go to school and get all of that education if a person could be a second grade dropout and make the same money?

QUESTION: How would you feel about making incomes more equal than they are now?

TERRY: Well, I believe a person would work harder for a person that didn't have as much income as they would for a person that had [a great deal more]. Say, if you are working for a person and he has more income than you, say, not that much more—he would work more for him than he would for a man that had millions of dollars. He wouldn't waste as much material doing the work, you know. Well, if a person is working for a man that has millions of dollars who buys the material, if he cuts it wrong, no big deal, you know. If a person is working for a person who is not so rich, you are going to try to get him by as cheaply as you can and make him more so you can make more yourself, and pay more attention to what you're doing. Like Multicorp, you know, they waste more in drawers and tacks than they do down at Johnson's. At Multicorp they might make a hundred drawers extra but at Johnson's they might not make but five. [Terry has just quit his job as a case fitter at Multicorp and moved to Johnson's. He is bitter about management and pay policies at Multicorp.]

Dave's feelings are similar to those of Junior and Lewis. He agreed with the rest of the group that totally equal pay would be unfair and a disincentive for hard work. Any movement toward equality might be desirable, but it would not last because those who do work harder will inevitably end up getting more. He is more positive about the justice of our present system than are either Kevin or Junior.

DAVE: I don't think it would be right. Me out working or you out working just as hard as you can work eight hours a day about to kill yourself [this is a real possibility for Dave because he runs a lathe, one of the more dangerous machines in a furniture plant] and then another fellow over here just counting toothpicks or something making the same amount of money that you are just wouldn't be fair. [He agreed that people would not work as hard.]

QUESTION: How would you feel about moving toward more equal incomes or do you feel people get pretty much what they deserve as it is now?

DAVE: Well, uh, I'd like to see it closer than what it is, but I've got my doubts. There's always going to be your separate classes: your lower, *your middle, and your upper. People get pretty much out of life what they put into it. They make their own life.*

Of the four men who believed equal incomes would be desirable, Mark and John expressed enthusiasm and Eddie and Albert favored the concept only mildly and with uncertainty. Mark expressed some doubts about having equal incomes for all, though his doubts are directed more at feasibility than at desirability. John was the most enthusiastic.

JOHN: *It [equal pay for all workers] would be beautiful. I know that.* [He went on to say that it would be "hard to tell" if people would work as hard, but that it would be nice to take some things away from the rich "who make sure that some people never have nothin'."]

MARK: *Well, I tell you, everybody is spoiled so rotten that it wouldn't work, but Marx had a good idea as far as everybody being paid the same. That won't work now. Not now. Everybody is spoiled. They're too used to making high wages, like a doctor more than a bricklayer. So I think if wages were balanced out, it would be better. I would think so. And so would the economy. . . . Even the president the same.*

QUESTION: *Do you think people would work as hard?*

MARK: *Well, look at China. Everybody over there is making about the same wages. Everybody works hard. They worship their leaders because they get out and work with 'em. Mao did.*

This extremely knowledgeable and radical rhetoric that distinguishes Mark from the other men stems from his brief association with a radical left-wing group. Beneath the radical veneer, however, many of his views are in concord with those of others in the group. In fact, he is one of the most anticommunist of the fifteen, except for his advocacy of the idea of equal incomes!

Eddie, the unambitious do-it-yourselfer, feels that if incomes were equalized at about $15,000 many more people would be helped than hurt, which is fine with him. But he expects that jealousies and suspicion would arise toward anyone who saved and bought things others do not have and that some would work harder and some would not. Albert also sees some problems with the idea, though he could not define them.

ALBERT: *Well, I don't think [equal incomes] would be right. Well, I don't know.* [He pauses.] *I never give that much thought—I guess it would be all right. Well, like at Multicorp. Well, a person that sweeps and cleans up and picks up papers and stuff, just doing little jobs like that. I don't see any reason why they shouldn't make a decent living from doing it. . . . But you might run into problems no matter how you did it.* [Making a "decent living" does not necessarily mean equality, but Albert's words imply support for significant movement toward equality.]

In his study of fifteen blue-collar workers living in New Haven during the 1950s, Lane found that they unanimously rejected the idea of income equality. His analysis concluded that this was more than a mere rejection, but a strong statement of fear of the idea of equal incomes, because the ideal threatened values that were important to the sense of security and self-identity of the men in his group.[12] To some degree, most of the Furntex workers in my small group also fear equality, but there are significant differences.

The first obvious difference is that almost a third of the men in this group find some merit in the idea and are willing at least to consider it. In this sense, they are more open to ideas of social change than were the sample of blue-collar workers of the 1950s.

A more important difference is that these southern workers of the 1970s are much less sure about the justice of the present social structure than were Lane's workers. Lane defined his workers as "traditional man," who finds a sense of security in knowing that the important things are as they should be, even though some daily suffering may be experienced. They did not favor even moderate redistribution of wealth: "The feudal serf, the Polish peasant, the Mexican peon believed that theirs was a moral and 'natural order'—so also the American working man. . . . And almost none followed up the suggestion that some equalization of income, if not complete equality, would be desirable. The fact of the matter is that these men, by and large, prefer an inegalitarian society, and even prefer a society graced by some men of great wealth." [13]

A few of the workers in my group feel that they and most other men get pretty much what they deserve. A few feel that others get what they deserve but they themselves have been treated unjustly. Most feel that though some of the very poor may suffer poverty because they lack moral virtue and a willingness to work, they themselves and other workers (sometimes just other workers) deserve a greater share of wealth than they receive.

Albert showed a good deal of compassion in talking about the just desert of those who work and do the best they are able.

ALBERT: *Well, I would like to see everybody living—well, I figure that I live below average. I figure that if everybody could live, I guess you might say, below average, it might be all right. But you have people that live way below me, the way I do. I mean, I live in a four-room house. It's not much, but I can look at people that don't have what I have, you know. If people could live as average as I live, I think things would go a lot better. I think you'd still have people that still want to live as high as the Filburns [a wealthy local family] or as high as, you know, but I think if people could come up to a level where they could kind of live with it, things would be better.*

Lane suggests that workingmen reject equal incomes or any movement toward more egalitarian incomes partly because it threatens their self-identity. Were incomes to be made more equal, then the day-to-day struggle these men pursue would become meaningless. This struggle is central to the self-identity and esteem of the worker. It gives him a sense of worth and is one of his few sources of pleasure.

Lane found his workers to be generally grim and stoic and to have few pleasures outside of material consumption. He described them as having "sacrificed their hedonistic inclination, given up good times, and expended their energy and resources in order to achieve and maintain their present tenuous hold on respectability and middle status." He reported that some could not remember having had a good time out in the evening "for ten or fifteen years" and what good times they did report were not "remarkable for their spontaneous fun and enjoyment of life." [14]

As we have seen, the furniture workers in my group based a good deal of their pride and self-esteem on the belief that one makes it on his own, that one is relatively independent of others, that one is able "to get by," as Albert put it. In short, the men in this group gain self-respect through the belief that they achieve the values of individualism. But this pleasure is not the only joy in their lives. They enjoy activities with friends and family, especially with family. All, except for Brent and Rick, remembered having a good time out in the evening within the past six months. Albert, Jim, Lewis, and Paul had been to parties, dancing, or outings with their wives. John goes bowling with his wife every week and sometimes more often. Kevin had gone skating with his wife the previous week. Roy took his family out to eat and for a drive (a luxury since they own no car and must borrow one). Dave, Terry, and Melvin had been hunting in the past few weeks. Mark went over to his girl friend's house, listened to records, and talked. Eddie was simply "out" with a friend. These experiences, unlike those of Lane's group, are for the most part spontaneous and appear to reflect a real enjoyment of life. Only Junior seemed notably lacking in joy and spontaneity. He harbors a good deal of hostility toward everyone, including himself, and remembers the last good time as about six months ago when he and his wife went out to dinner to celebrate an anniversary. The next time they attempted a dinner out their little girl accompanied them, and the evening was spoiled when Junior lost his temper over her misbehavior. Brent and Rick find good times few and far between because both are lonely bachelors, though both frequently go to parties.

Psychological dependence on their modest material achievements tied Lane's men to support the existing reward structure in our society. My group found sufficient pleasures in their leisure time and family endeavors to make redistribution of wealth and status less relevant. But the end result is the same—little or no action supporting redistribution.

Values of family and pleasurable activities that replace material and work values may be seen to be part of what Parkin calls a "subordinate value system." He describes that system as "essentially *accommodative*; that is to say its representation of the class structure and inequality emphasizes various modes of adaption, rather than either full endorsement of, or opposition to, the status quo." [15] Emphasis on family and leisure activities is a value that serves to accommodate the existing reward structure by offering alternative satisfactions. This raises the question of the salience of the injustice of the reward structure for these men, which will be considered in the conclusion of the discussion of the wage issue.

Achievement

One important value shared by both the New Haven workers of the 1950s and southern furniture workers of the 1970s is belief in individual achievement. This value was also shared by the upper-middle-class Los Angeles suburbanites in Lamb's study of twelve families.[16] The principle that achievements should be rewarded is a fundamental value in what can loosely be called the American ideology. Time after time, the workers of Furntex affirmed the value of achievement in their rejection of absolute equality of income. They, like northern workers and western suburbanites, reject equality of result because, in Lane's words, "[it] would deprive people of the goal in life."[17]

Just as do Lane's workers, the men of Furntex get some measure of satisfaction in their modest fruits of achievements. Most of them feel they are doing somewhat better than did their parents. Paul is the only significant exception in that he is downwardly mobile and recognizes that fact.

Like the workers of New Haven, they recognize education as an important key to success, though they are not quite so certain about the inevitability of the relationship. Several mentioned that college graduates are working in the plants making no more money than they make. Nevertheless, they speak as though education is important. Nearly all claimed that they will push their children to complete school. Six of these workers are either planning to further their own education or are already doing so on a part-time basis.

Alternative Modes of Action to Implement Redistribution

Given that these men feel there is injustice in the reward system in Furntex, one wonders how they think this injustice could be resolved. In this section, we shall consider three possible modes of potential action: labor unions, political action, and personal action.

North Carolina has the second lowest percentage of unionized workers of any state in the nation.[18] Union organizing drives have always met stiff opposition in the state both from business and from many workers. Social institutions such as the church have been used to rally opposition against unionization, which was often labeled ungodly and communistic.[19] The sense of individual pride that leads men to believe they can make it on their own often has functioned to make collective action unthinkable and unworkable. But if feelings of relative deprivation caused by low wages are as strong in North Carolina and in the South as a whole as they are in the group of young furniture workers interviewed in this study, the state could be at the dawn of a period of significant union growth as these younger men replace older members of the work force.

Each of the men in the small group was asked several questions about unions. When asked whether unions would help increase the pay and benefits of workers around Furntex, all but three thought they would. Dave, who is the member of the group most opposed to unions, feels that any increases in pay would merely be consumed by union dues. Eddie agreed that dues would consume any extra wages. Terry, who at one time worked at a small unionized furniture plant in Furntex that no longer exists, does not believe that unions would work well in the furniture industry because wages were no higher at that plant than at any other in town.

Junior also worked at the unionized plant. He stipulates that to be of any help, a union would have to be "a real union and not just a little ole pretend-to-be [union]. If they was a big powerful union they could get $4 and $5 and $6 an hour for an experienced furniture worker."

The men were asked whether they thought they might join a union if an organizational effort were made at their plant. Of the fifteen, six indicated that they would definitely support a union, four that they would lean toward joining, one leaned away from unions, and four were definitely opposed. On the negative side, Terry, Dave, and Eddie were joined by Lewis, who reasoned that unionization would increase wages, but would not ultimately help the workers because then prices would increase.

Even though only Lewis used this rationale to explain his opposition to unions, the belief that price increases in local stores are directly connected to local general pay raises is widespread. The belief borders on a conspiracy theory that the economic system is arranged so that workers can never get ahead. Junior, who is one of the most distrusting and generally hostile members of the group, actually believes that local grocery stores know about pay raises a day in advance and have their employees stay up all night before the wage increase is publicly announced raising prices on all the goods in the store.

All the men were asked how their fellow workers feel about unions and whether they would support a unionization movement. Not surprisingly, most project their own feelings on their coworkers, expecting them to make about the same decision. Only Eddie differs here. He leans against a union himself because he thinks his own wages are pretty fair, but he assumes that other workers would probably favor unions because their wages are lower than his.

Wages and fringe benefits were not the only concerns these workers related to unions. Roy and John mentioned job security as a reason for supporting unions. Junior and Terry believe that unions would protect the worker from being made to do someone else's job when his own work is completed. Terry is particularly bitter toward Multicorp for their attempt to force cabinet room workers, who often wear relatively good clothes to work, to work in the finishing department when their own work is completed, where their clothes get stained.

One of the questions asked was whether older workers are more or less favorably disposed toward unions. Most generally feel older workers are more opposed. Rick, however, said that his own opinion on this question has changed. His explanation indicates a good deal of insight as well as a measure of compassion and understanding.

RICK: *If you had asked me this five years ago, I would have said that it's mostly older ones that are against them, but since I've returned since last year [from New York], I have found that we've got a good mixture. As a matter of fact, there is a lot of people that wants it, but they are not coming out in the open and saying it because of their jobs, right now. They're afraid of losing their jobs. Younger workers would talk about unions, but the older guys would not right out in the open. But they would talk about their jobs and conditions in a way that you would know that they were on your side. As a matter of fact, that is something that you got to look out for now, when you start talking about union. Cause you see an older guy, he's got a lot of debt, you know. He's buying a home and all, and he's not going to come out and say: "I want a union!" cause he know that might be his job. But a young guy like me, who knows he can go somewhere else and get a job, he might say it. But a lot of 'em really do want a union. Because they see they getting used. A lot of them beginning to wake up to that now. A young guy get a job doing the same thing an older guy does and they pay him the same thing. Well, an old guy, he resent that. They'll say, "Years ago, we never really got this—I don't know what is happening—changes is comin' about now." You see, in my opinion, in actuality, what they is really speaking about is unions. You see, a lot of them really don't know. They say "no" but they really don't know. But they is speaking about unions, because that is basically what a union is all about: job upgrading and job seniority and all of this.*

The next question concerned what would happen if an employee were openly to promote unions at his place of work. With the exception of Terry, who thinks management does not care because they "know" that unions are ineffective in small furniture plants such as Johnson's, and Melvin, who has never talked about unions, the answer reflected universal fear. "They would get rid of him." "I think they would find themselves out looking for a job." "Other workers would tell the management, and he would be dismissed." "I think that if it got as far as up at the front office there would be a little trouble. Maybe they would put him on a rougher job or somethin' . . . somethin' that would kinda drive 'em away." "You would have to go!" "I think he'd have to have a lot of money in the bank and get up early in the morning so he could be the first one in the unemployment line." "They would try to fire us." "I feel I'd be fired." "They'd probably get rid of you."

This fear was not groundless—many claimed to know of actual cases where someone lost his job because he talked about starting a union. Rick claimed that those who had worked at the small furniture plant in Furntex that had been unionized had difficulty securing work in other plants. This is a real fear whether or not it is justified on objective grounds. Several of the men were hesitant to discuss unions at all. Another called it a "very touchy subject." They seem honestly to believe that they would lose their jobs were they actively to support a union.

If the expressed fear accurately reflects their feelings, then the claims that they would support a union must be accepted with some skepticism. It seems unlikely that they would support any unionization effort unless they felt quite certain that it would succeed. As Rick astutely pointed out, family responsibilities and debts can be a powerful inhibiting factor. Should a union ever succeed in organizing in any of the large existing plants, the old adage that "nothing succeeds like success" might well be applicable. But the barrier of fear will be difficult to overcome. For the purpose of our discussion here, unionization is not a realistic means by which these men may right the felt injustice of their wages. For the present, the only impact unionization has on them is a spillover of increased wages and benefits from other higher paying industries that locate in the area.

A second possible means by which to bring justice to the reward system might be to engage in politics. This possibility goes directly to the heart of my central question of the potential for a populist-type political coalition. If such a coalition is to be formed around the issue of increased wages for the workingman, he must first see politics and government as salient to the issue of wages (even if neither is presently working to right the perceived wrongs).

A number of my questions were structured so as to give these fifteen workers an opportunity to relate politics and government to a more equal distribution of wages. When low wages were mentioned as a problem facing the nation, state, or community, each was asked what government could do to solve the problem. The issue also arose in discussions of electoral preferences, differences between the political parties, and ways government affects family and work.

In examining the content of our conversations on these questions and on a few others that also relate politics to wages, a noteworthy relationship emerges. Five of the fifteen men directly relate perceived differences between the political parties to a more equitable distribution of wages. They also volunteered this issue as an important difference between Ford and Carter in 1976. None of the others perceived party or candidate differences in 1976 as directly relevant to this issue. The five who did are the same five who voted in the 1976 election (Paul, Jim, Kevin, Rick, and Brent). All voted for Carter.

Paul and Jim both associate Republicans with rich people and with big business and feel that the Democrats and Carter will do more to help working people. Jim believes that more Democratic politicians come from poor or working-class families and therefore are more likely to empathize with the lower class. The two blacks who voted in 1976, Rick and Brent, echoed similar sentiments except that they emphasized blacks as well as the poor and working classes. Perhaps the clearest statement on the salience of politics and political parties was offered by Kevin. He feels that the tax structure functions to keep the workingman poor while protecting the rich, but harbors a strong faith that the Democrats and Jimmy Carter can increase the wages of working people through tax reform.

KEVIN: *I'd just say taxes. Oh, yeah, that's a good one there. During all this presidential thing, you know, changing presidents and all. I was watching the presidential rebates [sic] and all. The way it looks, the way Carter said—that's the man I voted for—the way he says, we're getting gypped, you know. . . . The way I look at it, the poor man is getting the bad end of the deal and that's me! Any poor man that votes for the Republican party has to be crazy in my book. You know, if I was rich and made a lot of money I probably would vote Republican because it would save me money. A man making twenty or thirty thousand dollars a year, he don't have to pay as much in taxes as I do. Just like these big companies and all. They might turn around and build a big park or something and then not have to pay nothing in taxes! They get out of it altogether. Then I'm turning around and having to pay all that money.*

Later, Kevin again linked his electoral choice to the issue of wealth distribution, saying, "I think he'll [Carter] make it better for the poor people. And he's going to make the economy better. . . ." The other four members of the group who chose to engage in politics by voting in 1976 would probably agree with both of Kevin's statements.

Several of the others view government as salient with respect to their wages via taxes, or inflation, or the economy, but they generally did not see any difference in how the parties or the candidates in 1976 would deal with these issues. Of these other ten men, only Mark saw any difference between the parties on the issue of taxes, feeling that the Democrats generally support lower taxes. But he was more concerned with moral issues, such as prohibition, and had heard that Carter raised taxes in Georgia while governor, so taxes were not a clear-cut issue for him in 1976.

Analysis of the content of the interviews uncovered an important element that helps to explain voting participation. Its strength relative to other factors will be considered in the section on the general question of political participation. These five men voted because they strongly felt that (1) net wages (after taxes) of working people are unfair, (2) government does and can have an impact on wage levels, and (3) there was a difference between the political parties and their presidential candidates of 1976 on this issue. These men are not simply voters; they are *issue-oriented* voters. They fulfill the prerequisites for issue voting outlined by Angus Campbell and his associates in their classic study *The American Voter*. They have an opinion on an issue, have some idea of government policy on that issue, perceive differences between parties and candidates on that issue, and care enough about the issue to make it relevant to their voting choice.[20] In this case, they may well have cared enough about the issue that it was responsible for their decision to vote at all. In comparing these five voters with the ten who did not vote in 1976, the important difference relative to our discussion of political action to implement income redistribution is that the voters perceived a choice between parties and candidates that is relevant to this issue. Merely favoring relatively higher wages for workers is not a sufficient condition for electoral political activity because most in the group favor some movement toward greater wage equality.

Some form of personal action is the way most of the members of the group attempt to resolve the felt injustice of the wage structure in Furntex. Since they all believe in the value of achievement, one obvious way to attempt to improve their present condition is to strive for greater achievement and the greater rewards that ostensibly should follow.

Several of the members of the group have chosen this tack. Education is seen as one means. Jim and Terry are taking night courses that they expect will enable them to get higher paying jobs outside the furniture industry. Paul, Rick, and Mark are planning to return to school and make an upward exit from furniture work.

Some are attempting to achieve upward mobility within the industry. Kevin believes his chances to advance in furniture production are good if he works hard to prove himself and is ready to accept a transfer if that means a promotion into the supervisory ranks. He is, however, showing some signs of impatience—he feels that his two years of hard work already should have brought him some advancement. But he is only twenty years old and still has considerable patience. "The way the man's been telling me is that you don't get opportunities over night."

Junior, who is ten years older, has been working in furniture longer and also strives for upward mobility within the industry but is much less patient and much more bitter. He has left job after job when he felt that increased achievement on his part did not lead to increased pay from the company or to promotion. He is a man caught in a dilemma that casts a dark shadow of unhappiness, frustration, and randomly directed anger in all corners of his life. He regards the value of reward based on individual achievement as a sham and a cruel hoax played upon the working class. Yet he stubbornly refuses to abandon it and continues in an almost self-fulfilling way to enrage himself battering against walls he knows he cannot climb.

Several live in an uneasy and uncomfortable balance between a belief in achievement and upward mobility in their work and the realization that hard work over many years may not pay off. Lewis mentioned a man he works with who has labored for Multicorp for forty years but has nothing to show for his work. Lewis hopes that his own present job is just a "stepping stone," but admitted that he may be fooling himself. He and others (Roy, Albert, and Brent) move from company to company for very modest hourly wage increases. Now that he has turned eighteen, Melvin will likely follow suit.

Several of these men exhibit an even more uncomfortable partial acceptance of their position in society. Albert tells himself that he has done about as well as anyone with his limited abilities can do and is content merely to "get by." Roy would like a few "luxuries" like a motorcycle, car, and house of his own, but claimed happiness in having a loving wife and family. Brent lives in a state of limbo between dreams that something will happen to change his life radically and the realization that these are merely dreams. Eddie rationalizes that he is well paid and cannot complain, yet he is deeply disappointed in himself because he was unable comfortably to cope with the pressures and responsibility of the management position he held for a short period at Multicorp.

Only two members of the group, John and Dave, seem to have come to a fairly comfortable acceptance of the static nature of their present economic condition. Both are among the highest paid members of the group, and both feel that relative to most other workers they do pretty well. Both have most of the material things they want and see themselves in the same job in the future.

Of the three alternative modes of potential action, some type of personal action is the dominant choice for the men in this small group of furniture workers. They either try to break out of the furniture industry, hope to advance within it, or come to an uneasy acceptance of their status and lower their expectations. They find alternative satisfactions to economic status either in family life or in unfulfilled dreams. Only a few see partisan political action as relevant to their problem, and that action is largely limited to the simple act of voting.

None of these conclusions should be surprising. For, as we have seen, these men embrace individualism as a central value and have little thought of or experience in collective action beyond family. In their experience, socializing institutions that teach partisan collective action for redistribution of wages are nonexistent or biased against such action. There are few labor unions in the area and none in their places of work. The Democratic party of the state avoids such dangerous issues as redistribution. Only George Wallace and some faint echoes from the national Democratic party and Jimmy Carter that touch upon a greater share of wealth and justice for working people have reached the hearing of a few of these men. As we shall see, the most significant politically socializing institution in their lives is the church, and it has emphasized issues that are either irrelevant to or contrary to any movement toward greater equality in wages. It is amazing that even a third of these men voted and that their voting choice was molded by considerations of economic redistribution.

Salience of the Wage Issue: Summary

Though these workers do not want a system of perfect equality in wages, they do feel that present working-class wages are too low, at least in the South. They would support some movement toward greater equality in wages as long as individual merit and responsibility were still rewarded. Even as ill-defined as this issue is in national politics, a significant proportion of them cited the issue as a determinant in their voting activities in 1976. Were partisan choices more clearly defined on this issue, a good many more of them might perceive voting as a relevant activity, especially if the costs of voting were lowered by such reforms as automatic voter registration.

A great number of pitfalls jeopardize this analysis, such as the possible low salience of the wage distribution issue (it may be much less important than other issues such as race or morality) and the difficulty of defining the issue to avoid regional resentments or violation of other values such as belief in reward based on individual merit.

As we have already noted, the five members of the group who voted volunteered rationales related to redistributive justice in explaining their partisan preferences. We might conclude that these volunteered comments are proof of the high salience of this issue, but we can draw no firm conclusions from their answers to questions where *I* rather than *they* raised the issue in asking about movement toward greater equality in wages. Instead, we must look at the problems and issues they themselves define.

Each was asked a series of questions concerning what he thought are the major problems facing his community, state, and nation. Thirteen of the fifteen men volunteered issue concerns directly related to wages. Six of them are concerned that high inflation is eating up all wage increases. Eight said unemployment is a major problem facing society. Ten volunteered low wages as a major problem, the very issue with which we are concerned. Five even volunteered the issue of the need for a more equitable distribution of wealth.

The only single issue that was raised more often than wages was crime and safety, which was mentioned by twelve of the men. This does not appear to be as potent an issue as wages, however, since most often crime was mentioned as being less of a problem in Furntex than in other areas. Indeed, the belief that there is relatively less crime in Furntex than elsewhere is a mainspring of community pride and identification.

If we include other issues volunteered and defined by these men that are also related to more equitable distribution of wages, such as unions (mentioned by two), energy (six), housing (four), job security (one), better community facilities for working people (seven), poverty (four), and elite control of society (seven), we find that the issue of wages is directly or indirectly a concern of every member of the sample. This statement cannot be made for any other issue they defined: race-related issues (mentioned by nine), individual initiative (seven), human compassion and greed (six), morality issues (six), Watergate and Nixon's pardon (five), national defense (four), health care (four), too much politics (four), government trust and scandals (four), Vietnam (three), women's liberation (three), excessive government control (three), foreign policy (two), foreign aid (two), amnesty (one), homosexuality (one), the Russian wheat deal (one), and weather—Melvin is angry that the government does not do a better job in forecasting. Thus it would seem accurate to conclude that the issue of wages and concerns related to relatively greater wages for working people is as salient as any for these workers of Furntex. Were these men to vote and make their voting choice on the basis of issue considerations, the political adage that "people vote their pocketbooks" might well apply.

Because these men do not view themselves as politically concerned public men and because they largely pursue private familial values, the strongest statement that can be made concerning the wage issue is that it has *potential* power. But the power of the issue lies dormant as long as these men view politics as irrelevant.

Health Care

In outlining a strategy for electing populist-type candidates in the South, Clotfelter and Hamilton argue that health care is a good potential issue for candidates for national office because "middle and lower-middle-income groups . . . believe that they are not being cared for properly."[21] The workers of Furntex share this belief. They compassionately feel others also suffer, and they are willing to support federal programs to achieve universal health care.

Though this study treats health care as an issue separate from wages, the separation may be somewhat artificial. Poor health and medical costs are really negative wages. Corporate and elite targets of resentment about low wages can also be targets of resentment about poor health care. In the minds of these men, doctors are not far removed from lawyers—both are businessmen who use their professional titles to get rich at their expense. Companies that do not pay workers well may also provide inadequate health insurance or try to avoid paying valid claims made by workers.

Though only four men volunteered health care as an important issue, the emotion with which these men responded to questions about national health care led me to conclude that it is a highly salient issue.

Looking first at the item in the economic liberalism index stating that the "government in Washington ought to help all people get doctors and hospital care at low cost," we find that all members of the group, save Lewis, who slightly disagreed, respond on the "agree" side of the scale (five "strongly agree," eight "agree," and Eddie would only "slightly agree"). Though the differences are small and would not be statistically significant, the average score on this item was higher than on any other for the group as a whole. Significant to the ear of this listener were the relatively firmer and more definite statements of agreement on the health care item.

Earlier in the interviews, I asked a series of open-ended questions dealing with the issue of national health care. The questioning began by asking the men how they feel about the existing Medicare system. This was followed by a comment that some people are talking about expanding the system into a national health care system covering everybody financed from general tax revenues. They were asked how they would feel about this sort of action. Then the question of how far such a plan should go was broached. The men were asked if it should go so far as to make doctors government employees with salaries fixed by law. Finally, they were told that such a movement toward national health care might be labeled as "socialism" by many people. They were asked if this would bother them. These last two questions were added after the interviews had already begun and therefore were not asked of the first three workers interviewed.

The present Medicare system that provides aid to older people in paying for medical care received widespread and strong support from these workers. All except Terry, Melvin, and Roy, to whom the system had to be explained, have generally accurate knowledge of the Medicare system. Several are personally aware of the system, mentioning that it has helped their parents or grandparents. Even Lewis, who is one of two members of the group to reject the concept of national health care, finds merit in Medicare.

LEWIS: *I think that's a pretty good thing, Medicare. I think that's all right, uh, I feel like no matter how technologically advanced you get, or, uh, how socially far you advance, I feel like there is still a need to take care of the old people. I feel like that should be a major concern, taking care of the old people.*

John, the other member of the group who rejects national health care, also embraces Medicare. His statement indicates a good deal of empathy; he mentioned that he, too, will get old someday and may need this kind of help to avoid too great a strain on his savings. Ability to look into the future and see oneself as old and in need of help was not uncommon. These men have no illusions of eternal youth or good health. The flavor of their comments is realistic in assessing their own futures. Jim best expresses this feeling.

JIM: *Maybe things are going smooth right now and maybe this is the majority of the people that are not having problems like this. But I'm sayin' that some day it's gonna happen. I mean it's inevitable you're gonna get sick and you're gonna get sick enough to die—maybe cancer or somethin'!*

The only dissatisfactions expressed about the Medicare system are that it is inadequate—it should do more. Junior, whose life is practically defined by medical problems over four generations from memories of his grandmother's suffering through his own migraine headaches to his baby's poor health, feels that Medicare does not pay enough. Jim passionately argued that we have let our old people down in providing benefits that are sufficient only to keep them in depressing and dehumanizing rest homes he visits with groups from his church.

JIM: *I believe that in the United States, the government, I don't know whose fault it is. But I believe we've let down our elderly people. I believe we've really hurt 'em. Not only financially, but as far as feelin' they're really worth something. I go to a rest home, maybe once every two or three months, a kind of mission of our church. We go out there and maybe sing three or four songs and read some scripture. And it's really disheartening to see these people, man. They really look like life's really passed them by. And who really cares, you know. Some of them have mental disorders, you know, and they're not really there. But some* *of them are in fine shape. And they still have that look of despair, like "who's gonna take care of me? Why am I here anyway?" And I believe that it's the fault of the government many times that these people don't have enough money to live on. If a lot of these people in these rest homes had the money to live, they wouldn't be in rest homes. That's the truth. They would be in an apartment by themselves and be quite satisfied and maybe have friends to come in and all like this. But they can't do that cause they don't make but maybe $40 a month off the government, and they can't do that cause they gotta pay these bills—they've got a pill to take every day and it costs $25 a month to get them pills. That leaves 'em $15 and they've gotta eat. I've read about old people that eat dog food—they'll just go and buy dog food! And, uh, this is bad, cause some day we're gonna get old [another note of realistic empathy].*

With only a few exceptions, the basis for this strong support of government-provided medical aid for the elderly lay in a realistic sense of empathy and in a belief that such care is more a matter of simple right than merit, though the idea of merit is not totally absent. All of these men believe that retired people deserve equally good medical care regardless of their levels of individual achievement while working. There may be an assumption that the elderly on Medicare did work before they retired, though none specifically stipulated a work requirement. Dave came closest to making this a requirement while at the same time showing considerable compassion.

DAVE: *I think it is good because, if, uh, I feel that if a person can work at the age of sixty-two or sixty-five or whichever one he's able to retire at, he's worked that long and I think he deserves it. . . . I don't think elderly people gets half as much time and being with than what they really ought to be, cause I visited several rest homes and it's just—I don't see how I could live in one. . . . I have a friend that I run around with and do a lot of hunting and fishing with and he's got grandparents in there, both of 'em. And it's really bad, I mean, the way the elderly people's treated.*

Eddie and others were less clear about any lifetime of work prerequisite.

EDDIE: *Well, I hadn't looked into it on any large scale, but grandfather has it and it seems to help him on his hospital bills and all. Now, who is payin' for it to start from, I reckon it's taxpayers. Really, I think that after a person gets so old, he should have something to fall back on, the confidence that it would be there if they needed it. I would have to say that right now I would be for it [Medicare].*
KEVIN: *I think it's [Medicare] just fine, and I don't mind paying tax money to that. It's good for those who can't help themselves.*
MARK: *That's a good thing cause a lot of these old people can't take*

care of theirself and they're [not] even getting enough on social security
to pay off the medical bills.
    PAUL: I think it is a good thing, because a lot of people who are older
and on fixed incomes can't afford medical care and they do need help
and it ought to be there for 'em.

It may be somewhat surprising that these men who so strongly embrace
the values of individual achievement and meritocracy do not more
closely tie medical care for the aged to individual merit. They seem to
view retirement as the time when competition is over and rewards are no
longer relevant to competition. In this sense, they are like the middle-
class Los Angeles suburbanites studied by Karl Lamb: "When the athletes
have hung up their track shoes, government concern again becomes appropriate: support for pensions and medical care for the elderly are welcomed. Some might say that a lifetime spent in the race, regardless of the
order of finish, earns a modicum of comfort in old age."[22]
    Even more surprising is the finding that, unlike Lamb's middle-class
Americans, these working-class southerners who share the belief in individualism and reward based on merit do not shy away from a national
health care system on the grounds that it may violate individualism. All
except Lewis and John endorse the principle of national health care. In
fact, most of them verbally support radical and far-reaching systems of national health care, even to the point of making doctors government employees. They believe from their own experience and what they see in the
lives of others that the need is so great that the principle of merit is irrelevant. Poor health is a matter of chance and may strike anyone, so sharing
the burden of cost makes more sense than placing it upon the unlucky
individual, be he rich or poor. Since an individual does not earn good or
ill health, why should he bear the costs alone? Another feeling that comes
through even more strongly is anger directed toward doctors and the present health care delivery system. The personally experienced and shared
delay of treatment in hospitals and emergency rooms while having to
prove ability to pay has not been accepted as a fact of life. These horror
stories have been perceived as lessons of injustice. Incidents where doctors and health care personnel acted more like businessmen than caring
humanitarians have eroded the special status that long insulated them in
public opinion against the threat of government regulation.

    BRENT: If things keep, if inflation keeps snowballin' you know, bigger
and bigger and your salary still remains the same so you get a, not necessarily a terminal type of illness, but you get some type of cancer, and
you got to stay in the hospital maybe half a year or a whole year at a
time. Your insurance is going to run out, I mean if you have any. Your
savings, I mean it's been rich people more or less exhausted all their
money trying to—trying to live.
    DAVE: They's a lot of people that, say, below average pay of what
average people get paid that has to go to the doctor and just really can't
afford paying it all their self. I think, it wouldn't break my heart if they

put doctors on government pay—not a bit. . . . I've been in Veteran's Hospital in Salisbury several times for the last three months to see a friend. He went in there for alcohol but there is a lot of people down there that has got holes blowed in them from bombs, been shot, and they don't get half the medication they ought to get. [His voice was rising in anger.] The last time I was in there, they had wrote a letter to Congress asking for more medication and for more help. They wrote to several congressmen, and uh, they were even thinking of writing to the president. . . .

JUNIOR: *They could do that [national health care] with all the money they waste up there on moon shots. That'd be fine there. I've got a lot of insurance myself, and it just seems like it don't never pay all the whole entire bill. You've got to dig money out of your pocket.*

QUESTION: *Should it go to the point where all doctors are government employees with fixed salaries?*

JUNIOR: *Yeah, because a lot of people, say, the wife tries and the little kids are sick and the daddy, he's a drunk and he wastes their money and they ain't got no insurance. I mean maybe the momma gets to the point where she can't help it and she's got to take it [the children] somewhere, and the first thing they ask for is money. And you fill in all those papers. Cause I know I've cussed 'em out at Furntex Hospital a dozen times for the same thing. I throw down the insurance card and I say I [will not] give you the information, you just know I got the insurance. Right there it is, proof that I got the insurance. You just get her [his wife] back there and work on her. If I hadn't of preadmitted my wife, I'd of probably had the law on me then. Cause I had done had her preadmitted [his voice was rising notably], and they wanted us to start the whole paperwork over again. She [the admitting nurse] said she couldn't find it. I said I ain't filling out nothin'. I said she goes up now or I push her upstairs one. Cause she wasn't in labor no time. I went all the way through with her. I took the classes to go all the way through with her just to see what it is like. And that girl didn't appreciate the language I used. Course, I didn't appreciate—I had it on paper that I had her preadmitted. I laid the insurance cards there, and I said you copy all you want to and we'll get her upstairs and then I'll come down here and we'll fill all this stuff out. No! She wanted me to fill it out before they would even roll her upstairs! I know a lot of people try to jump out and not pay their bills and stuff like that. Still yet you've got it and they know it and it's on paper right there in front of 'em, the dates and everything. . . . They ought to send 'em on up and they can just do the paperwork later. But they just act like they got to have that paperwork before you can go up them stairs.*

MARK: *That would be all right [making doctors government employees and fixing their salaries]. England's got it. And from what I have heard, they didn't have any problems. And as far as poor people paying off the hospital rates and everything, you know they set the payments. Like here you have to pay it all. You go to the emergency room, you got to pay before you get fixed up or either die. Socialized medicine is good.*

[He himself had said earlier that national health care sounded like socialized medicine—unusually knowledgeable.] At least you know you gonna be saved if they can save you. And you don't have to set there and write a check while you are bleeding to death. When I went over there when I had this accident and went through a windshield when I was fourteen, I had to set there in the emergency room and I was bleeding and I had to hold a rag up there. [He still bears a long scar across his forehead.] Ambulance took me there and everything and left me on a stretcher and left me there in the emergency room, still bleeding, and, uh, I had to call my parents and everything to get them over there and to pay 'em money before they would take me in there and sew me up. That made me mad, very mad, and my parents mad!

MELVIN: As rich as some of them are, that [making doctors government employees] would be all right also!

Seven of the ten men who were specifically asked if a national health care system should make doctors government employees on fixed salaries approved of the idea. Eddie, Paul, and Rick, who support the principle of national health care, do not wish the system to go that far. Paul, whose wife is a nurse and who is familiar with the beliefs of the medical profession, toyed with the idea and made a curious distinction between essential medical services, from which a doctor should not become rich, and inessential services that are luxuries, from which it is legitimate for doctors to make high profits. When the issue of socialism was raised, he decided that price ceilings may be a more desirable alternative than federally employed doctors.

QUESTION: Should it go to the point where all doctors are government employees with fixed salaries?

PAUL: From what I hear about what some doctors make, ha! My wife works at the hospital in the operating room and, uh, I have my own opinions on doctors, too. Some of 'em make too much and some of 'em don't make enough. Like I know for a fact, Dr. Hipri, in town, I know he's a dentist, but from what I hear he's the highest priced dentist in town. I know my wife had four cavities filled, and it cost her the same thing as it did for me to have thirteen. And I go to Dr. Fair. But, uh, then I hear things like he's [Dr. Hipri] got a new Mercedes and his wife goes to France once a year to buy a new wardrobe. He takes people that have to have their teeth fixed and he charges the heck out of 'em so he can send his wife to France! So if he wanted to live like that he should have gone and been an orthodontist or something where he could have gone and made the money legitimately.

QUESTION: Some say that nationalizing doctors would be socialism. Would that bother you?

PAUL: Doctors ought to be on their own like they are now. But what they charge, the government might ought to put a ceiling on that. The government has a ceiling on the prices of everything, and I don't see why it shouldn't have a ceiling on doctors—what they can charge. Now,

I do know that doctors have to charge a lot more lately cause their mal-practice insurance has gone up. . . . [He blames lawyers.] There ought to be some kind of federal protection for doctors on malpractice.

Rick totally opposes any form of national health care involving govern-ment control over doctors' salaries because it would be inconsistent with his own expressed strong belief in reward based on achievement. He said that nationalizing doctors would be getting "into communism, and com-munism is what this country is against." Rick is bothered by any move-ment toward socialism because he views this as also contrary to the ideals of democracy. He offered an interesting example. Rick, who is black, com-pared two doctors, one graduating from North Carolina A and T, which is a predominantly black college, and one from Duke Medical School. He argued that the graduate of Duke deserves to make a whole lot more sim-ply because Duke is a much better school, and this means that he had to be better to get into that school. He should be rewarded for his merit. "This is incentive—what our system is all about—what makes it work." Rick ended by saying that the nation can move toward a national health care system without entailing the dangers of socialism.

Eddie is perhaps the most interesting case in that his reaction clearly demonstrates the power of labels, such as "socialism," in national de-bates. Eddie moderately endorsed the principle of national health care and proceeded to lambast doctors for making high profits. But when the red-tinted flag of socialism was waved before him, he quickly reversed his position.

QUESTION: *Should it go to the point where doctors are government employees and their salaries are fixed?*

EDDIE: *Well, right now I don't think they should only pick up the doc-tors, they should pick up the lawyers, too! [He laughed.] I think doctors in particular. I could put 'em in a class with lawyers, because [a] law-yer's going to get his sum of money from anything that is settled. And he can even get it worked from both sides. He can get it from both sides. Doctors have, they have the knowledge, and they're charging you for that knowledge, too. I know they spent quite a few years pickin' it up. I can see 'em making a good livin'. The hours that they have to spend now—I don't know that all of 'em spend it—but the few that I know is busy every time you see 'em—they is busy. If they're not makin' hospi-tal calls, they're in the office. I would say they put in a, maybe, fourteen-hour day, average, maybe. They deserve a little extra. But I would say if it would be a good comfortable livin', put a ceilin' on it—dentists in-cluded. Dentists are gettin' outrageous really. It's a fixed thing. You go to the dentist, he takes the X-rays the first time. He makes you an appoint-ment so he can read the X-rays in two or three days. He makes an ap-pointment for you to come back. He charges you for the first visit. He comes back and charges you for what he does. And then if you've got one tooth on this side and you've got one on this [other] one, it's an extra appointment to come back for that. My daughter's at the dentist*

today. It was $22, and I don't know what he done. And she has braces
on her teeth by a different dentist—$1,200 and something dollars! It's
due the ninth of this month, I believe. Well, I'm payin' this dentist in
installments, $35 a month. Well, what he does, there's no cavity work,
no cleanin' her teeth. All he does is adjust her braces. . . . I can sit down
and figure $2,000 for teeth in no time at all!

QUESTION: Some people would say that if we went that far this would
be socialism. Would that bother or worry you?

EDDIE: Well, I reckon I'd have to put myself up there in that doctor's
shoes. In a way it would be. It would be what I say movin' too far out of
line. Because he spent his years—he took his time—he spent his
years—he trained his hands—he trained his mind. It ain't like nothin'
the average person can pick up and do. He should, I reckon, be able to
set his own price. But I don't think he should be in a union or organization where he says that this doctor over here can't charge $3 less for a
tooth than I do. If this doctor over here feels he can fill a tooth for a
dollar and a half, let him do it! Not just get in there where everybody
has to come up at one time. If this is the best dentist over here, or doctor
or lawyer for that matter, if that's the best—say, he's got his ability, if he
can do it, he charge you $10—if you like his work, you want to go to
him, that's fine. But I wouldn't put no cap on it that says that this man
over here can't do the job and maybe just as good for $3 less, or what-
ever. . . . I feel like if they ever moved toward socialism all the—it
wouldn't be just one dentist, it would be all of 'em in the city of
Furntex. . . . Each one of 'em would have a set price, and it would be just
like throwin' it up on the door when you walked in, extracted teeth: $10,
and it would be everyone that you walked in to.

The two members of the group who reject the entire idea of a national
health care system reject it for different reasons. John rejected the idea out
of a deep mistrust of his fellow citizens. He believes that many people
would take advantage of free medical care by going to the doctor for every
little ailment, and he, who goes only when it is really necessary, would
pay in his taxes for the medical bills of all these other people. Lewis's rejection of the idea of national health care is in line with the conservative
view indicated by his low score on the economic liberalism scale. He is
suspicious of any increase in government power.

LEWIS: I wouldn't want that. Cause, I think, uh, I believe if you start
doing that, uh, government might be getting too close to home. They
might be getting their—they've already got their hand in my front door,
you know. I feel like they might [be] slipping in a little bit more and a
little bit more every time they get in a little bit more of doing. But I'd
rather pay my own bills.

Both of the workers who reject national health care are blacks; all the
whites in the group support the idea, at least verbally. Though no firm

conclusions can be drawn that can be generalized to others, we may conclude that within this small group of southern workers, the whites are at least as liberal as the blacks on the issue of health care.

Although the vast majority of these men are dissatisfied with the cost of available health care and dissatisfied with the level of wages provided by their employers, they are, by and large, satisfied with the medical insurance provided them by their employers. A few, like Dave, were notably enthusiastic.

DAVE: *Multicorp is one of the best companies that I have ever seen for that. They have good everything as far as insurance. . . . They're the best company that I have ever seen.*

Most used terms like "okay," "adequate," "pretty fair," or "as good as most" to describe their benefits. It is worth recalling Eddie's statement that wages and benefits, including insurance, for all workers seemed to have "picked up" since some new industries had located in the area. Several of the others might agree with his assessment.

Benefits are in fact improving, even though they may be meager by national standards. Multicorp instituted a retirement plan during the time these interviews were conducted. The personnel manager of Johnson's informed me that medical insurance benefits had been increased and a retirement plan would soon be made available to Johnson's hourly employees.

Despite the general tone of approval of their employers' provision of health care, there was some significant minority dissent. Rick and Mark find the insurance benefits provided by Johnson's totally inadequate. Melvin, who had little to say about any subject, seemed to agree, saying, "I've seen better." Brent believes that Multicorp's program is inadequate for a long illness, though he doubts that any other company in the area is much better.

Junior, who apparently has had more medical problems than anyone else in the group, lodged the most serious complaint. Not only has the health insurance been inadequate to pay for his family medical bills, but companies in Furntex try to avoid paying work-related accident claims in a most unethical fashion. It should be noted that though he generalized, the story he told is not about Johnson's, but about another small company for which he had previously worked.

JUNIOR: *A lot of times you get hurt on the job and they try to bump you off if you're collecting a lot of insurance. We had a boy down there where I used to work at Silver Furniture lose four fingers and half a thumb, and they tried practically everything in the book to get that boy to quit before his insurance check come back so he wouldn't get it. Cause if you're not workin' to the day you get your check, they're not responsible to pay you even if it's twenty or thirty thousand. He got back eighteen thousand. They put every hard job on him that they could to* get him to go. And he struggled through long enough to make it to get that check. And the day he got that check, he quit, which I couldn't blame him. They put him doing jobs they knew he couldn't do.

QUESTION: Did that make you mad?

JUNIOR: It did! I had my hand hurt, which I collected off of insurance, which was not my fault. It was just an accident that happened. It wasn't my fault. It was more or less the equipment's fault. And they didn't want to pay me a simple little old three days for being out of work, and, uh, they wanted to pay my hospital bill gladly, but they didn't want to pay me for being out of work. And they didn't want to give me any kind of compensation or settlement for the hurt to my hand. But I ended up gettin' it, but they made it a little rough for me for a couple of weeks. They knew that workin' with one hand bandaged up was tough. After they paid off and I went back to work with both hands, everything was fine and dandy, but during the time I was with one hand I could tell the treatment they gave me was—they didn't want to pay off. I told 'em my hand my being out of work for three days ought to be worth $500 and they said I'll give you $150 and that's it. I said I wouldn't accept it. So I went and talked to a lawyer and he told me just to go and talk to 'em and tell 'em that I would take it to court if it come to that, and they were glad to write out the check for $500. They didn't want to have to go to court with it cause the lawyer's fee would have jacked the price up to about $3,000 and he probably would have got $700 or $800 out of it and I would have probably gotten $2,200 out of it and it would have took me a year to get it. And at the time I needed the money. I'd been out of work and my hand was bummed up—had to be sewed up three different times cause it busted open three times—had to have stitches three times over again.

For the most part, these men view the issue of health care as separate from the issue of wages. In talking about wages, targets of blame were usually their employers, who are also seen as the elites of the area conspiring to keep higher paying industries out so that wage levels will remain low. Except for an unfair tax structure that penalizes working people (this will be examined in detail in the section on class consciousness), the national government has little to do with wages. Health care is seen as a different issue. Employers and local elites (except for doctors and hospital administrators) are not held to blame, except when they renege on promises. The national government is seen as the appropriate agent for responsibility for adequate health care. They understand that the government runs Medicare, and they overwhelmingly support this program and even think it should be expanded. Having accepted Medicare, most of them are ready for the next step of a national health care system that would cover everybody. The day-to-day needs they see and experience are great enough that most are not bothered even if such a program were the "creeping socialism" that the Ford administration once talked about with great alarm. This acceptance of and support for national health care might be seen as a long-term strategic victory for those incrementalists who felt that Medicare had to be enacted and accepted in order to make national health care possible.[23]

The combination of personal needs for which company plans cannot provide (Jim's wife had a baby while he was unemployed and therefore uninsured) and acceptance of the national government's role and responsibility for health care together make health care a good potential issue for populistic coalition building. The only warning that need be given is that those seeking to use this issue should avoid allowing it to be defined in terms of socialism, though if these workers of Furntex are representative, such a label might not be a fatal blow.

Working-Class Identification and Consciousness

> Where a man has achieved a clear and strong social identity, anything that affects a group he has embraced and incorporated in himself makes him a partisan. He enters politics as a group member, finds his rationale for group activity in the (internalized) group values, evaluates success and failure in terms of group (and therefore self-) advancement. Where the social identity is diffuse . . . individual goals and purposes must serve as political motives, and since the relation of politics to these individual purposes is often obscure, the drive to participate in politics is often weak. Political participation unsupported by a strong social identity is difficult for the amateur to sustain.[24]

This quotation summarizes the conclusion of Lane's examination of the class consciousness of a group of New Haven workers in the 1950s. He found their sense of class awareness and solidarity to be very low and characterized their social identity as "diffuse." He postulated that one important reason for their diffuse social identity is the strong doctrine of "social mobility" that is an important element in the American belief system. This doctrine might also be labeled as meritocracy or reward based on achievement. It tells the individual that his success and rewards in life are based on his achievements and that in this society opportunity for achievement is open to all, regardless of class.

Lane found several consequences resulting from the combination of a strong belief in social mobility and the day-to-day reality of class existence that makes mobility difficult. The workers he studied were ambivalent about the existence of and importance of social classes. After talking about class differences and how they define their lives, often in an indirect manner, they denied the importance or relevance of class. Often they stressed moral equality as a more legitimate notion than class. This judgment would serve the joint function of affirming the doctrine of social mobility above class as well as compensating themselves for their own position of social inferiority.

Denial of class also meant loss of the social and political information that is often a part of a social identity. Lane found his workers lacking strong opinions or guidelines for interpreting events. Class denial prevented these cues from reaching them and ordering their perceptions of reality. They tended to adopt a version of middle-class values altered to enable them to live in relative psychic comfort in their position of lesser wealth and security. These alterations often were rationalizations emphasizing other values, since pure middle-class values did not fit their daily reality. Lane found that they emphasized the dignity of hard physical work and the joy of family living as well as middle-class material values.

Lane also found an air of fatalism among his workers that led them to accept their working-class status as the best they could do given their educational attainments. Most, however, felt a sense of satisfaction from the belief that they had done a little better than their fathers before them and that their own children would have more education and hopefully do better than they. Thus they were able to find some comfort in their own situation without abandoning their belief in social mobility. They may secure further comfort in that a posture of fatalistic pessimism is often a means of accommodating material deprivation and insecurity.[25] In a sense, Lane's workers' beliefs are much like those associated by Almond and Verba with the "subject political culture," where the citizen may have positive or negative affect toward what the political system does to him, yet he accepts it because he believes there is no alternative.[26] The ultimate political consequence for the New Haven workers was that political participation became irrelevant because the individual was seen as more important than the group.[27]

A populist political coalition is by definition class based. Therefore, for such a coalition to come about, its potential members must have some sense of themselves as a group with common problems, goals, and enemies. Should the workers of Furntex have a "diffuse social identity" as did the workers of New Haven, we can conclude that the prospects for a new rise of populism seeking movement toward greater equality in the reward structure are not favorable.

The fifteen young workers in the sample were asked a number of questions designed to tap their social identification, consciousness of that affiliation, and the impact of that identity on their view and interpretation of social reality.

Salience of Class

The first point of inquiry was to determine whether the idea of class is meaningful to these men. They were asked: "Sometimes people talk about the idea of 'social class,' like when they use terms like 'middle class' or 'working class.' What do you think people mean by these terms?" With the possible exceptions of Roy and Melvin, two of the least educated and least articulate members of the group, all have some meaningful idea of class differences. Even Roy has some perception in thinking that working-class people "work harder." Almost universally, the others define differences in terms of income. Albert, for example, sees social class as simply the "income bracket" to which one belongs.

Their responses to my "what else?" and comments in other portions of the interviews revealed that these men perceive other differences as well. To John, the upper class are greedy and always striving to make more money. Rick has a similar perception, except that he labeled it more positively and extended it to the working class. He believes that some upper-class people have worked hard to achieve their status and that the difference between working- and lower-class people is that those in the working class are striving, as he is, to achieve higher status. Paul made a similar distinction between the upper and lower classes, saying that responsibility as well as income is involved. Many rich people are really "lower class" because they waste their incomes on things like drinking. Several, including Rick and Junior, include educational differences, saying that the upper classes have greater achievements and opportunities. Mark and Kevin view the rich as having more influence in schools, feeling that upper-class children can "get away with more" and receive preferential treatment. Junior feels that more generally the rich are able to pay their way out of trouble. Lewis and Terry made manual/nonmanual labor distinctions between the working and upper classes. Jim added status and secondary group memberships to the list. Several men reported that the middle and upper classes go to different churches than do working people.

JUNIOR: *Clothing to me hasn't got anything to do with religion. If you want to be saved and live for the Lord, that's what counts. It ain't just coming to church for clothes, which I think a lot of the big churches do. . . . I've been to one or two of 'em. I didn't have a suit that quite went or a sports coat that didn't match, and I got stared at the whole time I was there. I tried to be friendly and nice, but the people just acted like they didn't want to have nothin' to do with me cause I wasn't in their class. Which I reckon they could look at me and tell that I wasn't. Course I really didn't care. I just went to be going one time to see what it was like in a fancy church.*

Jim said that most of the influential people in Furntex go to the First Baptist Church, and he rationalized that it is not as good as his church because he has found it to be "not as personal" and "cold." Paul echoed Junior in saying that many rich people go to the same churches merely to "show off" their clothing. Rick added that there is another First Baptist Church of Furntex, a black church that most of the influential blacks attend.

Perhaps the most comprehensive statement on class differences was made by Eddie, who sees income, prestige, life-style, work, and religious differences.

EDDIE: *I would say that the middle class is really the working man that is making a fairly good income. Maybe he does a little golfing on*

*the side. [He works at] something that he's comfortable with and it don't
really strain him. Your higher class is just more of the same. They got a
little more income and a little more prestige, and maybe they do a little
more golfin'. They're, uh, I would say probably up in church work pretty
heavy. The lower class I would say probably works forty-eight hours a
week, maybe a little at night on the side.*

Thus, for the most part, distinctions of social class are meaningful to
these men. They perceive differences in prestige, influence, life-style, secondary group memberships, vocations, educational attainment and opportunity, and goal orientation and striving.

Class Self-Identification and Acceptance

Life has taught these men where they belong in the social structure. All
but two placed themselves in what they either label or describe as the
working class. Melvin has no concept of class differences and said that he
guesses he is "middle class cause I reckon I can do just as good a work as
the next man." Dave feels he is middle class because he is better off than
most of his fellow workers and therefore, does not identify with them.

DAVE: *I really make more money than what most people down there
make and have been down there less time than they, so I can't complain.*

Though these men are aware of and openly admit their class position, a
few of them, like most of the workers of New Haven, turn around and
deny its importance and relevance. Paul, who recognized and admitted
that he has "taken a knock down" from the class of his parents, serves as a
good example. He recognized the reality of classes and even of conflict
between classes, but adhered to the norm of meritocracy that says classes
should not be important. He thus assured himself of his own personal
worth despite his status. He also stressed alternative values.

QUESTION: *How important are social classes in America?*
PAUL: *I think they are ridiculous. People are people! In the past jobs
I've had, I've had a rare privilege of talking on a person-to-person basis
with the extremely rich. Like when I was installing burglar alarms, I was
practically on a first name basis with people that were worth hundreds
of thousands of dollars. That's not extremely rich, but that's pretty rich
for around here. On the other hand, I've worked with people that's as
poor as they can be. So I've seen all classes, and people are just people,
if they let themselves be.*
QUESTION: *Does it bother you that you are "knocked down" from
what your parents are?*
PAUL: *No, it doesn't. I'm happier. I'm on my own. What I do have I'm
doing by myself. I know I've got less money to work with, and I can't
have everything I want. I appreciate what I've got a heck of a lot more. I*

know where it came from. I've got a wife that loves me and I love her. And we've built up what we've got on our own.

Rick made a similar distinction between the reality of social classes and the norm that they should not be important. He stressed values that enhance his status as a member of the working class.

QUESTION: *How important are classes in America?*
RICK: *They are, but they shouldn't be. [He paused, as though reconsidering his position.] Well, that's life. That's the way society is. That makes a person strive, too. That gives him incentive, too.*
QUESTION: *How do you feel about being in the working class?*
RICK: *I dig it! I thrive on it! I like a job that gives me challenge just like this communication.*

Though both Paul and Rick denied the importance of class distinctions as a norm, few others exhibited this ambivalence. In this sense, there is a difference between these men of Furntex and Lane's workers. Most of the rest simply acknowledged perceived class distinctions as part of social reality. In admitting their membership in the working class, however, many others stressed status-enhancing values. Terry, for example, explained that he likes being a member of the working class because being mobile is superior to sitting at a desk all day. He also expressed moral disdain toward white-collar workers who are "afraid to get their hands dirty." Kevin, who would like very much to move up in the class structure, nonetheless emphasized the positive value he associates with his class status.

KEVIN: *To me, there's only one good thing about it [being working class]. What I got I work for. Nobody else can't say they gave it to me. I've never wanted anybody to hand me nothing. What I got is mine. I got it. I worked for it. That's the only thing about it.*

Just as the workers of Furntex are less ambivalent regarding class than Lane's workers, they are also less likely fatalistically to accept their status, though their assessments contain a significant element of fatalism. Albert is perhaps most like the workers of New Haven in that he accepts his position in life as about the best he can do with the abilities and education he possesses. Brent, who lives in dreams that he knows will go unrealized, expressed a similar fatalistic acceptance of his class status. Lewis sounded even more fatalistic.

BRENT: *I feel like and know that I am missing something. It's not where I would like to be, but it's where society more or less dictates that I am. But it's a way of life and I get by.*
LEWIS: *I wish that it [being in the working class] was better, but I know that unless I do like maybe four years in school and take up a trade or unless I know somebody, I know that it will pretty much be the*

same as it is, you know, until I stop drawing breath. So, uh, I wish that I was in a higher income bracket, but it's all right the way I am cause that's the way it's gonna be.

Few of the others are willing to accept their station in life. Only Albert, Dave, and John expect to be in the same job in five years. As they stated in regard to wages, most desire at least moderate upward mobility through either increased education or hard work and advancement to better jobs within the industry. Even Junior, who time after time has been frustrated in his attempts, continues to believe that somehow and someday his hard work will pay off and he will get the rewards he deserves.

This generally less than fatalistic acceptance of their station in life may result partly from the simple fact that these workers of Furntex are much younger than were the workers in Lane's study and still believe they have time to advance. Their attitudes may well change with time and age.

Social Mobility and Opportunity

We have already found that the relative optimism displayed by these men involves individual strategies for advancement rather than group-oriented behavior. Most see themselves rising within their own group rather than seeing the group as a whole rise. Thus, in a way, their individual plans, which are a part of the doctrine of social mobility, may be detrimental to the class identity that is a prerequisite for the building of a populist coalition. On the other hand, the relative difficulty of individual mobility out of the working class may be an issue that could give these workers a sense of group identity even though it is not a salient issue in their own lives.

Lane reported that his group of northern workers were not greatly disturbed by the existing inequality of opportunity. They were satisfied by the existence of sufficient opportunity to make modest advances: "Most of my subjects accepted the view that America opens up opportunity to all people, if not in equal proportions, then at least enough so that a person must assume responsibility for his own status. . . . This is the constant theme: 'All men can better themselves.'" He reported that only three of the men in the sample expressed any significant anger at differences of opportunity that exist at birth.[28]

Each of the Furntex workers was asked whether he thinks it is "hard to move from one class to another." A slim majority of eight feel that moving up in the class structure is almost impossible. The others feel that it is possible for them and for others in their class, but only with hard work.

Yet even some of those who view interclass mobility as nearly impossible for most believe that special circumstances may make it possible for themselves. Junior, Terry, and Mark all feel this way. Junior believes that his ability to work hard gives him an advantage over the average furniture worker, whom he views with some contempt, but also with sympathy.

JUNIOR: *All these things he [the average worker] wants, and there is no way for him to get ahead unless he can get to be a manager, or, uh, go to college for some special course or something that he thinks he can make plenty of money on. But just going out here and working like a regular furniture worker, it's almost impossible, unless you don't owe one thing to start with —which sooner or later you're gonna owe for something. . . .*

Terry said that it is very hard for a working-class person to move out of his class because to do so requires a good education, and most people cannot afford educational opportunities, though he is lucky enough to have the G.I. Bill to help. Mark feels his parents' support gives him extraordinary advantages.

MARK: *Well . . . it would take a little luck plus a little influence, somebody to back you up. [He feels his parents back him up.] If you got that, you might could do it.*

The other members of the group who feel that mobility is extremely difficult tend to apply that belief to themselves. John, Brent, and Lewis, all of whom are black, cited educational, racial, and class biases that radically reduce their opportunities for interclass advancement. Eddie thinks special connections are necessary.

Albert, who is black, is not disturbed by discrimination, blaming his own shortcomings in ability. Like some of the others, he gains satisfaction from the belief that he does better than his father did in caring for his family and that his child will do better than he because of a better education and more family encouragement. He regards mobility for others in his class as extremely difficult, however, saying that "in order to advance, you would have to be in a whole lot better position and either work awful hard or know somebody that can help you out." Since he thinks most people could improve their situation by working harder, he must be regarded as the weakest of the eight who believe that social mobility is almost impossible.

Brent and Lewis are the most pessimistic in the group about the availability of opportunities. Brent made what is perhaps the strongest statement: "In order to get rich you either have to steal a lot of money or you have to know someone who can place you in a real good job." He sees little way for someone like himself "in the working class to go out the next day and get a real good job." He does not even feel that education helps much because he claims to know many college-educated furniture workers who do little better than he. Lewis, as most others, views education as the key to success, but, along with Terry and Junior, feels that educational opportunities have a heavy class bias.

LEWIS: *I think it's [moving up to another class] very hard. [It takes] anywhere from eight to eleven years in medical school, just so you can make it as a resident doctor. I think that's pretty hard, you know, and, uh, going from, uh, one class to another, you have to spend money to make the money. And, uh, a man in, uh, lower class doesn't have that money to spend.*

These eight men represent a bare majority. And even their views are somewhat mitigated by their own special circumstances, skills, or belief that at least intergenerational mobility is possible. Their main concern is with achieving moderate mobility within the working class.

We can conclude that membership in the working class has not been very effective in teaching these men of Furntex about the difficulty of upward social mobility. Nor is this a concern that unites these working-class members. Even those who view it as extremely difficult often tend to stress social adjustment problems rather than the economic climb. Eddie, for example, said it would be difficult for him to learn to play golf on Saturdays and abandon his usual habit of watching television. This may be a kind of rationalization by which these men avoid facing the reality that they probably cannot advance into the upper class regardless of how hard they work. Great concern over interclass mobility leads to frustrations and unrequited dreams, as witness Brent and Lewis.

Man, however, is a complex creature and quite capable of pursuing more than a single strategy. Even though modest individual economic mobility dominates group advancement, group interests could still be an important concern of these men. The reader should remember from the discussion of the wage issue that they did desire some group movement toward greater equality of income in society.

I am suggesting that other class-related issues than one's own personal economic salvation may be salient enough to these men to draw them together in a populist coalition.

We have already seen that class is meaningful to most of them. Now the question is exactly how it is meaningful. Does class membership provide them with opinions and guidelines for interpreting social reality? It was precisely these kinds of class-based truths that Lane found lacking among the workers of New Haven.

The Question of Social Blame

One issue of interest might be labeled the question of social blame, or the enemies question. Identification with the working class, if that identification is meaningful, would presumably teach these men that their enemies and those who are to blame for such social ills as low wages and high prices are the corporations and/or the rich who own corporations.

From their comments during the interviews, I would judge that ten of these men blame either the rich or the corporations for their economic condition. These men feel that local and corporate elites hold wages down, prevent better paying industries from locating in the area, and keep the cost of living high so that they can continue to make large profits on the products they sell.

MARK: [Poverty is caused by] the gain of the man that already has the success. He's taking all the money and not distributing it out in the right way where the poor people can at least make a living and live right, comfortably, anyway, and have the necessary things, just the necessary things.

BRENT: [People are poor because] people are born into poverty. Most are unable to escape out of it, but those who are rich do not want them to escape—even those who make it out of poverty themselves then join the rich in trying to keep themselves rich and others poor.

EDDIE: I don't know, it's what I would say the upper class that's really got their weight into it [keeping wages low in Furntex]. . . . Because, I don't know, a man lives in a $40,000 house and he's got houses around him that are equal in stature. I don't say that they feel they are any better than anybody else. But when they speak, they want to be heard. Even in talking to some—it's not all of 'em—but I know some that really carry expensive houses, and they could talk to you standing in a dog lot if they wanted to! [He laughed.] But it's the ones that give you the impression that they are a step higher and they are going to keep you where you are at so don't try to get up!

John feels that those with money are always trying to hold others back. Rick referred to the rich as "feudal lords" who run things and make important decisions in their own interest.

After saying that it's "big industry versus everybody else," Paul raised an issue that was highly salient to the entire country in the winter of 1976–77—the energy crisis. This is another issue that entails the question of blame. Five of the men mentioned the energy crisis and all five blamed the oil corporations for increased prices. Paul's comments are typical.

PAUL: The gas price increases [made me mad]. I keep saying to myself, why in the heck do the oil companies want to keep raising the prices when they already are making more money than they ever have? They can afford to absorb some of this. If their costs are going up, then certainly with tremendous profits they can afford to absorb it.

Among those five (Dave, Junior, Lewis, Melvin, and Roy), two are not sure who to blame for low wages and high costs or blame only individual employers or the workers themselves, but are nevertheless sure who to blame for the energy crisis. They think the oil companies created the shortage artificially in order to raise prices.

DAVE: I really don't believe that there is a shortage of it. I feel the major companies, I mean the biggest companies as far as gas companies go, is holding more theirselves for more money than anything. It's just like this, well, they's been either two or three big tankers that they claim is busted or in the ocean now, coming in. And, uh, you wait, and mark my word, before it is over with, our gas will go up again on account of that just so they can get more money back on account of that. And I don't think it is fair really, having to pay for stuff like that. [He went on to say that the government can do little because it is ineffective.]

LEWIS: There might be a whole lot of people that make more money off of importing oil than getting it domestically, you know. So they, uh, I really don't think there's that much of an energy shortage. Cause back when gasoline was in short supply, prices went sky high. So then, uh, after a while, there was plenty of gas around, you know, and they act like it just pumped up out of the ocean, you know. I felt like it was around all the time, you know. They were just trying to fix it where they could just charge higher prices for it. And like they say that natural gas is a shortage. I don't really believe that it is. [He went on to blame government for not doing anything as well as the corporations.]

Taxes

Another issue that class interests would define as salient is taxes. Each of the men in the group was asked if he thought income taxes are fair in the sense that people in all income brackets pay their fair share. Eleven of the Furntex workers expressed strong feelings that the tax system is biased against the working class. Several of the men touched on this subject in their discussions of wages, but here, when the specific subject was taxes, their statements were much stronger.

Brent feels the poor pay too much and the rich are able to avoid taxes. Jim thinks that tax reform is the most important issue facing the country because "the average man needs to know that everyone is being taxed fairly." Paul argued that the rich are able to avoid taxes and added that they also do not pay a fair share of social security. Mark's comments are typical.

MARK: The rich people are not paying as much as they are supposed to. You can see that. You read it in the paper, where, you know, like Rockefeller writes off these deductible tax things, you know. He's not really paying but maybe a hundred dollars of all his millions—something like that. There's so many loopholes that the rich people can pay for, and it won't cost 'em but a third as much as it would to us if we paid the whole amount—you know, the employee, who has to work, really work for a living.

Perhaps the most interesting comment was made by Junior, who began by acknowledging the necessity of taxes and exhibiting a good knowledge of some of the services provided through taxes before he got to the point of interest here.

QUESTION: Does the income tax system seem fair to you?
JUNIOR: Well, I reckon it does cause they gonna have to take the money out if we gonna have the roads fixed and all this kinds of stuff they spend the money on, which I don't know where all of it goes. I know a lot of it goes to these old age homes and insurance and every-

thing like that, and roads and highways, schools and all this. I know all
that money goes to that. And if they didn't have it they couldn't do all
this with it. . . . It probably seems like too much when they take out on
you, but still yet there's a use for it that they've got. I think they overpay
a lot of the, uh, senators and stuff like that. I mean just like the president
right now retiring. He doesn't have to do a thing but get out and play
golf and he's going to get $84,000 a year from now on out of our money.
That's to me completely wrong! . . .

QUESTION: How about taxes being fair so far as all income brackets
paying their fair share?

JUNIOR: Well, more than likely the person making the large salary,
uh, at the end of the year he's got enough evasions so that he can get
most of it back where a workin' person, just payin' regular bills, unless
he is payin' interest or support or something like that, he's stuck. It
doesn't seem fair because they say they give so much to this and so
much to that and they may do it intentionally just to not break even on
taxes. Which we read in the paper all these millionaires been, some of
'em, this guy they showed on "60 Minutes," an Arabian millionaire, turn
around and give so much money every tenth month so he wouldn't have
to pay no taxes, knowin' he would have to pay more taxes than the
money he would give, but he give that money to break it even, which
doesn't seem right for a person making $250 than it does for a person
making $1,000 a week. Cause at the end of the year that guy's got some
kind of interest, deductions, or something that he can say that money
went on, whereas a person working just to pay his bills ain't got nothin!

Though somewhat off the point, this lengthy statement merits a few observations. First, Junior was not the only member of the group to display a
knowledge of government services that affect his personal family life. But
he, like most others, was unable to give such a knowledgeable response
when directly asked, "How does government affect you and your family?"
Many of these men drew a mental blank on this particular question, giving the impression of a total lack of political awareness and sophistication. Yet often their knowledge would emerge at other times in the interview in talking about such topics as taxes or getting to work or health
problems. This seems to indicate that many of these men were intellectually intimidated by abstract and academic sounding questions. Any
judgment of their political knowledge and sophistication based on their
responses to such questions is likely to be misleading because what is
really measured is their self-confidence in confronting and dealing with
abstractions rather than their political knowledge and awareness. This
may be one reason why mass surveys find working-class members to be
almost totally lacking in political awareness.

A second observation also relates to political knowledge of the working
class. Though this study was not specifically concerned with identifying
from what sources in the media they acquire political information, I did
learn that few of these men regularly read the newspaper (other than
sports and comics) or watch television news. About a third of the group,

however, spontaneously mentioned the television news magazine show "60 Minutes," and each remembered and related specific details of stories. News programs with an entertainment format seem to have a great deal of appeal and potential as information sources for men in this socioeconomic group.

A final observation, which is more directly related to the question of taxes, is that most of these men do not seem to mind paying taxes if they feel that everyone is paying a fair share and that the money is being spent wisely. Some object to specific taxes or specific exemptions. Eddie, for example, objects to land taxes, and John feels that people who do not properly care for their children should not be allowed a deduction for them as dependents. But the strong majority sentiment is that taxes are necessary. All agree that it is necessary and legitimate for the government to use force in collecting taxes, even though many generally oppose the government forcing people to do things against their will. Though these men are not happy taxpayers, they do seem to be willing and responsible taxpayers.

Of the four men in the group who do not perceive a class bias in the tax system, only Lewis and Melvin see no other bias of any kind. Lewis feels that income taxes are fair to everybody and, moreover, that he, as a low-income earner, gets quite a few tax breaks that enhance the fairness of the system. Melvin has no thoughts at all on the subject. The other two see no systematic class bias, but are disturbed by certain events. Dave is upset that Nixon did not pay his fair share in taxes, and Roy is angry about a report he claims to have heard that Ford Motor Company did not have to pay any taxes. But these men do not generalize their complaints into a systematic tendency explained by class as the others seem to do.

Perception of Class Conflict

All of the men in the group were asked directly about conflicting class interests: "Some people say that the various social classes want different things and come into conflict with each other. How important do you think this class conflict is in America? Have you come across any evidence of conflict of this kind?"

Upon examining and distilling the answers offered to this question and to a few others when the subject arose, I found that their responses can be grouped into three fairly distinct categories.

The first type of response is that they see little or no class conflict in society. Four men (Albert, Lewis, Melvin, and Roy) fall in this category. Lewis was the only one to give a complete explanation. The other three would probably agree with his analysis.

LEWIS: *I don't think there's that much conflict between the classes. I think, uh, I think all of us are after the same thing, but some of us already have, and some of us don't. But I don't think there's a conflict. See, cause, uh, a man who's making $50,000 a year, he wants a nice car* *to drive back and forth to work in just like I do. But he can get it and I can't. Or he has it and I can get it, but I don't have it yet.*

Some of these men may believe that wages for the working class are too low, but they do not perceive this as a purposeful injustice—they do not view economic social life as a zero-sum struggle between social classes. Injustices are individualized, as are successes. The most one can ask for is more individual compassion and sharing, as Albert requests when he says, "If people thought more about one another, I think it would be a better world to live in. I guess you could say that people don't care whether you're making it if they are makin' it. If you got more than enough, and if you could share with other people and try to make them have just a little more, then the world would be a better place."

At the other extreme, five members of the group (Brent, Kevin, Mark, Paul, and Rick) believe that class conflict is pervasive and generic to society. Several even defined politics in terms of class conflict.

BRENT: *As I said earlier, money's one of the main influences, or major influence in America, and everybody's doing everything they can to get that dollar. Poor people steal and rob, and rich people have to lose money on it in the process—it's a fact.*

KEVIN: *You'd have to be going to you different governments to find out—you'd be talkin' about the same thing right there as your Republican and Democrat. Because a Republican would want, you know, or a rich man would want the Republican party to save hisself taxes.*

MARK: *It [class conflict] has a lot to do with our economy, and, uh, the unemployment rate, because, uh, the middle classes is a lot more apt to get a job than the poverty-stricken people, I think. [He went on to talk about the job advantages of the middle and upper classes.]*

PAUL: *The class conflict, I feel, is not just important. That is America. I feel that's what politics is basically. Your Republicans are thought of to be the upper-class, richer people. Democrats are people that don't have as much. Now, I know that's not [completely] so cause there's rich Democrats and there's poor Republicans, but just in general what the way the parties feel, uh, keepin' up with the upper class or what have you. It's what keeps people going.*

RICK: *Yeah, it's [class conflict] important. Like right here in Furntex there is a lot of conflict over how much money for programs is to be spent. I'll give you a good example, the old theater. [The city was being asked to help fund the transformation of the theater into an art and cultural center.] You don't have too many lower-class people who are into that type of, uh, art. They're not into that kind of, you know, shows, plays. Most of 'em around Furntex, you know, don't—you have a few, but you don't have any many blacks as you do whites, you know, in proportion, the ratio is low. Course you got more whites, but in proportion it is still low. . . . Cause I think the emphasis should be based on need, and, uh, the majority need, that is. And the majority need is to get*

those black kids some recreation on the south side, maybe an outside
theater or a gymnasium or something like that. . . .

Five men among these fifteen workers of Furntex voted in 1976. Four of
them, excluding Mark, are in this group who view class conflict as important and pervasive in our society. These four also see Republicans and
Democrats in class terms. Brent and Rick think the Democrats better represent the interests of the "average" man. Kevin and Paul, as they told us
above, associate being rich with Republicanism. Mark is the only worker
who has a strong sense of class conflict but does not view the major political parties in class terms. Perhaps one important reason he did not vote in
1976 was because the conflict he sees in society is not expressed for him
in partisan differences.

The other voting member of the group, Jim, is in a third category that
falls between those who see class conflict as pervasive and those who see
it as unimportant. These six (Jim, Dave, Eddie, John, Junior, and Terry)
have a moderate view of class conflict. They either see it in only a limited
context, or, like Jim, feel it is important, but cannot really explain how or
give examples.

Dave perceives class conflict in the fact that the city is building and
maintaining a municipal golf course because he feels the game is only for
the upper class. Eddie feels there is only a little conflict: the lower-class
resent the middle class because of wealth inequalities. He went on to say
that this resentment is unfair because those in the middle class worked
"so much harder to get where they're at." Though he earlier considered
himself in the working class, he now seems to consider himself middle
class. Rather than focusing upon his own potential resentment of those
above him, he focuses on the resentment of those below him. John feels
some conflict with those in the upper class over access to private schools.
He said he would like very much to be able to send his children to private
schools.

Junior and Terry focus on work-related conflict over wages and job
tasks. Junior thinks that workers often are in conflict with their bosses
over raises. Terry said that bosses often ask workers to do tasks they themselves would not do. This job-related conflict is closer to the societal
conflict found in the first category, but it is qualitatively different in that
these two men see class conflict as more limited, particularized, and individualized. They did not go far beyond their own personal experiences in
their discussion of the subject.

Jim's comments also place him relatively close to the first category. He
stated that class conflict is important, but was unable to explain how or
offer a good example. He finally landed on a most curious example that
reflects his own aspirations for mobility into the upper class. He said that
middle-class members are not always fair to rich people in attributing
to them unfavorable characteristics and ascribes this to jealousy and
envy. Moreover, he added that many rich people have worked hard and
merit their wealth. Considering the wrath he expressed toward the rich
and their efforts to suppress blue-collar wages and toward their "cold"

churches at other points in the interview, we must conclude that Jim is ambivalent about class conflict. He recognizes it and at the same time denies its legitimacy because of his own aspirations to join the upper or at least the upper middle class.

One might argue that we are incorrectly categorizing those who could not discuss or give concrete examples of class conflict when specifically asked this fairly abstract question in the same way that mass surveys underestimate political knowledge. Perhaps Melvin or Roy might have some notion of class conflict that would show itself in answers to other questions. Conscious understanding of conflict between classes, however, is precisely what I was looking for. Conscious recognition of class conflict is an important element of class consciousness, whereas unconscious recognition is not. The potential of unconscious recognition has already been considered in probing these men's perceptions of class differences.

Happiness of the Rich

Another question that has an impact on class consciousness, conflict, and the potential for a class-based political coalition was asked in a series of questions about income: "Do you think that people who are very rich are happier than those who are just average?"

A view of the rich as happier would tend to heighten the salience of class differences, increase the intensity of class conflict, and greatly increase the sense of relative deprivation felt by those who live in a society that values "the pursuit of happiness." Such a view would increase the potential for a political coalition whose aim would be a more equal sharing of wealth and therefore happiness. On the other hand, the rationalization that the rich are no more happy or even less happy would tend to compensate these men and decrease the salience of conflict and deprivation.

Lane asked the workers of New Haven this question and found that they tended to generalize their own unhappiness as possessors of small amounts of money to assume that even greater worries must accompany larger amounts of wealth. He concluded that the combination of this generalization and reassuring rationalizations had "a conservative effect on the social outlook of these plain workingmen."[29]

The workers of Furntex also tend to reduce the potential for unhappiness and conflict in their own lives by attributing lesser happiness to the rich. Paul echoed the workers of New Haven in saying that greater wealth only means greater debts and worries. Others offered a variety of similar reasons why the rich are less happy than average folk: "money cannot bring happiness," worry about retaining wealth, having things "too easy," the frustration of being driven by an insatiable hunger for greater wealth, and loss of privacy and joy in the simple things of life. Perhaps the most interesting and tortured rationalization was given by Lewis, who tediously explained how the rich are less happy with their wealth than he would be (thereby implying his own moral superiority).

LEWIS: No [the rich are not happier], they have some of the things that I was talking about, but I also feel like they also have like, uh, uh, I guess you might say too many vices. They might have a car and house and all like that, but I hope that if I ever get those things that I would be basically the same person that I am now. But a rich man who already has what I'm trying to get usually takes on a lot of extra drinking, maybe. He feels like his social standing is very important. If I can get, well, what I'd like to have is a Thunderbird, a '77 Thunderbird—that's what I would like to have. If I had one and was paying on it and had a fourteen, eighteen thousand dollar brick home, you know, not extravagant, you know, paying for that. I would probably be the same person that I am now. But a rich man that would probably go and pay cash for that same car that I have, he might feel like, well, before he got all those things, he might have been the kind of person where he let his kids play with black kids, maybe. Or, he didn't care too much who his kids ran around with. But now that he's rich, he feel like he has to be extra good, you know. Not only can't his kids hang around with black people anymore, but not substandard white people either. You know, send 'em to a private school, not to a public school, you know. So, you know, I figure a rich man, he might have the things that I want, but he's got more problems with what he's got than what I intend to have.

Although the dominant feeling is that the rich are less happy, a significant minority believe that the rich are indeed happier than average people. Five of these workers openly admitted jealousy with no compensatory happiness. Jim, Junior, Melvin, Kevin, and Rick all confessed that the rich are at least as happy if not happier than they and their peers. They certainly do not see excess wealth as a cause of excess woe. Jim feels they are happier because they don't have the money worries of average people—they can afford anything they want. Kevin and Melvin agreed. Rick and Junior offered the most interesting comments.

RICK: I don't really have any thoughts on that because I don't see why he wouldn't be happy if he were very rich. Why wouldn't he be happy? If he's not happy because he is too rich, I'll take some of the burden off his shoulders! [He laughs loudly.]
JUNIOR: Well, I think that if I had a lot more money I would be a lot happier. I don't know if anyone else would be. Cause it would reduce my worry and I would probably feel different toward my wife, and I probably wouldn't be near as irritable as I am now. I wouldn't be as nervous. 'Bout my worst habit is chewin' my nails, and I've had that habit for about nine years now, and it's been so bad I can't quit. And I've just been smokin' about two years. I try to keep off my fingernails, but I still chew 'em too much. If I can't chew 'em, I'll take a pocket knife and cut 'em.

Three of these five men (Jim, Kevin, and Rick) are among those who voted in 1976 and who explain their partisan preferences in terms of class differences. Another possible impact of their conscious economic jealousy is increased liberalism, which is consistent with the effect found by Lane. Jim, Rick, and Junior are among the five members of the group with the highest scores on the economic liberalism scale.

The Impact of Class Consciousness

Thus far in considering class consciousness, concepts of class and class differences, class self-identification, social mobility and opportunity, the question of blame, tax burdens across classes, the perception of class conflict, and the relative happiness of the rich have been examined. The next task is to determine how these men's class-consciousness attitudes relate to other major variables considered in this study. To determine possible relationships, a simple index of class consciousness was constructed utilizing all of the above attitudes. (See Appendix Table A, Table 2.) The index allows the men in the group to be ordered from the most to the least class conscious and that ordering to be compared with orderings on other important measures.

The first notable point is that race does not appear to be a significant factor in explaining class consciousness. Salience of class and concern with class-related issues bridge both races—blacks and whites are evenly distributed throughout the group.

Those workers who exhibit the greatest class consciousness include three of the five who voted in 1976, suggesting that concern for and awareness of these issues motivate voting. Class consciousness, however, is not by itself sufficient motivation to bring these men to the polls. The four nonvoters who had relatively high class-consciousness scores do not perceive that the major political parties offer any choices relevant to class-oriented issues. These class-conscious nonvoters saw neither the Democratic party nor its 1976 presidential candidate as meaningful in terms of their concerns. All of the voters, on the other hand, found either Carter or the Democratic party expressing their economic issue preferences.

A positive relationship was found to exist between class consciousness and union support. The relationship becomes even stronger if union support is related to both class consciousness and voting. Four of the five class-conscious voters expressed unequivocal support for labor unions. Only two other men in the entire group exhibited such complete support. Speculating beyond the data, there may be a commonality between the ability to make a strong and definite commitment to collective action for higher wages (even if it is merely a verbal commitment) and to participate in an election. Both of these actions are based on an unambiguous set of issue preferences and choices perceived to be relevant to those preferences.

A rough positive relationship exists between the ordering of these men on economic liberalism and their ordering on class consciousness. (Compare Appendix Table 1 with Table 2.) This should come as no surprise because there is a logical consistency between a sense of working-class consciousness and a desire for the government to play a strong role in providing services, regulating industry, and guaranteeing jobs. Such a logical consistency is noteworthy, however, because a number of students of public opinion have argued that there is little consistency or even content to the political belief systems of members of the working classes.[30]

Conclusion

In this chapter, a lengthy and detailed examination was made of the attitudes of fifteen southern furniture workers toward a number of issues about which a populist-style political movement might be constructed. With regard to government guarantee of jobs, these men feel that government has some responsibility to seek to provide jobs, but this view is greatly mitigated by a strong belief that the individual should be responsible to seek out and accept almost any other alternative means of survival.

On the question of wages, the beliefs of these workers seem more in harmony with the themes of populism. They feel they have been cheated, that hard work does not pay off as fast or as much as it should, both for themselves and for others. They compare themselves with workers in other states and regions and with some of the workers in newer industries that have moved to the area. Blame for low wages is placed on local businessmen, elites, and corporate interests. Though they do not espouse the radical goal of total equality in reward for all (that would compromise their strong belief in individual merit), they do strongly support some moderate movement toward greater equality as long as reward based on merit is retained. Wage and wage-related issues were found to be among the more salient issue concerns of these men.

The discussion of health care aroused a strong element of anger based on the bad experiences these men have had and observed in obtaining medical services. They are also disturbed by costs that seem to be rising faster than their ability to pay or to get insurance. They seem willing to support radical solutions, perhaps even including government control of doctors' salaries.

On the question of group identification, these working-class men exhibited a greater degree of class consciousness than seemed to exist among the workers studied by Lane in the 1950s. They are aware of class differences, correctly identify themselves, blame those classes above them for economic and social woes, and a majority seems consciously aware that class conflict exists and is important.

All of this information bodes fairly well for those who would wish to involve these men in class-oriented politics focused on redistributive issues. Much was discovered, however, that would not seem so favorable for their involvement. Though the men were concerned about jobs and wages and see the government as properly playing an active role in each, their own alternative private interests, satisfactions, and strategies may outweigh their public, group-oriented concerns. These include family satisfactions that may compensate for not being rich, the pride they derive from surviving and making it on their own, a belief that they will rise at least within their own class if not to another class because of their own special abilities and circumstances, a belief that moderate intergenerational mobility does take place, some fear of measures that can be labeled as radical or socialist, and a very notable lack of perception of any link between their issue concerns and partisan politics.

This last finding may be the greatest obstacle. In beginning this discussion, I asked whether these men translated issue positions into support for Carter and whether this was sufficient to explain their decision to vote. In looking at all the issues covered, the perception that the election involved some choice that was relevant to their issue concerns was a prerequisite for voting. Thus if it is not sufficient, it certainly seemed necessary, at least for the men in this small sample. In Chapter 5, the question of participation will be examined in greater detail, seeking to explain why some of these men perceived this link between preference and electoral choice and why others did not. Certainly anyone who would hope to appeal to these men on populist themes must make them realize that political choice involves these kinds of issues. Since party labels do not evoke such issue differences in the minds of many of these men, a populist candidate may do well to disassociate himself from the insiders of a political party. This is precisely what Carter did in 1976, and it apparently helped him in obtaining the votes of men such as Jim.

One other positive finding for those who would wish to see a populist coalition built and succeed was that blacks and whites seem united on most of these issue concerns. The only significant difference found is that blacks believe that racial discrimination is a significant factor adversely affecting jobs and wages for blacks, whereas whites do not. As shall be seen in the next chapter when the general topic of racial discrimination is examined, this very important difference may overshadow the commonality of black/white interests on the other issues.

CHAPTER FOUR

The Social Issue—
Racial Prejudice

You are made to hate each other . . . because upon that hatred is rested the keystone of the arch of financial despotism which enslaves you both. You are deceived and blinded that you may not see how this race antagonism perpetuates a money system which beggers you both. [Tom Watson quoted in David Leon Chandler, The Natural Superiority of Southern Politicians, p. 213.]

We have seen that the men of Furntex for the most part hold issue positions on political and economic questions that are at least potentially compatible with carefully directed and worded populist appeals. These issue positions are relatively consistent across racial lines. Both black and white workers desire jobs, better wages, low-cost health care, access to schools, and equitable taxes. Nor do many of either race object to government programs and taxes to bring about these goals as long as such programs are cost-efficient and the burden is equitable across class lines.

The likelihood of any such coalition aimed at attaining these goals is low, however, unless these men can unite across racial barriers. As long as working-class whites are more concerned with maintaining social and economic superiority over working-class blacks than with the distribution of wealth and rewards, the politics of racism will prevail, even if it is disguised by code words such as "busing" and "welfare."

In this chapter I will examine the racial beliefs of the ten white and five black furniture workers of Furntex and will attempt to ascertain the depth or centrality of any racial antipathies they hold. If this judgement can be made, functional prejudice will have been distinguished from folkways prejudice. As was noted in Chapter 1, functional prejudice, which emanates from deep within the personality and serves such important needs as a sense of high self-esteem, is a much stronger potential motivator for political action than the more superficial folkways prejudice. The latter is more of an etiquette system that lacks behavioral cues because it serves no important psychological needs.[1]

First, the racial attitudes of these workers will be examined in detail in specific social contexts, in terms of interpersonal relationships, in a political context, and in their views of idealized racial relations. As we have already discovered, these men's attitudes betray themselves in subtle ways as well as in their direct answers to questions. Careful examination of their words gives many clues as to the nature of their prejudices. Differences between black and white attitudes on race relations are important to consider in light of a recent study that found a movement toward polarization and a good deal of distrust and antagonism between "social control" oriented whites and "social change" oriented blacks.[2]

Racial Stereotypes

The attitudes toward blacks of the ten white workers in the group can be measured by their responses to three questions: (1) By and large, do you think that white people are more dependable than blacks? (2) In general, do you think that whites behave better than blacks, blacks better than whites, or are they about the same? (3) On the whole, do you think that white people try to get ahead more than blacks?[3]

A study done in the 1960s found that an overwhelming majority of southern whites tended to affirm these negative stereotypes.[4] A similar response was made by a number of the white workers of Furntex. Six of the ten white workers in the sample agreed with all three statements, feeling that generally, compared to whites, blacks are less dependable, less well behaved, and make a lesser effort to get ahead. Four, however—almost half—(Mark, Paul, Roy, and Terry) register strong disagreement with these stereotypes, raising serious questions about the continued universality of these beliefs. Paul showed a firm sense of differentiation, insisting that each man must be judged individually and therefore generalizations cannot be made. Mark, Roy, and Terry feel that none of the stereotypes are true. Roy stated that in his own experience many blacks are more dependable than most whites, and Mark thinks that black people are trying harder to get ahead than are most whites. He views this as a positive sign of societal progress.

A few of the others showed some hesitation in accepting the stereotypes. Jim carefully explained that blacks do not behave as well in that, when a large group of blacks are together, they tend to make whites feel "left out" and "different." On an individual basis, he feels they act about the same as whites. Eddie predicts that blacks may soon improve their efforts at getting ahead because they seem to be learning more in school, though he still feels whites generally try harder. As blacks mature, he said, their behavior seems to improve.

Some of those agreeing with the stereotypes added other racially stereotyped ideas in the course of our conversations. Eddie has qualms about allowing his little daughter to play with young black boys because they learn about sex earlier and become sexually active at a younger age than do white boys. Kevin says that blacks play a different style of basketball than do whites, that they are more concerned with "moves" and "faking you out" than with winning. He attributes black athletic accomplishments to his notion that "they have three more muscles in their legs than a white guy even has. So they got more ability to run and jump and all that jazz, you know."

Perhaps the strongest stereotype is that of the "lazy and shiftless black." In talking about welfare or unemployment, several men added their own version of the idea that blacks don't try as hard to get ahead as do whites.

KEVIN: *A black person, if they had the chance, they would draw off the government. They wouldn't work at all if they didn't have no other way, you know. To me, well, you have some of them, some blacks will work for a living, you know, some blacks. But I would say a percentage of them, if they had the chance, they would live off the government. I would say that there are some whites that are that way also, but it is not as high as the blacks in percentage.*

JUNIOR: *A colored person, as long as they can get welfare, that's all they worry about, even the ones makin' good money.*

MELVIN: *They's a lot of people on welfare, you know. And it seems like these colored guys and people, it seems like they can just get on the welfare, easier than the white guy. Which most of them does, you know. They drive around in these fancy cars. You've probably seen a lot of them, you know, driving around in these fancy cars. I just don't see how in the world they get on there. I mean they just seem to get on there faster than the white guy. On top of that, they get on there, you know, these husky niggers, they get on there and they won't work at all. Young guys, you know they won't work. They get on there, and I don't see how they get on there. And these people that really needs to get on it, seems like it really makes it hard for them to get on it.* [He finished by describing a white family he knows that needs more government aid; he believes that lazy blacks on welfare deprive the truly needy.]

JIM: *In my own life I've seen people that were able to work that wouldn't work simply because of laziness, yet they were drawing a welfare check every month. And I've known of instances where people, well, not especially blacks, but I guess especially, where they would have children just so they would send 'em welfare checks every week.*

The flavor of these comments indicates that a significant number of working-class whites strongly believe that blacks are lazy and that government-sponsored welfare and subsidy programs are designed to help these undeserving blacks almost exclusively. Melvin touched on an important element in this view—preferential treatment or reverse discrimination in these programs. We shall soon see that this fear of reverse discrimination applies to areas other than welfare, such as jobs and promotions.

The potential political impact of belief in these stereotypes is detrimental to the building of a biracial working-class-based political coalition, for it means that whites have fears and resentments that could work to the advantage of opponents of such a coalition. The image of blacks driving "welfare Cadillacs" is given at least lip service by many working-class whites, though the image may not be as universal as it once was.

Schools and Busing

Massive white resistance to school integration has been an important element in southern politics since the first significant efforts were made to desegregate schools following the 1954 *Brown* decision. White southern political candidates have often used that issue in rallying white support in Democratic primary campaigns as well as in general elections. By its very definition, school integration has separated whites and blacks politically to the detriment of attention to common economic problems.

The issue of busing has become the recent political descendant of the school integration issue. Many people in both the North and South had easily paid lip service to the ideal of school integration and in fact have only token integration by drawing school district lines to reinforce and emphasize existing segregated residential patterns. When the courts began to strike down the legality of these evasively designed districts, the battle against the reality of school integration became a national issue. It may even be said to have had a national presidential candidate in George Wallace, who used the resentment of court-ordered busing to gather support of many whites in both the North and South.

By 1976, the crusade against forced busing was over in much of the nation. It was certainly over in most small towns, at least at the high school level, where it had never been a legitimate issue because single high schools had always served these communities. Busing simply meant that all students were bused to a single school, not all white students to a white high school and all black students to a black school. Busing remains an issue in areas that still retain the traditionally smaller neighborhood-oriented grammar schools and in cities with populations large enough to require several high schools, each located in a racially homogeneous community.

Though the forces against busing may have lost the battle in the South and in most of the rest of the country, the war against segregation is by no means lost. Many white families have abandoned the public school systems and set up their own private schools and so-called "Christian" academies so their children do not have to share classroom space with blacks. As a result, many public school systems in the South are facing increasing financial trouble because they have been abandoned by the wealthier white segments of the community, who will no longer vote for financial support of these schools. Many public school systems in the South find their clientele restricted to blacks and poor and working-class white children whose parents cannot afford private school tuition. This is especially true in the deep black-belt South, where whites fear being relegated to minority status in the public schools.

Furntex is not in the deep South or in the black belt. Demographically, it is like the border South: the black population is above the national average but poses no realistic threat of gaining majority status.

Furntex has no significant private school system, perhaps because its blacks pose no threat to the majority status of the white citizens. The public school system is now completely integrated; every public school has a white majority. Like many other cities, Furntex chose centralization of grammar schools and reduction of the number of grades at each location rather than retain the traditional neighborhood schools with a large number of grades at each. Mixed housing patterns would have made impossible the drawing of district lines that satisfied both the courts and whites who were fearful of black majorities. The end result is large-scale busing but preservation of white majorities. Centralization and accompanying economies of scale can be used as the stated rationales of busing, rather than integration and court pressure.

The road to this solution was a long and difficult one. Like most other towns in the area, Furntex successfully ignored integration requirements or appeased federal demands by tokenism until the late 1960s. Only in 1967 was the school system reorganized so as to bring about significant integration. Integration ended such traditions as the annual senior class trip to Washington, D.C., and New York City. It also temporarily made life difficult for school board members who found they could not retain the sacred neighborhood school concept and maintain strong white majorities within all the schools.

When I interviewed fifteen furniture workers in the winter of 1976-77, they and their families had lived for about ten years with the reality of school integration. I asked them several questions about the integration of their schools in order to learn how they evaluate it and how well they have accepted it. If they evaluate it negatively and refuse to accept it, school integration and busing may yet retain potent symbolic power that could be used to divide any black/white coalition. Both the whites and the blacks in the group were asked: "How do you feel about what the government has done to promote school integration?" From their answers I could get an idea of how they evaluate school integration and also tap their feelings about government actions to promote it.

The overall evaluation of the ten white workers may be characterized as one of acceptance, containing both a flavor of strong approval and some ambivalence about the effect of integration on the schools. The men could not be categorized clearly because several entertained both feelings simultaneously. A representative sampling of their comments follows, beginning with those who are unequivocally positive about school integration and working toward those who are more ambivalent.

Mark, Terry, Roy, and Paul are the four members of the group who express firmest support for school integration. Roy simply said, "I don't see nothin' wrong with it." He later added that going to school with blacks in the seventh and eighth grades helped him get along better with blacks. Terry said that school integration is good because "we're all created equal" and emphasized that both races need to learn to get along with each other. Mark echoed similar feelings.

MARK: *Well, [the government's] done good so far as trying to, uh, put discrimination out and just by sending blacks and whites in schools together . . . but back in the eighth or ninth grade I wouldn't have said that, but now I do.*

The suggestion is made that school integration was a learning experience for whites, that it may have reduced hatred, distrust, and prejudice. Though the four men named above did not explicitly say so and may well not consciously hold this attitude, another member of the group did. Paul, whose knowledge and beliefs no doubt are influenced by his middle-class background as well as by the cultural experience of integration he shares with the others, stated explicitly that school integration was purposely designed to reduce white prejudice.

PAUL: *I personally feel that they [government officials] have tried to do what they think is best. At first I couldn't understand it. I thought that was interfering with people's rights and freedoms as Americans. I mean a person ought to be able to say that I want my son or daughter to go to so-and-so school. But I feel that what they're trying to do is if they can get the kids in school together at a young enough age, black and white, that they won't think anything about it. Being brought up side by side it would be like anything else to 'em. And I feel in the long run it might pay off. At first I was totally against it. That's something that my opinion changed after I thought about it. It took a couple of years to change this. But when it was first being done I thought it was stupid and interfering with rights. But after you think about the long-term results, like if I started to school. I never went to school with a black child till I was in junior high school. And when I got to the seventh grade, this is what changed my mind [as I am] thinking back on it. When I got to the seventh grade and started going to school with blacks, I was more or less afraid to associate with 'em. They were like different forms of life. Whereas I feel like if I had been brought up with 'em from nursery school, they'd just a been like anybody else. And I feel like that's what the government had in mind.*

Several members of the group are ambivalent about school integration, though they seem to have accepted it as a fact of life that is essentially just. Eddie accepts the fact that his children go to school with blacks and to a limited extent is willing to allow them to play with blacks after school. He is, however, upset by government actions, such as busing, that have forced integration.

Kevin, who attended an integrated school, said that he has always gotten along well with blacks in school and elsewhere and sees nothing wrong with racial mixing in schools. But he is upset by what he described as reverse discrimination in schools, saying that blacks are able to "get away with more things" than whites. As an example, he cited a case when a black and a white were given the same punishment for fighting, but the black had started the fight.

Jim and Junior are perhaps the most ambivalent in the group. Both are greatly disturbed by discipline problems in school and tend to associate black entrance with these problems. Their expressed concerns echo those of many anxious and fearful white middle-class parents. After expressing doubts and fears, however, both concluded that they approve of school integration. Their comments merit quotation at length.

JUNIOR: Well, when I's going to school there were colored boys in my room. Maybe the colored people belong in their own school. [But] they could go together to school okay, I think. Maybe there's one or two in there that causes a little bit of trouble. I think they ought to be got out of the school somehow, one way or the other—either straighten up or get out! Because most of the time it's just one or two that starts trouble. But I don't see no reason why they can't go to school wherever we do or the same school or whatever, long as they don't cause any trouble. But 90 percent of what you hear about is trouble the whole time that they're going to school with us. They slap a white girl. They pull her hair and then they got mommas and daddies from both sides mad. . . . Some say they ought to be in the same schools together and some say they ought to be in separate schools. If they're gonna do that, then they might as well stop the colored people from working in the same factory as the white person does, which they'll never be able to do. Due to unemployment discrimination they can't do that. If they can do it in a furniture factory, they can—kids had got to go to school so they can learn something so they can get out and be something or at least make enough money to make a living on—they might just as well let 'em go to school together and quit arguin'.

JIM: That's [integration of schools] a touchy thing. I believe that integration is good, but—I'm not a racist, you know. I'm not what you would call prejudiced. I have a lot of black people that are friends. But as far as schooling, I think that integration has hurt our schools more than anything. I have a sister-in-law that teaches high school. The things that are going on at that school are unbelievable, the kids, the way they act, and most of 'em are blacks. And it's discouraging to me. I believe that, uh, the blacks have the right to go to school. [He pauses as though to think.] Well, I guess I don't believe in integration. I think we should go back to the way it was. You know, that may sound contradictory or hypocritical than what I said about equal rights and caring for black people, helping them with their houses. But, uh, many black children, you know, from what I gather, in high school especially, instead of the white culture influencing them, the black culture is influencing the white culture. . . . [A little later when we were talking about busing and neighborhood schools, he continued on the subject.] You have more and

more black people moving into white neighborhoods and it's not as violent—it's not as opposed as it used to be. Course you've got restricted
areas. Restricted neighborhoods are very popular now. You must make
so much a year and you must pay so much for your house. You know,
you take a black guy that makes $60,000 a year and buy him a $45,000
home, he's not going to live like normal black people.

QUESTION: So who would go to the neighborhood school in this
neighborhood? Would blacks be allowed to go if they had homes there?

JIM: I believe they would go to that school—the same school. Cause I
believe, it has a lot to do with the way that kids are raised, the standards they are raised with. I think a lot of your kids, and black kids as
well as whites, that are troublemakers in school, are raised under an
environment of, mistrust, you know. . . . [He talked about bad home en-
vironments for a while.] Of course, there are poor black children, very
poor, that are very well behaved and well disciplined. . . . Well, [he
paused] I guess if you went into that, you would have to go into the
well-to-do families where the parents are high all the time, or where
they are separated. It happens there, too. And they're going to be
troublemakers maybe, too, someday. I guess the whole thing comes
down to maybe integration is good. Maybe the schools need more discipline in 'em. [He spoke of trouble in his sister-in-law's school and ended
by advocating the need for corporal punishment in school.]

Only two members of the group may be fairly categorized as being completely against school integration. Dave responded to the question by saying, "I can't say that I like the way it is being done because, my last two
years of high school [after integration] I didn't learn nothing. I mean, my
last two years of high school was a paper-backed book. . . . And we never
had homework and we seen a lot more films and movies in school than we
did anything. I mean that it really wasn't pertaining to the basic school-
work that you're really supposed to do. I think they should go a lot stricter
on the schools now than what they are really doing." When pressed on
whether this marked decline in school quality was related to integration,
Dave refused to answer directly. Nor would he give an overall evaluation
of school integration. He fatalistically accepts integration as something
there is "nothing you can do about" and seeks to minimize his contact
with blacks. He answered several questions about black/white relations
by saying, "I have nothing against them. They don't bother me and I don't
bother them." He dealt with racial questions to which his answers might
label him as a racist in the same way he deals with blacks—avoidance.

Melvin is the other member of the group who evaluates school integration negatively, but he is openly negative and seems to have no fear about
conclusions that may be drawn from his answers.

MELVIN: I feel like they shouldn't mix them up. [Later, in talking
about why he liked Nixon, he strengthened his position.] Well, I don't
know if it was him that said it or not, something about school buildings,

you know, these niggers going' to nigger schools, gettin' their own school. I think it was him that said that. That would be nice if he could do that—get their own school for 'em.

In addition to asking each white worker for his overall evaluation of school integration, I asked each a series of questions about how high a percentage of black children he would be willing to have in school with his own children (Jim and Terry were not included because their interviews had been completed when the questions were added). The questioning began with 10 to 15 percent and ended with 75 to 90 percent.

The answers tend to confirm earlier findings. Most of the men are willing to accept low percentages of blacks in their schools, even if only reluctantly as in the cases of Dave and Melvin, who both feel that there is no other alternative than acceptance. But at around 50 percent and above their attitudes begin to change. Fatalistic acceptance turns to open defiance. As whites become a minority in schools and the black proportion approaches 70 percent, both Melvin and Dave vowed that they would refuse to send their children to school. Kevin joined them, saying that it would be as though one were the only white guy on a basketball court— one would feel "out of place."

The other five men stated that they would be willing to accept as high as 90 percent blacks in school with their children. Roy, for example, said that he would be bothered if his children were in the minority, but that he would accept the situation if teachers were good. Junior added that even "colored teachers" would be all right as long as the kids were not mistreated.

JUNIOR: *They're going to school to learn, and it doesn't matter who is sitting beside you.*

What is surprising here is not that some of these men are opposed to school integration and fear minority status, but that so many of them willingly, if not even enthusiastically, endorse and accept school integration. The fact is that school integration is a dead issue for most of them. It is a fact that is to be lived with and adapted to rather than opposed. Even Dave, who personally opposes it, knows that outward verbal opposition is no longer acceptable.

"Forced busing," which has been a more acceptable form of and code word for opposition to school integration, generates only a little more enthusiastic opposition among the white furniture workers of Furntex. Only three of the workers expressed any opposition to busing. Jim and Eddie are the most vocal.

JIM: *I don't believe in busing people explicitly just for the purpose of equal balance of race in school. You know, when we went to school we went to the school that was the nearest one to us, and we knew all the kids. We grew up with 'em. And I believe that's the way it should be, you know.*

EDDIE: *I think they went way overboard with it, especially on busin'. I don't know how much it is really costin' the taxpayers. It's bound to be gettin' in their pockets. I think that the colored and the Indian and what-not should have as good a schools, as warm a schools, and really, I think it should be up to them. If you have a family down here that wants to go to Furntex, and Furntex is capable of handlin' that many pupils, well, then, I think it should be all right, say, first-come first-serve basis. I don't see the law just reachin' out and sayin' this section goes to this school and this section goes to that school. And they look back and say, "Now, wait a minute, now, that won't work. We'll bus you from here over to here." It's just gettin' in the taxpayer's pockets.*

Is busing a code word for school integration to these two men? Both were ambivalent about school integration. Jim's statements in opposition were offered with a great deal of compunction. He was torn between general principles he professes to believe and his perception of the terrible conditions in schools after integration—so torn that he talked until he found a source of these behavioral problems other than integration—discipline in the home and in school. Eddie's children attend an integrated school, and he claimed that there has been no "trouble" as a result. He even claimed that he would not mind his children being a racial minority in school, though he admitted that as the percentage of blacks approached 90 his emotions might get the better of him. Thus he, too, exhibited some compunction about his expressed opposition to school integration.

The answer to the above question seems to be a guarded "yes"—busing is a code word for integration. By opposing school busing rather than school integration, these men may oppose radical forms of school integration, especially sending their children to school with blacks from the lowest economic classes, without violating their own self-image as non-prejudiced persons who do not advocate segregation. One may safely oppose busing on grounds other than race, such as cost or the traditional sacredness of neighborhood schools, as do Eddie and Jim. Neither of these men are hard-core functional racists, but nevertheless, the busing issue (and by implication school integration and related issues like school discipline) could sidetrack them from the central economic concerns of a biracial populist coalition. Their fears and apprehensions can still be used to distract them from class-related economic issues.

Another white worker who expressed strong opposition to school busing took such a different position from those of Eddie and Jim that he must be considered separately. Roy's words on the subject clearly indicate that busing cannot be a code word for opposition to school integration, but might distract him from economic issues.

ROY: *I don't agree with that [school busing]. Kids should go to the school that is closest to where they live. Like where I live there is a colored school near and that's where my kids go. That's just the way I feel. [Roy lives adjacent to the largest black community in Furntex. The elementary school to which he referred was at one time the only black* elementary school in town. Now it is integrated and houses only three grades; because it is in the quadrant of the city with the largest proportion of black population, its black enrollment is higher than in most other schools, though not a majority. It has retained the stigma, however, of being a "colored school."]

Three of the white members of the group are either indifferent to or do not perceive busing as a racial issue. I had to explain the racial significance of school busing to Melvin, and then he expressed his opposition to the idea. Dave is more concerned about the practice in North Carolina of allowing students to drive the buses than he is about any implications for integration. Junior views busing as a means used by authorities to split up troublemaking students and a means of moving students from overcrowded schools to less crowded ones. He sees few racial implications in the practice.

These men's lack of perception of busing as a racial issue, especially for Melvin, may be partly due to their overall lack of political awareness and knowledge. But also taking a bus to school, at least after elementary school (and during elementary school if one lives on the edge of town), is such an accepted practice in their lives that busing per se is not an issue. The destination of the bus may be an issue, but riding a bus across town is not; many of them did this long before schools were integrated. That their children should do so is no great shock.

The other four white workers in the group expressed either support for or acceptance of busing for the purpose of school integration. Kevin and Terry said it is necessary if there is to be school integration and accept it as they do integration itself. Not surprisingly, Mark and Paul, who were the strongest advocates of school integration, are also the strongest supporters of school busing.

We may conclude that school integration and the means for bringing it about have been accepted as a fait accompli by a majority of the white workers of Furntex. There seems little need to explore in detail the views of the black subsample on this issue in search of ways their opinions conflict with those of the whites.

The unanimous opinion of all five blacks is that school integration has been beneficial, especially to blacks, whom they believe experienced inferior educational facilities where schools were segregated. Brent said school busing is a blessing, remembering that before integration and busing, he had to walk across town to the black school. Now his children can comfortably ride. He also evaluated school lunch programs and special educational programs as side benefits of integration. He and Rick both remember being too hungry in school to stay awake or learn. As did only a few of the white workers, most of these black workers see school integration as a purposeful means of improving race relations and reducing prejudice. Brent thought the planners were "farsighted," that eventually children will learn from contact that racial stereotypes are not true, and that someday people will no longer choose schools for reasons of race so that busing will not be needed. Even Lewis, who is otherwise consistently conservative in his opposition to any national government actions that interfere with local and individual freedoms, agreed that in this case people needed to be given "a shove."

On the issue of busing alone, however, those whites (Jim and Eddie) who claim to know blacks who oppose busing could justify that claim on the basis of two of the blacks in my small subsample. Albert and Lewis, though favoring school integration, oppose school busing. Their reasoning is similar to that of Eddie or Jim—Lewis invoked the rationale of transportation costs, and Albert paid homage to the ideal of neighborhood schools.

LEWIS: *As far as busing goes, you know, I don't feel like that's right. I don't know what could be done, but I feel like other arrangements could be made besides busing, because, you know, why get a bus load of black people, you know, and ship 'em ten miles across town, you know, when the white people over there don't want them over there in the first place. I think some other arrangements should be made, you know, like, well, say, like, uh, I don't know what the figures are, but, like, say, if it costs, uh, $10,000 a year to bus black people to another school. Well, why not spend, uh, $50,000 and build a centrally located school where both of them would have to go to? And then, I mean like it would take, maybe five or six years to show the difference so far as money goes, you know, but you wouldn't have to bus anybody, you know.*

ALBERT: *I got a little girl and we got a school, I guess two hundred feet from my house. It will make me angry if when she get ready to go to school they make her go to Pike school which is over here [on the other side of town]. It would make me angry if they made her come way up here when I got a school right down there. I don't think it makes any difference about the busing. I just don't think it is right to make her come to school up here when we got a school right there. [The school that Albert wants his children to be able to attend is the same "colored school" that Roy thought his children should attend.]*

Within this small sample, black opinion on the potentially divisive issues of school integration and busing is much like white opinion. Though the blacks are markedly more favorable toward what they see as positive results, both groups accept integration of schools as an accomplished fact. It has even been accepted as a just norm and has considerable appeal on that ground alone. Even those who have some qualms about the results of school integration, such as Jim, Eddie, and Junior, exhibit compunction about their negative statements in the face of this norm that they have internalized. With some surprise (from this observer's liberal point of view), I found that black and white opinion on busing is even more congruent. A group of whites agree with Rick that busing is not a radical innovation— they rode buses to school themselves. Other whites are like John in feeling that busing is necessary for school integration and accept both as facts of life. And others agree with Albert and Lewis that integration is desirable without busing.

On the issue of busing alone black and white opinion is most divisive. Indeed, one could argue that this is precisely the question that Wallace used to separate the races in the Democratic party in recent history. The loss of whites who are honestly opposed to busing alone (perhaps Eddie and Jim) along with those who seize this issue as an outlet for their hostility toward blacks (perhaps Melvin and Dave) would decimate the ranks of any biracial political coalition.

As one can learn from listening to these men, the best way to nullify this potentially divisive issue is to succeed in building school systems that are integrated and have rationales for busing other than integration alone. For small towns such as Furntex, the answer may be centralization of schools at all grade levels. For larger areas, concepts such as magnet schools whose facilities are designed to offer so much more than neighborhood schools that all races are drawn to them might solve the problem.

In either case, the ideal of the small, homogeneous neighborhood school must die. This seems to be happening in Furntex, though it is a slow and painful process even in an area where school busing had the advantage of some a priori legitimacy. Once fully integrated schools are established and gain the sanction of legitimacy that comes with time, and parents are assured that their children are physically safe in school, which also would seem to require a period of successful integration, busing will have lost its potential as a divisive issue. If Furntex is an example, areas of the South that are successfully implementing integration without white flight to private schools are accomplishing this defusing. In other areas, where middle- and upper-class whites have abandoned the public schools, successful integration of blacks and lower-working-class whites might defuse the issue, thereby increasing the potential for a stable biracial coalition.

Jobs—The Fear of Reverse Discrimination

Any political coalition that is concerned with economic redistribution will inevitably be concerned with job opportunities. As long as blacks perceive white workers as engaging in and supporting job discrimination and as long as whites see blacks as trying to gain unfair advantage in promotions and salaries with the aid of federal programs, the prospects for a biracial populist coalition are not at all favorable.[5]

Black furniture workers in Furntex feel that prejudice and discrimination adversely affect the career opportunities of their black peers. Many of their comments on this subject have already been heard. Rick believes that a closed, informal communications system excludes blacks from knowledge of job opportunities, thereby eliminating them from competition. John claimed to know of many furniture plants where blacks are given all the most unpleasant and lowest paying jobs.

Kevin inadvertently supported John's contention when he remarked that blacks seem to like certain types of jobs: "Your blacks like to work in the rough end. I don't know why, whether or not they like to work near them saws or what. And your blacks like to work in the finishing room. They like it. I don't know why—finishing and packing."

Lewis feels that even the poorest whites have advantages over blacks. Brent blames poorer educational facilities, white paternalism, and brainwashing for the fact that blacks are either unable or unwilling to fight for economic advancement. Only Albert does not believe that black opportunity is reduced by job discrimination or prejudice. He feels that this is merely an excuse used by too many blacks for their own personal failures.

When asked if the government should make sure that blacks get fair treatment in job opportunities, the black workers were nearly unanimous in agreement. The only deviant case is Lewis, the black conservative, who fears any increases in government power and believes the problem should somehow be handled on an individual basis. He went so far as to say that government action may be necessary in some places where things are really bad, like "Watts or Harlem or Brooklyn," but he does not think the situation is that bad in Furntex, where, with extra education and effort blacks can advance.

Seven (perhaps only six due to response set bias in Melvin's answer) out of the ten whites in the group also agree that the government should in principle see that blacks do not suffer discrimination in job opportunities. On the other hand, most of these men feel that blacks should not be given any extra advantages. Those three (Dave, Eddie, and Kevin), who were ambivalent or against government actions in the area of job discrimination, spoke about their fear of reverse discrimination in other parts of the interview. Some of their comments are bitter, as were Dave's when he said that blacks are "gonna get whatever they want." Eddie was the clearest in expressing his resentments.

EDDIE: On a lot of occasions, if you've got a colored guy and a white guy working together right now. Well, there's no reason why they shouldn't be paid the same wages. None whatsoever that I can see. There's no reason why they shouldn't be treated equal. But if it comes to movin' one of these people on, I think they should look at their record instead of maybe their color. I'd say that if the colored guy's got the best record, then move him up, not because he's colored, but because he's got the best record. But if you know and you're workin' with him and you know that you do a better job than his, and you know more about the next job than he does, I don't see pullin' him out because he's colored because I would say that the government says that they have to be equal. I don't see no law that says you have to pull him out. Promote him because he's colored so that your foundation can say, "Well, we have a colored superintendent or vice-president or whatever." But a whole lot of this is comin' up. It's in furniture. I know for a fact that it's in furniture. And I could call some by name that I know don't know *their job. And they've got that position because they were moved up in order to fill a position with a colored person. . . . It don't matter, black, white, or whatever, if a man's qualified, promote 'em!*

Paul, who approves of government action against discrimination, also volunteered concern over reverse discrimination.

PAUL: *I have mixed feelings so far as race. I feel it is a good idea to try to get things together right. I feel we should give 'em all the chances we've been giving them. [But] I don't dig the way they've taken it. . . . You give 'em equal rights and now it seems to me that they want more than equal rights. . . . You give one a job. All right, he's going to get the same money and everything that—well, soon he might want more money and more favors, and I've noticed . . . they practically demand more favors. . . . You know, they've got to the point where now they think they are better and they demand more rights. If a man's going to have equal rights with me, that's fine, and everybody gets along with each other, there's no reason why all of this "I want more and I want your job." But, uh, I just get the feeling that a lot of black people say, "You know, we've got our rights, let's take over now!"*

If we add to this group Melvin, who does not wish to associate with blacks anywhere, including at work, and who resents giving any opportunities to blacks, and consider that some of the others feel that government should not grant special advantages to blacks, we find that more than half the white workers are concerned with what they perceive as reverse discrimination.

Thus we have found that black and white workers in Furntex are divided on what actions the government should take to abolish job discrimination. As we have already seen, both groups believe in the value of individual competition, in meritocracy. But blacks believe that under present conditions they have not yet been given a fair start in the race. Whites, on the other hand, tend to view federal government pressure on industries to seek out and advance qualified blacks as plans to change the rules of the game placing whites at a competitive disadvantage.

In this sense, the views of these working-class whites resemble those of the middle-class whites in Lamb's study of residents of a Los Angeles suburb. Lamb quoted one member of the group as representative: "This business of trying to bring the Negro up to their proper place. It's going to take time, and they have to earn it. It's not going to be handed them on a silver platter." [6]

These opinions indicate a great barrier to the realization of any biracial working-class political coalition. The position of working-class whites in the South may well be closer on this issue to that of affluent middle-class suburbanites of the West than to their black working-class neighbors. Given the centrality of the values of achievement and meritocracy, such a conflicting interpretation of the status quo could be of great value to those who may wish to separate and polarize the working classes along racial lines. Such an issue could easily be used to capitalize on existing racial prejudice to spread and perpetuate its ill effects.

Religious Worship and Integration

We have already noted that even though only a few of these men are formally religious in the sense that they regularly attend church, many of them come from religious backgrounds. When asked about religion, most feel that one can be religious without attending church. Thus they are able to view themselves as being somewhat religious. Religion seems to be an important symbolic value to which they pay verbal tribute, if not contributions of their time and money.

Because religion has such an important symbolic value, their views on the propriety of interracial worship and membership might shed some light on the nature and depth of racial prejudice in Furntex. Because so few of these men are church members, however, we must consider their answers with some slight skepticism because their statements can only be hypothetical until they become active in church.

It is noteworthy that biracial church attendance and membership was an issue of national interest in the winter of 1976–77. This was when presidential candidate Jimmy Carter was embarrassed by his home church's reluctance to admit blacks as members. The well-known and well-publicized incidents in Plains, Georgia, were referred to as a preface to questioning these men about blacks and whites attending the same church. These questions were salient to the workers of Furntex because all had heard about the controversy surrounding Carter's home church, and all had some opinion on the issues involved.

The black workers' views were definite. John summed up their feelings best in what was perhaps his most articulate statement of the entire conversation.

JOHN: *It's all the houses of the Lord. There's not one that is better than the other. Why should I not be able to go into the house of the Lord? Now, that's His house—that's His church. Why should I have to get permission to go to His house or His church?*

Rick and Lewis have attended integrated churches, Rick when he lived in New York and Lewis in Furntex at the only integrated church in town, which is primarily a working-class church and not one of the "first" churches of the town. These two men do not think integrated churches are anything out of the ordinary.

Albert was the only black worker to hesitate in answering the question. He began by saying that it would be better for each to go to his own church. Then he reconsidered and decided that it is really no different from school, and integration should be acceptable. He finally remembered that his sister attends the integrated church in Furntex and commented, "It's just a house of the Lord."

Six of the white workers of Furntex believe that blacks should be permitted to worship and join whatever church they please. Their positions on this issue are surprisingly strong, unequivocal, and unconditional.

JUNIOR: *They should go to whichever one they really believe in . . . in God's sight it would be the same. Course a lot of white people don't like goin' with the colored people to church, but still yet, I don't think they got any say so about that. . . . I believe if the people were really church-believing people I believe they would let 'em in. Now, the rest of the church [his church] might not completely go along with it, but as far as the preacher and, uh, the board of directors, I believe they would get in. They'd have to be an awful good reason for 'em not to. Now, they may be some other members to drop out of the church due to the point that they wouldn't like colored people in the church, but in my eyes they wouldn't be living for the Lord if they did drop out. It would be just a sorry excuse.*

PAUL: *I feel that it was totally ridiculous that they barred blacks from the church [Carter's church in Georgia] in the first place because religion is the worship of God the Lord, and, uh, He created all of us, and, uh, to keep a man from worshiping the Lord seems totally sacrilegious. And if a church is going to bar a black man they are totally against what a church should be for.*

Kevin remembers going to revivals with blacks and can therefore see no objection to integrated churches.

Two of the white workers equivocated a bit in their acceptance of blacks in chuch. Eddie thought other white members might experience discomfort, and Roy does not want troublemakers in church.

EDDIE: *I don't see nothin' wrong with a white goin' to a black church or a white church if that's what they want cause the church is supposed to be the Lord's house. If one wouldn't be welcome, I can't see why not really. . . . I feel like that down there [in Carter's church in Georgia] might have been political motivated. I don't feel that something like that [is good], but I feel like if a colored man feels like he has to go to a white church—I don't know. I'd have to go somewhere on the middle line because there's gonna be a lot of people in that church that might not feel comfortable with him there. Still yet, I feel like it's the house of the Lord. [Eddie ended by noting that he doubts a black would be allowed to join his church and used this as an example of the hypocrisy of those who regularly attend church—he does not.]*

ROY: *I don't see nothin' wrong with it [blacks and whites together]. It's like on this program that I watch on Sunday mornings at nine. There's this preacher that heals people and all. I mean that when you go to heaven or hell or wherever you're going, it's not going to make any difference to God what color you are. There's going to be colored people and white people all there together. . . . It's okay if they are going there [to church] to worship God, but not if they're just going to cause trouble.*

These responses are interesting in that the speakers sometimes take a different position in principle than they might assume in actual practice. In principle, Roy and Eddie can see nothing wrong with integrated churches. Advocacy of this principle makes them feel that they are unprejudiced, a value that seems to carry a positive self-image. This enables them to criticize whites who oppose the integration of churches, thereby bestowing moral superiority upon themselves. But in actual practice, they are free to oppose any specific black application for admittance to church membership on the grounds that the individual is only seeking to "cause trouble" or that he is "political motivated." Because any black application for membership in an all-white church can easily be interpreted this way, blacks can be effectively barred without sacrifice of principle.

One might argue that though these men seem genuinely ambivalent about the question, such an equivocating position is what one would expect to find among many middle- and upper-class white southerners. They outwardly appear to be above the racist lower classes by accepting the principle of open membership, but then appoint committees to screen applicants and weed out those who seek to join for unworthy motives. All blacks are effectively barred because the "only possible motive" one could have for joining would be to seek publicity by being the first black to join an all-white church. In fact, this is precisely what Carter's church accomplished. The principle of integration was accepted and a committee formed that then rejected the applicant. This ploy seemed to satisfy Roy and Eddie, as well as many of those white middle-class Americans who had been critical of Carter's church.

Only two out of this group of ten white workers expressed obvious hostility to the ideal of integrated churches. Melvin feels that things are at present as they should be, with each race having its own churches. Dave was evasive. Though the content of his words is similar to those of Roy and Eddie, his tone of voice and obvious annoyance with the question showed a lack of ambivalence on the issue. His feelings of fear and resentment far outweigh any dedication to principle. His mouthing acceptance seemed more a half-hearted attempt to mislead the interviewer than a subconscious attempt to convince himself that he is not a racist.

DAVE: *Well, uh, they do everything else together.* [*He says this with obvious disgust.*] *Like I said before, as long as they don't bother me, I'm not going to bother them. If they want to get along with me, fine, I'll get along with them.*

QUESTION: *So you wouldn't mind if they came to your church?*

DAVE: *It wouldn't bother me a bit, if, you know, they acted like, just a regular person and not just try to pull more and more blacks in and make it, just end up making it be just solid blacks in church, you know, and all whites leave out.*

In a subtle yet significant sense, Dave's reaction is very different from Eddie's or Roy's. The latter two have internalized the principle of integration so that any feelings of racism they may harbor are engaged in a silent internal war with this norm. They enhance their own sense of self-esteem by embracing liberal values, all the while making behavioral concessions to prejudice. Dave has not internalized the liberal value of integration. He merely recognizes it as a societal value to which he must pay lip service or else be evaluated negatively by others.

Yet Dave's actual behavior may be much like that of Roy or Eddie. Each would find some grounds to oppose any specific black application for church membership. Therefore, in terms of actual behavior, about half of the white workers of the sample, when we include Melvin, would probably *act* in a prejudiced manner when faced with the question of an actual black application for membership in a church they attend.

These ten white workers might be seen as illustrating several stages of socialization of the liberal value of integration. Melvin openly espouses the countervalue of segregation. Dave, who prefers segregation, recognizes that his position is not socially acceptable and pays defensive lip service to integration. Eddie and Roy have begun to internalize the value and feel genuine ambivalence. The rest seem to have resolved the internal struggle and to have fully accepted the value of integration with respect to religion.

A number of conclusions can be drawn about working-class prejudice in Furntex. Most working-class whites accept in principle (and probably in fact, if faced with a fait accompli) what nearly all working-class blacks accept completely: the integration of churches should not be opposed. That is, in at least some areas of social life, liberal, integrationist, nonracist values have become a significant part of the belief system of working-class southern whites. The majority of these men seem to be no more racist in this area than are the middle- and upper-class whites of Furntex who attend lily-white middle- and upper-class churches. Many of these men would feel as uncomfortable in those churches as would their black economic peers. Some working-class blacks and whites do in fact worship together. In a social environment where blacks and whites work and worship together, prejudice and racism may well be in decline.

Housing

The question may be raised whether acceptance of working, attending school, or worshiping with a member of another race extends to acceptance of living next door to him. Relations between neighbors are often considered more intimate than those between workmates. Living beside someone is a stronger statement of social equality than sharing work space or worship space. What is being shared is much more private and closer to one's primordial sense of identity. Public relationships are qualitatively different and imply much less about status.

The views of the men of Furntex about integrated housing were probed in a number of ways. They were asked where they live, how race relations have changed, and how people should live ideally.

We should not be surprised that Melvin and Dave, who are hostile toward public racial mixing, are also hostile to blacks and whites living near each other.

One of the other whites draws a clear public/private distinction. Junior, who is willing to accept integration of public spheres of life and who has even internalized that value, draws a clear color line when it comes to integration of more private spheres. As shown in the following passage, he is even willing to condone subversion of the law in order to maintain a segregated private sphere.

JUNIOR: *I don't think a colored person should really live in a white neighborhood unless—I don't think he should really live in the same neighborhood. He just wouldn't feel at home. He'd want to be around his type of people knowin' that the white people feel bad toward him. I don't think he should live anywhere [near] a white person really. Ideally they'd be better off with their own people. . . . They gotta go to school, so we can't be too choosy about that. But where they live, they could be a little choosy.*

QUESTION: *How do you think race relations will be in Furntex ten years from now?*

JUNIOR: *It will probably get worse. They will probably be right beside us, probably . . . cause they're gettin' everywhere now. A person building new houses, he can't refuse 'em for no reason at all even if it is an all-white section. If they've got the money for the down payment; they get turned down; that man's in trouble. He'd better have an awful good excuse or lie about the house being sold one. And I know as a fact that they do lie about the houses being sold to keep 'em from gettin' in. They do it in White Rock, the neighborhood I'm trying to move into. One was wanting the house beside me, and they told 'em the house was already sold and it's not. Cause a buddy of mine is going to buy the house. They'd tell 'em anything. They showed 'em a legal contract made up that it was owned to keep 'em from filing for it. But it just so happened that the niggers [it is significant that here he changes the label he uses from "colored," who do not threaten him, to "niggers," who threaten his private turf] didn't want the house that bad or they probably would have pushed it and they probably would have got it. Cause he made a barefaced lie about it.*

The rest of the white workers in the sample tend at least partially to accept integration in the private realm of housing. Kevin made the qualification that it is acceptable only if whites maintain a majority. He fears becoming a minority, as did Dave with respect to church membership. Eddie said that he would not mind living near blacks if they could afford to buy the home near him, but that ideally he would have "separate and equal" housing for each race in districts with the provision that people could freely move about where they wish and where they would be accepted as friends. "It would really be up to the individual then to make friends or enemies." Once again, Eddie manages to have it both ways. He accepts the principle of integration, thereby enhancing his own self-image, while avoiding any of the practical consequences by stressing other values—individualism and choice.

The other five white workers are more positively inclined toward integrated housing. Roy lives in an essentially integrated neighborhood and can see no reason why it should be any other way. Terry remembers having had black neighbors with whom he got along well. Paul feels that integrated housing would promote better race relations and better understanding. He generalizes from his own change in attitude that came from contact with blacks. Mark made a similar argument, saying that it would promote compromise between the races. Jim feels, as does Eddie, that where a man lives should depend only on how expensive a house he can afford. Unlike Eddie, he feels that ideally neighborhoods would be integrated.

Two of the white workers went beyond the question of integration to volunteer comments on the consequences for blacks of segregated housing. The comments of Jim and Paul echo many of the complaints of the black workers.

PAUL: *The blacks for the most part now really live in the slummiest part of town. Like I ride through there, and I'm appalled at some of the houses these people are living in. I mean, right under our nose—little shacks. It could probably be a little more integrated and generally the people just put forth a little more effort to get along better.*

JIM: *How many churches care about how the black people live? Not a lot! . . . There are houses in this town that do not have plumbing inside the city—black people living in them. Things need to be rectified. They need to be changed. Black people beginning to notice these things and beginnin' to come out with them. Like in [a nearby city], I saw on the news a couple of weeks ago, some black people talkin' about, "Man, we can't live in this mess no more. You ask us to get out of it, but how you help us?" . . . The normal southern white person says, "Aw, shit, they wanna stay in that mess anyway. They been raised in it, they gonna stay in it." That's not true! Your younger blacks, people my age and your age, they don't wanna live like that no more. They're tired of it. . . . I believe the majority of black people are beginning to say, "Okay, I've got my rights and I want to be equal to white people, right. I've gotta show 'em that I can be just as clean as they are, too." Because, black people, you know they notice it. You know without a doubt they notice the homes the white man live in and the homes they live in!*

Jim is certainly correct. The blacks of Furntex do notice that blacks have worse housing than whites. Nearly all the blacks in my small group volunteered statements to this effect. Perhaps the most angry comments came from Lewis, who lives in extremely poor housing.

LEWIS: *I would say housing is a real bad problem. . . . As far as black people go, when you move into a house, eight out of ten times you have to remodel the inside. When you move into a house, you don't know if it's gonna have hot water or cold water. You don't even know if it's gonna have water. This boy that lives around the corner from me, he moved into his house [and] he had manure wiped all across the walls from where the last person had gotten mad or something and moved out and on the doors. And it wouldn't come off the doors so he had to take all the doors off and throw 'em away and buy new doors, and he painted over the walls. That's what the average black person has to go through when they move into another house—IF THEY FIND A HOUSE!*

With the exception of Albert, who prefers separate housing for blacks and whites (like Junior, he makes a public/private distinction and favors segregation in the private realm), all the blacks feel that integrated housing would be the ideal situation and might improve housing for blacks. Only one member of the black subgroup, John, feels there is no substantial white effort to maintain segregated housing in Furntex. The rest regard white prejudice as an important factor in determining housing availability and conditions for blacks.

Thus, with respect to housing, we have found a little more difference between black and white opinion in Furntex. As a whole, whites seem a bit more racist and opposed to integration in this area of social life that is more private than work, school, or religious worship. Nevertheless, around half of the whites agree with the blacks that housing integration is at least acceptable to them if not desirable in the ideal. It may be somewhat like emphasizing that the glass is half full rather than half empty, but to find that a significant proportion of working-class southern whites are willing to live near blacks is a surprising finding in a socioeconomic group that is often stereotyped as a hotbed of racism.

Friendship across Racial Lines

Thus far we have mainly examined casual contact between whites and blacks of Furntex that do not threaten existing superordinate-subordinate relationships. Only when residential integration is discussed do interracial contacts necessarily raise doubts about the assumption of white superiority. In a comprehensive study of prejudice, Allport labeled such contacts as "equal status" contacts. After reviewing studies on the effect of different kinds of contact, he concluded that such equal status contacts tend to reduce racial prejudice, unless that prejudice is deeply rooted in the personality. Prejudice is reduced especially if contact is aimed toward the achievement of common goals.[7]

One might argue, as Allport does, that on-the-job contacts among blue-collar workers are equal status contacts in pursuit of common goals. But, as we have already seen in examining the issue of job opportunity, such contacts may be perceived so that prejudice is reinforced or even increased. The white worker may regard his black coworkers as inferior craftsmen who are seeking to use their minority status to gain an unfair advantage in wage increases or promotional opportunities.

In this section, the focus is on how these men define personal relations across racial lines. Each was asked if he has any black or white acquaintances whom he considers friends.

When asked whether they have friendships with blacks, six of the ten white workers (Eddie, Jim, Kevin, Mark, Paul, and Terry) specifically mentioned black friends at work with whom they joke, eat lunch, play cards, and share experiences. Some of these relationships extend beyond the workplace. Terry reported going hunting and fishing with black friends. Paul has a black friend with whom he goes "out drinking." Kevin plays ball with black friends and said there is a black couple with whom he and his wife frequently share meals at each other's houses. Jim and Terry both remember having very close black friends while in the military. Jim added that he shares a love for "soul" music with black friends and highly regards this black contribution to our culture. Another member of the group, Roy, did not specifically mention having black friends at work, but reported that he used to ride motorcycles with a black friend.

All of these relationships can be regarded as equal status contacts having a positive impact on how these men regard their black economic peers. The friendships reported by the five black workers in the group are similar to those reported by these whites. Rick, Brent, and John had close white friends while in the military. Albert has white friends at work and others with whom he plays ball. Lewis, who has few friends in either race, reported that he socializes and often shares meals with some white friends. All the blacks and over half of the whites in the sample (seven) have significant equal status contacts and pursue common goals of pleasure in these contacts. Assuming the validity of Allport's hypothesis that such contacts are impossible if prejudice lies deep within the personality structure, we may take this as evidence that these seven men do not suffer functional prejudice, though they may indeed harbor more superficial kinds of prejudice.

The contact of the other three members of the group with blacks is more limited. Of the three (Dave, Junior, and Melvin), Junior seems to have the most positive contact, yet that is limited to a single black at work whose car Junior helped fix one day so he could go home. The man reciprocated the favor once when Junior ran out of gas. But, as Junior said, "That was about it. We talk at work and play cards." This contact is different from those of the other men in that Junior regards it as unique and limits it to a single acquaintance.

The remaining two white workers have no contact at all with blacks that they perceive as equal status contact. In fact, Dave and Melvin go out of their way to avoid contact that would imply any equality in status.

Melvin spoke of a black at work whom he regards as typical in that the man "bugs" everyone else. He said he has never had any black friends and comes into contact with blacks only occasionally when he plays football. Dave shows extreme sensitivity to even the idea that he might have some close black friends. His contacts are purposely kept casual. Such an admission would be an admission of equality and would do damage to his self-esteem.

QUESTION: *Have you ever had any blacks as friends?*
DAVE: *Oh, yeah.*
QUESTION: *How did that happen?*
DAVE: *Uh, there's a lot of blacks that acts just like a white person, just like they's a lot of white people that act like black people. I mean, as far as, you know, just going up and start talking to. They's a lot of friendly [blacks].*
QUESTION: *Have you ever known any blacks that you could really feel close to as a friend?*
DAVE: *Yeah—well, now don't go saying "pretty close to!" . . . Playing football about three months ago, I got messed up running the ball and tore into a tree and I had to get ten stitches right across there [his head] and knocked two teeth loose and a collar bone and messed up my shoulder blade and knocked a hole in my temple right here and the day that happened was Sunday and when I come into work the next day on Monday, there was one down there at the plant that always picked and carried on and aggravated me about saying that my wife done it, stuff [like that], just picking and just really being friendly. But don't misunderstand me. I don't go up and beg 'em to talk to me!*

The positive contacts implying equality in status enjoyed by many of these white workers may have as their roots a long history of such contacts that date back to childhood experiences. Some, such as Paul and Mark, experienced their first contacts when schools were integrated. Others, such as Jim, made the first meaningful contacts in the military. Some had contacts with blacks in childhood.

Family members often interpreted the meanings of these contacts in subtle ways showing approval or disapproval. For example, Eddie's grandfather, whom he holds in extremely high esteem, directly interpreted the meaning of interracial contacts for him in such a way as to lay the groundwork for future equal status contacts. Eddie's earliest memories of contact with blacks are when he was a child working with them around the farm. Eddie related an interesting incident from his childhood.

EDDIE: *Well, colored people's chopped wood for Grandpa up there [at the farm]. All [of us would] set down to the dinner table and eat dinner. And, uh, well, my cousin, he got up and left the table. We all come in and set down and he was already in, already washed up and eatin'. [We] come in and set down and Grandpa, well, they [the blacks] weren't going to set at the table. They wanted a plate and they'd go to on the porch. My grandfather told 'em, he says, "No," he says, "when we eat, we eats in the kitchen around here. Get you a plate over yonder and set down." My cousin just got up from the table and walked off. He told 'em, he said, "You don't let that bother you. I run this household and you set down and eat." They acted like they were uncomfortable to begin with. But as things progressed they went on and everything was all right. Now, he didn't mind splitting wood out there with 'em, but he didn't want to eat with 'em. Well, you ain't going to eat out of one plate nohow. I wouldn't'go over to maybe eat out of their plate, but I don't mind eatin' with 'em, as far as settin' with 'em.*

No doubt Eddie feels there is some disparity in his status with blacks, but the lesson he seems to have learned is that sharing work with men across racial lines implies a very definite sense of equality in both status and interests. This is precisely the sense of commonality that must exist in order for a biracial political coalition to be successfully constructed.

Sexuality

Allport contends, "There is a subtle psychological reason why Negroid characteristics favor an association of ideas with sex. The Negro seems dark, mysterious, distant—yet at the same time warm, human, and potentially accessible. Sex is forbidden; colored people are forbidden; the ideas begin to fuse. It is no accident that prejudiced people call tolerant people 'niggerlovers.' The very choice of the word suggests that they are fighting the feeling of attraction in themselves." [8]

The most intimate of all social relations are sexual relations, and the most definite statement of equality that can be made across racial lines is to advocate the acceptability of interracial marriage. The workers of Furntex were asked how they feel about interracial marriage and whether they think they could maintain a good relationship with a friend who married across racial lines.

The black workers in the group are tolerant toward interracial sexual contacts. Brent summarized the positions of most of them in saying that "love is blind." The consensus seems to be that such decisions are the business of the individual involved.

The only significant dissent came from Albert and Lewis. Albert thinks that though it is an individual matter both races are "better off staying with their own." Lewis raised a rational objection that does not necessarily imply prejudice—the problem of the social stigma and handicaps placed on both the parents and any offspring. [9]

LEWIS: *I feel like if the two parties involved have a full knowledge of what they —of what they're doing, and know completely well and realize the consequences that might result and they still want to do what they're going to do, I think they ought to be allowed to. . . . To be a little extreme, if, uh, a black dude were to marry a Japanese woman, the kids they would have would have to go to school. And it's no tellin' what kind of names black people would think of for 'em and white people would call 'em. You know. Like the close-mind[ed] blacks, whites, and Japanese would all be against 'em. He wouldn't feel like he had anybody.*

The white workers are much less enthusiastic about interracial sexual contact and marriage. Only one member of the group, Paul, has no qualms about the question. The rest can best be described as fatalistically tolerant. They personally would not want to marry across racial lines, but they realize that such marriages are no longer infrequent and feel that they must be accepted as a fact of life. Roy went the furthest in expressing a belief that he could conceivably fall in love with and marry a black woman, even though he does not presently believe in interracial marriage. Mark displays considerable compunction in stating his position: "I'm sorry to say that I don't believe in it." Eddie's evaluation is similar to Lewis's—he expressed concern for the problems the children might face. Most of these men said that they feel they could probably remain close to a friend who married a black, though it might cause some strains in the relationship.

Three of the men do not exhibit even a limited degree of tolerance. Junior very strongly disapproves of interracial sexual contact and characterized the worst possible race relations as "datin' one another's daughter . . . and all of 'em livin' in the neighborhood together, associating together, and going to bed with one another's wife and husband all this. . . . It's that way now in a few areas." Junior earlier drew a clear line where he thought interracial contacts should end in talking about his little girl being in school with blacks.

JUNIOR: *I don't care, as long as they don't bother her. They can talk to her, or—I wouldn't want her to ever bring one home, now! But I mean she can talk to 'em in school, or whatever she has to do to get out of school, and then get out of school and go their separate ways. I don't think they should associate otherwise. Now, when they get older there ain't too much they can do about it. Cause I know a lot of white girls and niggers [again he has shifted his form of address from "colored"] date around here, and some of 'em are married to 'em. Well, I guess they figure that if they can work together they can get married. [Earlier, he used this same line of logic to argue that they should be allowed to go to school together. He explains how this case is different.] But I just couldn't see it. They go to school because they got to go to school. And they gotta work and you gonna have to work together somewhere, but you sure don't have to get married and live together!*

Dave and Melvin also expressed strong disapproval along with an air of fatalism that one can do little today to prevent such unfortunate relationships. Melvin made about the strongest negative statement in saying that he could not possibly be friends with anyone who was married to a black.

The significance of this combination of statements is that most of these white workers seem to be slowly accepting the fait accompli of interracial marriage that is informally thrust upon them by society, just as they accepted the fait accompli of integrated schools and workplaces that was legally thrust upon them by government. No doubt this is a long, slow process, but it seems to be happening. Only three of the men can be considered diehards on the matter, and even they have resolved themselves to the fact that they have little choice except to shield themselves and their own families.

Personal approval of interracial marriage is not, of course, a necessity for a biracial "political marriage." To achieve the latter end, all that would seem necessary is tolerance for the freedom of others to do as they please so that resentments and fears surrounding that issue do not cause erosion of any such coalition. To argue that complete personal acceptance of interracial marriage is necessary for the existence of a political coalition would be the logical equivalent to arguing that blacks should be kept in slavery and given no rights or they will intermarry with whites. Allport pointed out that Abraham Lincoln had to deal with this latter argument in attacking slavery. Lincoln saw this as "counterfeit logic which presumes that, if I do not want a Negro woman for a slave, I do necessarily want her for a wife." [10] One might argue that working-class whites may be able to conceive of and pursue common political goals with working-class blacks and yet not personally approve of marrying any of their political allies.

Idealized Race Relations

During the course of our conversations, the men were asked to describe as best they could how relations would be between the races in Furntex if they had the power to structure such relations. After they described idealized race relations, they were asked to describe what they would think to be the worst possible race relations. Finally, using their own descriptions of "best" and "worst," they were asked to rate race relations in Furntex as they are now, as they were ten years ago, and as they will be ten years from now on a scale of one ("worst") to ten ("best").

This series of questions was designed to reveal several aspects of racial attitudes in Furntex. The answers tell us whether these furniture workers are oriented more toward integration or segregation, whether black and white views differ, how they evaluate government actions that have promoted integration, and whether they are more oriented toward the past with its tattered banners of white supremacy or a future that transcends racial conflict.

Looking first at the five black workers in the group, we find them united in believing that ideal race relations involve integration. Brent spoke about breaking down racial stereotypes; John said the "habit" of living in segregated neighborhoods would no longer exist; Rick feels merit rather than color would become the single criterion for all of life's rewards. Lewis, after talking about how things would be integrated, offered the most insightful example. He said that ideally, if a black man and a white man had a fight and called each other names, it would not occur to either to use any racial slurs in the course of their insults. Only Albert thinks of idealized racial relations in terms of segregation, and he limits this to segregation of the more private spheres of life. He is fearful that trouble would result if blacks and whites live too near each other.

Taking the other side of the question, most of the blacks feel that the worst kind of race relations are those that existed in the past—forced segregation. Two of the men, however, Albert and Rick, feel that the next worst situation is forced integration. Given the choice of forced integration or forced segregation, their dislike for segregation (at least in the more public spheres of life) outweighs their disapproval of the use of force.

Working-class whites in Furntex differ from the blacks in their characterization of ideal race relations. Only about half the whites wanted anything approaching total integration. Not surprisingly, those who earlier in the interview expressed disapproval of school and housing integration or fear of reverse discrimination in jobs tend to see ideal race relations in terms of segregation (Dave, Eddie, Junior, Kevin, and Melvin). Yet once again, we might take the more optimistic view and look at the glass as half full, for half of the white men see almost total integration as a desirable ideal.

On the question of the worst possible race relations, however, one of the more important issues that separates blacks and whites in Furntex arises—the use of government power to bring about integration. The white workers define the worst kind of race relations as forced integration, not forced segregation. In fact, many of these men do not believe that segregation even involves the question of force. Of the ten white men, only three (Jim, Paul, and Roy) thought segregation was worse than forced integration. The rest agree with Mark, who says that the worst thing to do is "putting white and black people together that don't care one way or the other if they're there or not and don't want to help each other at all . . . just more or less forcing them to be together. I believe that they should keep them separate if it was gonna have to do all that, because you can't force people to like each other."

When asked why he approves of forced school integration and not of the use of force in other areas, Mark retreated to the now familiar public-private distinction used by others.

MARK: *But as far as living together, that's more, I mean living in the same community, that's a little more distressing there, because, uh, I mean, well, you know, going to, being bused together, going to school, you don't spend your whole time there with 'em when you go home or whatever you do.*

Their evaluation of government action designed to bring about integration colors the way these men rate past, present, and future race relations in Furntex. Most of the blacks believe that past government intervention was necessary and beneficial. Though a few are somewhat less than enthusiastic about future government actions, they do not fear them or view them as threatening. All the blacks in the group think race relations have improved in Furntex over the last ten years, and most see this trend continuing into the future.

The whites are somewhat less optimistic. Melvin said race relations have been bad in the past and present and expects they will continue to be bad in the future. Kevin and Junior feel that race relations were better in the past, when there was no trouble. Eddie and Dave remember that the civil rights movement began to have an impact in Furntex about ten years ago and therefore they rate that troubled period as worse than the present. Eddie sees worse relations in the future because of anticipated government action. Dave feels things will continue as they are now, unless blacks become politically active.

DAVE: I don't think it will get no worse unless that there is blacks votin' in the government. I think that the blacks would try to run things if they could be voted into office.

The other half of the white subsample shares with the blacks more optimism and the goal that relations will improve and be defined by greater integration.

The answers to these questions reflect attitudes similar to those expressed in other parts of the interviews. Blacks approve of past government actions and are integration-oriented. Though most whites have at least grudgingly accepted past government actions, some of them would journey back to the tranquility of the segregated past were they given the choice. Moreover, most do not wish government to force any additional integration upon them. Those who do see more integration as a desirable goal (about half) hope it will come about slowly, tranquilly, and voluntarily.

We might conclude that the white workers of Furntex live both in the past and in the future. They seem to have one foot in each world. This may be the natural reaction of members of a generation that has experienced both segregation and integration. Most acknowledge that the official norms of their society have changed. Such acceptance in itself should be comforting to those who would wish to build a biracial political coalition. That their own private visions of the ideal community do not conform to official norms and that their fears make *direct* government-initiated integration, especially in private spheres, a nonviable overt policy for such a coalition are simply two facts that must be accounted for by any would-be architects of a biracial alliance of the working classes.

Political Manifestations of Prejudice—
The Klan and Wallace

If the white workingmen of Furntex are hard-core racists, one would expect them to express some sympathy for, if not openly embrace, the goals of the Ku Klux Klan. Each of the men was asked what he knows about the Klan, whether he thinks it should be outlawed, or whether the group conducts worthwhile activities.

The Klan has had a long and active history in the Furntex area, though in recent years it has been confined to infrequent rallies outside of town and a few cross burnings. This decline in Klan activity is reflected in the responses of these men. Most seem to regard the Klan as an anachronism, a kind of joke involving people who are out of joint with the times. Interestingly enough, this feeling that the Klan is composed of a small group of ineffective fools is even stronger among the black workers. Most feel that the Klan is irrelevant because they "don't do much anymore."

Beyond this dismissal of the importance of the Klan are some statements that shed light on the racial attitudes of white Furntex workers. After Dave commented that the Klan is relatively inactive, he resentfully noted that "I don't feel it's no worse than, uh, the black people having these Black Panther clubs and things that they've got, I mean. I think if one was to be outlawed the other one should be outlawed." Eddie expressed some sympathy for the Klan, saying he had once considered joining but had decided that the Klan was wrong because "the colored man should have his rights, too, really, cause he's in the United States and he's supposed to be a free man, too. Really I don't see as the white man can say too much."

The rest of the men have little sympathy for the Klan. Most are in favor of outlawing the group. Two (Paul and Terry) gave a more libertarian response, saying that perhaps the group should not be outlawed, but its practices should be. Junior's response is fairly typical.

JUNIOR: *I think if anybody knows who is a member of the Klu [sic] Klux Klan is they should be told [reported], to the authorities—or if the Klu [sic] Klux Klan would ever get me out for something, or something like this, and I could know definite who they were and the law didn't seem to want to do anything about it, I'd just go out and find 'em myself. . . . They've [the Klan] been known in other states to get 'em out and beat 'em up. But to me it's wrong. You can't take something over just because you hate somebody. You can't dress up like, put a sheet over your head and blow somebody's brains out and hang 'em from a tree and whoop 'em for two weeks or some junk like that, just cause he done something wrong.*

We might have expected Melvin, who is the most openly racially prejudiced member of the group, to have expressed some sympathy for the Klan. In fact he did not. His only comment was that he has heard one may hire the Klan to destroy an enemy's property, and he does not feel this should be allowed. He and one other member of the group, Roy, who said he has never heard of the Klan harming anyone, seem genuinely ignorant of the Klan's racial activities, difficult though that may be to believe. Given that these are also the two least educated and sophisticated members of the entire group, if any are ignorant of these matters, they would be the ones.

An element of consistency appears in the logic of these men in condemning the Klan. They have once again rejected the use of more obvious and visible forms of force. Just as they reject the government's imposition of integration, they reject segregation imposed by an active Ku Klux Klan. They do not, however, seem to comprehend the more subtle and even more effective force that exists in social norms and practices of a white majority. These forces of tradition, with all their accompanying self-fulfilling beliefs and assumptions, have made the counterforce of government necessary for social justice.

A more contemporary political phenomenon associated with racial prejudice is support for George Wallace. One comprehensive study of Wallace support in the South in 1968 concluded that it "was based on simple opposition to civil rights." The study concluded that though there was a certain "share the wealth" populist flavor to the Wallace campaign, this was much less important than the white working-class fear that government actions would cost them a status loss to unfairly advantaged blacks.[11]

Four of the ten whites in the sample, (Eddie, Jim, Junior, and Roy) expressed some positive affect toward George Wallace. Three of those four (all but Jim) claimed to have been strong Wallace supporters at one time. My question here is whether these men were responding to Wallace's famous stand of defiance in the school doorway or to the Wallace who in 1970 told an audience, "The affluent super-rich in this country are more dangerous than the militants. . . . Citizens' power will right the wrongs perpetrated against the middle class and lower class in the United States. . . . No government is administered according to the objective and intent of the Founding Fathers . . . unless it is administered for the weak, the poor, and the humble as well as the powerful."[12]

Eddie is the strongest Wallace supporter of the four. He is the only one who claimed ever to have voted for Wallace. When asked about how he had voted in past presidential elections, he asked, "What year was Wallace shot?" After being told that Wallace was shot during the 1972 primary campaign, Eddie laughingly said, "I hadn't voted since '68. When he got shot he wiped me out!" Given that Eddie was registered as a Republican, the ending of Wallace's third-party efforts and his return to the Democratic party virtually ended Eddie's chance to vote for his favorite candidate unless he changed registration. Instead, Eddie simply dropped out of politics and no longer considered voting. When asked to explain his support for Wallace, Eddie was somewhat defensive and raised the subject of racial relations with no prompting.

EDDIE: *I have to admit that he had some stands on racial problems that I don't know what would have come out of 'em, but I don't feel that he was exactly right on everything. But it seemed to me like . . . he could speak to the public. It seemed to me like he could get more done and in a direct way. I just feel like I would have liked to seen him up there, to give him a chance. And he just didn't make it. So I don't know how it would have turned out. It might have been the worst decision I ever made.*

Eddie, who has internalized the norms of racial equality and integration, feels compelled to explain that his support of Wallace was not racially motivated. Yet many of Wallace's principles that related to racial issues no doubt have an appeal to Eddie: a firm stand against school busing, opposition to integration forced by the national government, and firing government-hired bureaucrats and social scientists who have nothing more useful to do than meddle in people's lives or work out new busing schemes.

Junior and Roy were less helpful in explaining their support for Wallace. Junior simply remembered that Wallace "had a lot of good issues in 1968," and Roy said that "the way Wallace talked I liked him better," but could say little more. One might easily understand Wallace's appeal to Junior. Though he is not strongly against school busing, he is extremely hostile toward government action that might bring blacks into white neighborhoods and greatly resents government welfare programs that he interprets as having rewarded blacks for being lazy. He hinted that the shooting may have been a conspiracy to keep Wallace out of office because "they felt like he could do more than the rest of 'em could." Roy's stand is more difficult to explain, even hypothetically. He is one of the least racially prejudiced men in the group, even on a superficial level. The most plausible link to prejudice would be that Wallace's stand against school busing coincided with Roy's. But, as we have seen, Roy's opposition to busing is not heavily racially motivated.

Earlier in the interview, Jim said that he liked Wallace in 1972 because he was saying some of the same things that Carter later said, for example, about welfare and tax reform. Such rhetoric may have had some appeal for Junior and Roy as well, especially Junior. Jim, however, found Wallace less appealing than Carter because Carter had greater credibility and Jim was disturbed by some of Wallace's positions on racial issues. He stated with some measure of pride that he disapproved of Wallace's barring the doorway of the University of Alabama, but then said that he might have supported Wallace in 1972 because "he seemed to have calmed down on racial issues." Yet, later in the interview, Jim indicated that though he accepts the principle of school integration, he has many doubts and resentments about its ramifications. No doubt Wallace appealed to these fears on a subconscious level.

Thus far, Wallace seems to be an appealing political figure for a number of reasons, including racial prejudice. Except for Roy, who seems to be an accidental Wallace supporter, Wallace's thinly veiled racist appeals struck a harmonious chord playing on both conscious fears (Junior) and unconscious racial fears (Eddie and Jim).

Other kinds of appeal can also be identified. No doubt regional identification with a southerner was a factor. More important are some of the issues of populism. Eddie likes the way "he could speak to the public" and feels "he could get more done . . . in a direct way." Junior echoed this idea, saying that Wallace seemed to scare the establishment into believing he could accomplish more—"he could do more than the rest of 'em." These men seem to be saying that Wallace appeals to them as common men, and therefore they identify with him and find him credible. Moreover, he is antiestablishment, and his policies would help hardworking average citizens like themselves. This is what Jim sees in welfare and tax reform. The fact is that these men feel threatened by rapid social and economic change and no longer believe that hard work pays off as they were always promised in the great American Dream. Wallace reassured them that it does, or at least it *should*, and he would right the situation. His position also reassured these men that they are important and valuable individuals—he reinforced their senses of identity and worth that were being lost in a time of social turmoil.[13]

The opinions of these white workingmen were by no means unanimous. Though three of the four found some appeal in the racist elements of the Wallace candidacy, four other whites in the group (Kevin, Mark, Paul, and Terry) totally refused even to consider supporting Wallace because of the racist elements in his program. Three of these four (Mark, Paul, and Terry) exhibit considerably less racial prejudice than Eddie, Jim, or Junior. Kevin seems about as prejudiced as any, and yet he, too, rejects Wallace because "him saying bad things about blacks causes me not to want to vote for him cause I wouldn't want him to say bad things about anybody else." The two men who might be expected to be most likely to support Wallace on racial grounds, Dave and Melvin, claimed to know nothing at all about Wallace.

Though Wallace does appeal to racist sentiments (remembering that those who expressed support for Wallace harbor more fears and hatreds than those who reject him), racist appeals alone are not sufficient to gain support. In fact, racist appeals turn away both those who are less prejudiced and some of those who may harbor some prejudice but accept nonprejudiced norms. Moreover, racist appeals seem to cause some discomfort in the minds of those who are still working out their own cognitive dissonance over integration—Jim and Eddie felt compelled to explain away any racist appeal that Wallace may have had. This discomfort would tend to reduce support for a candidate such as Wallace were other viable options available. If a biracial populist coalition were to be built, it would have to provide these kinds of options.

Conclusion

We began by asking whether the racial prejudice of the white working-men of Furntex is of such a quality and depth that it lies deep within the ego structures of these men. If so, prejudice would be functional to their personalities and would be a much greater obstacle to the building of a biracial populist political coalition than more superficial or folkways prejudice that manifests itself mostly as a habit or etiquette system. Having examined the racial attitudes of these workers in some detail in many different areas, we can now venture an answer to this most difficult question.

Racial prejudice certainly exists among the workers of Furntex. It is very much alive even if it is not well. Not a single white man in the group was found to be totally without any prejudice in the areas examined. Roy came perhaps the closest in that his only concessions to prejudice were an admission that he would be bothered if his children were to become a racial minority in school and an avowed disbelief in interracial marriage. Yet he would send his children to school even if there were 90 percent blacks in attendance and can conceive of the possibility that he might fall in love with and marry a black woman. A variety of attitudes indicating prejudice were distributed among the others: negative racial stereotypes of blacks, some concern over government actions that might force integrated housing, ambivalence over the results of integrating the schools, concern that whites could be relegated to minority status in schools and neighborhoods, a small amount of concern over blacks joining and perhaps even taking over white churches, disapproval of interracial sexual contacts and marriage, and a very strong concern that the national government has changed the rules in life's game giving blacks an unfair advantage in gaining jobs, promotions, housing subsidies, and welfare benefits.

Despite this long list of fears and hatreds, for the most part blacks seem to serve as the main target simply out of habit, because they always have been a target, not because denigration of blacks serves significantly to raise the status of most of these working white men. Many socialize with blacks whom they consider as close friends. Most of these men want more from life than simply being one step above working-class blacks—most have some middle-class aspirations. Only a few of the men display their prejudice without compunction, and most seem to have accepted the norms that blacks should at least be integrated into all public spheres of life.

Allport distinguishes several signs that indicate the type of prejudice that is functional to one's personality. One is avoidance of members of the disliked group.[14] Melvin, Dave, and Junior go to the greatest lengths to avoid contact with blacks.

Another is an extreme "threat orientation" toward the targeted group.[15] Several of the white workers see blacks as posing certain threats, but only a few seem obsessed with these observations. Dave fears that blacks would try to take over churches were they allowed to join and fears that blacks would try to take over the political system if they became politically active. Melvin sees blacks as threatening him personally no matter where he interacts with them and consequently wishes to segregate them totally from his life. Junior sees blacks as threatening in sexual and neighborhood contexts. Blacks who wish to sleep with whites or move next door to him become "niggers." Only he and Melvin used this disrespectful label. Kevin fears blacks might threaten whites if they were ever to gain majority status. Dave, Eddie, Junior, Kevin, and Paul feel threatened by blacks using the government to gain unfair economic advantage, but the expression of this threat seems much less intense than the other fears.

Another test for intense prejudice is the spontaneous injection of racist comments into irrelevant contexts.[16] Melvin was the only member of the group to do this. Twice during the course of our conversations he made the point that "I don't care nothin' about the niggers myself" at a point where the comment seemed totally out of context.

Judging from these few tests as well as from the general tone of the conversations, the members of the group who seem most likely to suffer from functional prejudice are Melvin, Dave, and Junior. In intensity they probably should be listed in that order, though, given Junior's acceptance of integration of public spheres of life as a just norm, he probably is much less prejudiced than either of the other two.

Three other members of the group could probably be described as exhibiting folkways prejudice. These men are relatively free of intensely felt threats, feel and express compunction about any prejudiced statements they make, have close and pleasant social relations with blacks, and avoid vulgar racial labels in mentioning blacks. In order of decreasing intensity, Eddie, Kevin, and Jim exhibit significant prejudice, but it seems best characterized as folkways rather than functional prejudice.

The last four members of the group do exhibit some prejudice, but they merit separate listing from the above three men, because they seem to have gone beyond an etiquette system that assumes the veracity of the traditional negative stereotypes applied to blacks. With the exception of Roy, who is probably the least prejudiced member of the group, it is difficult to order these four men. Paul, Mark, Terry, and Roy displayed very little prejudice in the course of these interviews and would seem to be the least prejudiced members of the group. Certainly the prejudice they do feel should not inhibit them from a political alliance with their black working-class friends.

The fact that about half this small sample is largely free of racial prejudice indicates hope for the construction of a populist coalition. In order to command a substantial majority, however, such a coalition would necessarily have to include many with significant prejudice if it is to succeed.[17] Those with functional prejudice are the least likely candidates for recruitment. Therefore, efforts must be focused on those who exhibit only folkways prejudice. Happily for those who would wish to see such a populist coalition constructed, functional prejudice is so limited that a substantial majority could be formed in this small group excluding these men. Given the intensity of his economic concerns, Junior might even be recruited into this majority if he saw no threat to the racial purity of his private life. To generalize well beyond the statistical limits of this small sample, we might say that if these men are at all typical (realizing the gross inexactness in using such a term), the prejudice of blue-collar workers in the border South does not rule out biracial populism.

A related question also asked at the outset was whether these men live more in the past or the future with respect to their racial attitudes. Put another way, the question is one of generational change in the South. Are young working southerners growing away from the prejudice and paternalism of their fathers and grandfathers that made them such easy prey to demagogues? This question cannot be answered directly because we cannot speak to the forefathers of these men. But ample evidence of change has certainly been uncovered.

The first point is that the prejudice of most of these men is quite different from the bigoted, working-class, redneck stereotype held by many well-educated members of the middle class. Few exhibit simple and deep-seated racial hostility. Most are troubled by and even thoughtful about their prejudice. Their attitudes are much more complex than I expected them to be.

A second and less subjective observation is that they discuss their own attitudinal changes. Some, such as Roy, Mark, and Paul, were conscious of these changes. They remember having altered their views when they learned what blacks were really like when schools were integrated. Others, such as Jim and Terry, were less conscious of the changes. They learned they could be friends with and relate to blacks when they found themselves in contact with blacks in the military and at work.

The fact that about half of the sample seems to have altered their views away from prejudice points to the possibility that these men may well be in a transitional generation. Practices and official norms changed just as they were maturing. The norms of integration and equality that were thrust upon them by government are the norms that they will teach their children, though no doubt much of their prejudice will be passed along in subtle ways. But for their children the socialization forces will be much more heavily weighted toward racial tolerance and integration than they were for these young workers of the 1970s. The end product should be men who are even less oriented toward the notion of white supremacy.

This points to another factor that has brought about the change, perhaps the most important in that it is causally prior to the learning process these men have undergone. In fact, a few of the men recognized what had happened, though they fail logically to pursue its implications. Mark says he approves of government action in forcing school integration because the resulting contact has reduced prejudice. Yet he turns around and argues that integrated housing should not be forced because one cannot legislate morality. Of course, he sees these as different issues because housing integration is still alien to him whereas school integration is not, despite the distinction that he and others try to make between public and private spheres of life. The point is that one *can* legislate morality. These men's very lives belie the idea that one cannot. Time after time—at school, at work, in the military, in eating places, and in theaters—once faced with a fait accompli, most of these men accepted it as a just standard and learned racial tolerance from initially forced contacts. They have learned that they share with those of other races common concerns, senses of humor, and pleasures. It is this learning of equality that may gradually erode the stereotypes that linger beyond any functional purpose in the etiquette system of many white workers.

In the introduction to this study, I described two competing theories that seek to predict the outcome of any effort to build a biracial populist coalition in the South. One theory suggests that working-class racism is exaggerated and views the mass participation of the working class in southern politics as having a liberalizing influence.[18] The alternative theory views racism as a stronger element than economic liberalism in the beliefs of southern workingmen and argues that an increase in electoral participation only provides additional cannon fodder for those who wield the guns of racist politics.[19] The question is which of these two theories best fits these men of Furntex. My detailed examination of the views of these men on both economic and racial issues allows me to attempt an answer.

Given that only a few hard-core racists were uncovered and an equal or slightly greater number of men were truly tolerant, the answer would seem to turn on the probable behavior of those who exhibit moderate levels of prejudice. If I have been correct in the judgment that the prejudice they feel serves little functional purpose for their personalities, then it seems likely that these men would respond to their more functional economic interests, if they perceived that these were their options. Thus their behavior, were they to participate, would depend on how the issues were defined to them. All other things being equal, economic self-interest should win out over racial prejudice. But if issues involving race dominate the attentions of these men, they will make the same voting choice as will hard-core racists.

Campaign strategy over how to define issues becomes of paramount importance. As we have seen, the most troublesome issues with which the architects of a populist alliance must deal are those that raise the question of reverse discrimination. Many white working-class southerners who are otherwise fairly moderate and tolerant on racial issues are greatly disturbed by what they perceive to be an effort by the national government to change the rules of the game so that the darkness of one's skin is more rewarded than is hard work.

This issue is so potent because it draws upon two otherwise separate sets of values held by these men. First, it appeals to their lingering racial prejudice and especially the stereotype of the shiftless, lazy black. Second, the issue calls forth a strong sense of self-righteous indignation that the very important value of individual merit is being violated. In an economic setting of low wages and few opportunities for significant upward job mobility, there is a real danger that the issue of reverse discrimination can transform what is only habitual folkways prejudice into a functional prejudice that protects the hardworking individual from threats against his hard-earned rewards. The small return he gets on his work investment can be blamed on blacks who collect greater rewards for lesser investments, thereby salving his own ego. Such an issue splits the races, rejuvenates functional racism, alienates workers against the central government, and does nothing to alter the present distribution of wealth among the classes.

One cannot overemphasize the importance of selecting a political strategy that avoids defining antidiscrimination laws and affirmative action plans as efforts to implement reverse discrimination. If such a strategy is not possible, then those who would hope to realize an effective biracial populist coalition must resign themselves to wait until the passage of time allows that kind of morality to have been effectively legislated. They must also hope that the national government can maintain enough support to sustain such a policy until the fait accompli is fully accomplished. This may well postpone any political battle for economic redistribution for many years.

In a thoughtful article that confronts this problem, James Clotfelter and William Hamilton suggest strategies by which those who would like to construct a populist coalition might seek to skirt this potentially disastrous issue. They, too, recognize that many with some significant degree of prejudice must be included in the coalition if it is to succeed in commanding a majority. They offer the following advice to those who must engage in the struggle to define coalition-building issues:

> Candidates should emphasize the general benefit of social programs, trying to avoid code words that say "blacks only". . . . To meet his constituents' need for scapegoats, a nonracist candidate might identify *new* targets for attack, more rationally chosen, to replace blacks. The most appropriate targets would be powerful economic groups, perhaps local businesses that pay low wages. . . . To his black constituents, a populist talks fair government employment practices and, more generally, jobs and prices and taxes, not race. To his white constituents, he says similar things: We will revise the tax structure (moving away from dependence on property taxes while increasing corporate taxes) and see that you get a fair share of government benefits—hard work *does* pay off, there is justice for whites as well as for blacks.[20]

My judgment is that an appeal of this nature could win a majority of the workers of Furntex. Whether it might succeed in other areas of the South requires a very great leap of faith from this extremely small sample. Even if we make this leap, there is a very important caveat. The relatively low level of extreme racial prejudice found in Furntex may differ substantially from that of other areas of the South where blacks compose a higher proportion of the population. The fear of a black ruling majority was found to exist in Furntex, but it is not a very likely threat in this town of the non-deep South. Because prejudice tends to increase as one moves into areas with relatively larger black populations, a threat orientation toward blacks would be a much more likely response in the deeper South.[21]

Of course, the success of any political coalition depends on the participation of its members. A striking fact that must be recognized as a great obstacle to any political coalition is that most of these men have never participated in any meaningful way in politics.

CHAPTER FIVE

The Problem of Participation

. . . the vote is a resource of every group in its struggle against the rest, and the most effective resource of less affluent groups, who have the greatest numbers. . . . Apparently the sole reason for retaining a restrictive registration system in many locales—especially in the South—is to manipulate the electorate. . . . Indeed the restrictive laws have been enacted by governmental bodies controlled by wealthy conservative businessmen—not "rednecks"—who view the political potential of lower-income whites with almost as much disquiet as that of blacks. [Chandler Davidson, *Biracial Politics: Conflict and Coalition in the Metropolitan South*, pp. 53–55, 82.]

Even if populist-oriented political candidates choose the right economic issues and are able to avoid the many pitfalls of racism, they must somehow solve the problem that their constituency is underrepresented in electoral politics. The workers may not be listening, and if they are listening, they may not vote.

This problem was briefly touched upon in the discussion of the wage issue. The five workers who voted in 1976 seemed to fit the requirements of "issue oriented" voters. They expressed issue concerns, had some idea of how voting choices reflected those concerns, and voted accordingly. Many among the other ten had similar issue concerns but saw little or no reflection of their positions in candidates or political parties. In pursuing this matter further, I will search for reasons why the nonvoting men do not have the same perception of and interpretation of partisan politics as those who did register and vote. In this chapter, we will first examine the pattern of political participation of these Furntex workers and then explore the environmental and attitudinal factors that may be associated with political participation. Understanding more precisely why most of these men fail to engage in politics even to the point of voting may give clues as to what, if anything, may be done to encourage greater participation.

Patterns of Political Participation

For the purpose of this discussion, the concept of political participation includes all behavior that directly involves the expression of political opinions.[1] One dimension of political participation is that concerned with electoral outcomes. Several actions are relevant to this dimension.

The first is talking politics. By simply engaging in political discussions, people acquire, reinforce, modify, or pass on political opinions. They acquire information about political candidates and political parties and learn the political values of their peer group. This is the most fundamental form of political participation. It is the easiest—one can do it virtually anywhere and anytime. It would seem to be a prerequisite for other, more complex and difficult forms of behavior—in order to vote, campaign, or hold office, one must first be interested enough to talk politics. It is also probably the most widespread form of conscious political behavior. Politics is a great spectator sport in the United States. People talk about political events, personalities, and campaigns in much the same way they talk about sports. This is reflected in the grain of truth that exists in the political maxim that a presidential campaign cannot gain much interest and attention until after the baseball World Series. People simply cannot concentrate on two "sporting" events at once.

Evidence of the popularity of talking politics and its sportslike attraction is found in the behavior of my small group of Furntex workers. Junior, who claimed to talk politics very rarely, apparently does talk and think about campaigns to the point where he placed a five-dollar bet that Carter would win the 1976 presidential election. Even though Junior does not perceive himself as ever talking politics, his betting on an electoral outcome is an indication of widespread casual interest in politics.

The workingmen of Furntex were asked two questions concerning talking politics. They were asked how often they engage in political discussions and then to describe the role they play in these discussions—a passive role of mostly listening or a more active role of attempting to convince others of the correctness of their own position. Four men in the group (Rick, Mark, Brent, and Jim) see themselves as frequently and actively engaging in political discussions; one (Paul) occasionally but actively discusses politics; six (Eddie, John, Albert, Dave, Lewis, and Roy) occasionally and passively discuss politics; and the other four rarely or never engage in political discussions. Thus we see that this limited form of political activity is fairly widespread among the workers of Furntex. If others, such as Junior, engage in political discussions that they consider are not serious enough to merit the label of political discussion, the actual extent of political discussion may have been underestimated. Though a placing of wagers on who will win an election is doubtless more casual than a discussion of the relative merit of issue positions, it is by no means necessarily barren of the expression and conveyance of political opinions and values. The explanation of why someone is going to win an election, which usually enters into such a discussion, may convey all kinds of political information, opinions, and values.

A second form of political participation directly related to electoral outcomes is voting. Voting is not as simple an act as is often thought. It requires a considerable expenditure in terms of foresight, time, thought, and even money. The main reason voting is so complex is that in most parts of the United States, including Furntex, citizens must register well before the time of an election.[2]

Registration is no great obstacle to the middle- or upper-class citizen, who may easily leave work and get to the place of registration. For the average member of the working class, however, it is not a trivial matter. Given that he generally has lesser education and fewer dealings with bureaucracy, he has more difficulty gaining information and understanding rules and procedures. He may not know where to find out about registration procedures. He might also fear that registration makes him more vulnerable to authorities, salesmen, and bill collectors. His living patterns are likely to be less stable than those of the upper classes, thereby making reregistration a more frequent necessity as he moves from one rental unit to another and from job to job. This pattern of instability in life makes the planning for the future that is required to register a more extraordinary and therefore more difficult act. Local registration laws may require one to take time off from work in order to register. A matter of mere inconvenience for salaried employees becomes an economic loss for hourly employees. Given that many working-class people lack private means of transportation and in many places public transportation is unavailable, getting to the place of registration becomes a problematic and costly factor. A de facto poll tax remains in existence.

In looking at the lives of this small group of furniture workers, one can see that many of these obstacles could be a barrier to registration. Certainly their career patterns reflect a high degree of instability. These men's lives are oriented to the present. Their jobs, places of living, family relations, and many other aspects of their lives are all relatively insecure. They have learned not to plan too much for the future because often things do turn out to be "a matter of luck or good or bad fortune." Most are unable to save much money and say they do not worry about financial security even though they admit a yearning for security. They must be present-oriented because it is largely irrational for them to expend too much planning effort for the future over which they have very little control.[3] This mental set makes them less likely to think about registering to vote until the stimuli of election rhetoric are upon them, and then it is often too late because registration books close thirty days prior to elections.

The problem of transportation is also nontrivial for many of these furniture workers. Four (Brent, Rick, Lewis, and Roy) have no means of private transportation and a fifth (Melvin) has a vehicle that is unreliable at best. To go to the place of registration, these men must either get a lift from a friend, walk, or pay cab fare, for Furntex has no public transportation. Although many of the men live within walking distance of the board of elections, the usual hours of registration coincide with their working hours, and the plants are located in other parts of town. Distance aggravates another cost, that of lost working time. In addition, local values are such that one simply does not walk off a production line job for this reason. It is amazing that any of these men are registered (Brent and Rick did manage to register), not that so few of them are!

Changes in residence are also a problem for the workers in this study. Eddie claimed to have been registered and to have voted for George Wallace in 1968. He said he has not voted since because Wallace has not run, but, of course, he is wrong. Wallace has run since 1968. Since then Eddie had moved, and he failed to reregister in his new precinct. Had Eddie been properly registered, he would have been able to vote once again for his favorite presidential candidate in the primary held in March of 1976. Registration seems to have been as great a barrier for Eddie as the rationale he offered—the fact that Wallace had been shot. Eddie is not alone. Well over half of the rest of the men in the group had changed residences during the two years preceding the 1976 election.

Given the publicity surrounding most elections, especially presidential elections, the relatively long hours that polls are open, and the free transportation that is often available to the polls, voting would seem to be a relatively easier act for those in the working class than the prerequisite of registration. There is some evidence that this is indeed the case in Furntex, though it is by no means conclusive because I did not conduct a controlled experiment. Five out of the six who claimed to be legally registered in 1976 did in fact vote. Only John, who feels that his vote will somehow get lost in making its way to Washington, claimed to be registered and did not vote in 1976. He limits himself to voting in selected local elections where he feels his vote has a better, though still poor, chance of actually being counted.

The next most difficult form of electoral-related political behavior is that of engaging in campaign activities. Jim regretfully spoke of his failure to volunteer to work on behalf of Carter's election. Persons in his socioeconomic class seldom undertake this kind of activity. In fact, only one member of the group reported ever having been involved in campaign activity in any election, and the exception reinforces the point being made. Paul worked to help a candidate in 1968, when he was in high school and was vice-president of the Young Republicans Club. But Paul was living at home with his upper-middle-class parents. He had plans to go to college and become a middle-class professional. At that time he was in no way a member of the working class. Given the context of Paul's campaign activity, perhaps it should not be considered, except possibly to illustrate the seeming naturalness of such activities to those in the middle class as opposed to those who are born and reared in the working class.

The next and final step in electoral participation is actually running for political office. This is both the most difficult and least likely type of participation. It is no surprise that no one in this small group has ever had this experience. Such activity requires excessive commitments in both time and money and is usually reserved to those who have proved their moral worth by becoming members of the economic and social elite.

These men find it practically unthinkable that they should engage in such activity.

Discounting running for office, I have discussed four types of electoral-related political participation: talking politics, registering, voting, and working in a campaign. Each activity seems to depend on the preceding activity, and in that sense each is more difficult. A person who talks politics may not register or vote or engage in campaign activities, but one who votes certainly has registered and he probably also talks politics.[4]

Since all of these activities are forms of political participation and all focus on electoral activities, they can be put together as a scale of political participation along which individuals can be scored and compared. I used their responses to rank my small sample of fifteen furniture workers on such a scale.

Before discussing this ranking, however, we should consider that political activities not related to electoral politics are also dimensions of political participation.[5] These include participation in the political activities of formally organized groups and citizen-initiated personal contacts with government officials. The first involves cooperative activities for collective goals that may or may not involve campaign activity, and the second involves individual action for personal goals. These activities are relevant to the discussion because, though logically independent, they are often associated with and have an influence on electoral-related behavior.

Americans are said to be joiners, but the propensity to join an organization is not equal across the entire population. Studies of organizational memberships have shown that those who are more educated, wealthier, and in higher skilled jobs are also those more likely to join formal organizations. That is, all those factors that indicate status are positively associated with memberships in groups that could have a potential impact on political opinions and behavior.[6]

Since these workingmen of Furntex are of relatively low status on most of these indexes, one would not expect them to have many ties with formal groups. This expectation is more than fulfilled. Very few of these men have ties to any formal groups, even if we count past memberships and church memberships. Brent is a member of the American Legion; Terry holds membership in the National Rifle Association; Rick was once involved in a now defunct "club" of young black men who tried to pressure the city council for greater funding of community social and recreational projects; Mark was once associated with an antiwar group; Paul was in a Young Republicans Club in high school; and Mark, Jim, and Junior all attend church regularly enough to consider themselves active members (though Junior regards his membership as marginal since he has not been "saved"). This is the total extent of their group memberships. Nationwide, about two-thirds of all unskilled laborers have one or more group memberships, not including church memberships.[7] Even counting church memberships, less than half of these men belong to any formal group, and no one holds more than a single active membership.

The significance of this unusually low incidence of membership in voluntary associations is twofold. First, their low level of group activity is but one more factor in a pattern of life that indicates low status and social isolation. The same rugged individualism and independence that gives these men a sense of pride in surviving and keeping their families together separates and prevents them from collective associations with each other for any public purpose. Their backgrounds and beliefs make them private men, who pursue private goals in very private and individual ways. Since group activity is strongly associated with other public activities, such as voting and political actions, we should not be surprised that these men who belong to almost no groups are also very unlikely to vote or be otherwise politically active.[8]

Second, low incidence of group activity means that there is little opportunity for these men to compensate for their backgrounds. Organizational memberships may be a way for the poor and ignorant to break out of a pattern that leads only to greater political impotence. Group memberships tend to be associated with increased political knowledge and political efficacy, both of which are positively associated with greater political participation.[9] Given the paucity of such ties among these men, they must seek other roads to political potency. In addition, as we shall see later, the one organization having the greatest impact, the church, tends to steer them toward political concerns that are irrelevant to their economic condition.

The other dimension of political participation concerns individual contacts with public officials. Discounting contacts with police, which will be considered as a separate but certainly not unrelated topic, only two of these men can recall ever having contacted any elected public official for any purpose. While in service, Rick wrote Senator Sam Ervin several letters in an attempt to avoid completing a tour of duty in Vietnam after having been wounded. Ervin was not helpful, but Rick was able to avoid completing the trip back to Vietnam with the help of a friendly doctor who had his orders and Rick held in Guam—through private action. The only other contacts were made by Mark, who claims to have written his United States congressman several unanswered letters, and Lewis, who once called city officials to complain about his electric bill. Though these men are perhaps not unique in the paucity of their contacts with officials, we do see once again some emphasis on private individual coping and adjusting actions reflected in one of the few contacts that were made.

In Table 1 all fifteen workers in the group have been arranged to indicate their relative levels of political participation. Six forms of political participation are listed, the first four of which are on the electoral dimension, and the last two on the other dimensions, organizational memberships and contacts with elected government officials. On the electoral dimension, the logical dependency of each form of participation on the preceding participation form is seen to exist, except for a couple of errors. Kevin registered and voted in 1976 although he claimed rarely to talk politics. Eddie is a similar case. He claimed seldom to talk politics, but he registered and voted at least once, in 1968, when he voted for the third-party candidacy of George Wallace. The active interest in politics that underlies electoral activities seems to carry over into the other two dimensions. Those few with some activity in these areas precede that activity with at least some electoral-related activity. The single notable exception is Terry, who explained his membership in the NRA by a single issue interest—opposition to gun control laws.

The fifteen workers have been divided into three subgroups. The first includes those who have been fairly interested and active in politics, including voting in the 1976 election. The large number on the bottom of the table are those who express little interest or activity in politics. In the middle are two deviant cases: Mark, who is very interested in politics and has participated in nonelectoral forms of behavior but did not vote, and Kevin, who is just the opposite. He registered and voted in 1976 but claimed and exhibits little interest or other participation in politics.

A total score for each individual was computed by scoring each "yes" or "some" as a 1 and each "no" as a 0. (See the last column in Table 1.) Two of the men have near perfect scores of 5; at the other extreme two men have perfect scores of 0. As one would expect for this group, the mean score, 1.9, indicates that they generally do not participate to the point of voting.

Table 1. *Political Participation*

Name	Talks Politics	Ever Been Registered	Voted in 1976	Cam-paign Work	Organization Member-ships	Contacts with Government Officials	Overall Score
Paul	Some	Yes	Yes	Yes	Yes	No	5
Rick	Yes	Yes	Yes	No	Yes	Yes	5
Brent	Yes	Yes	Yes	No	Yes	No	4
Jim	Yes	Yes	Yes	No	No	No	3
Mark	Yes	No	No	No	Yes	Yes	3
Kevin	No	Yes	Yes	No	No	No	2
John	Some	Yes	No	No	No	No	2
Lewis	Some	No	No	No	No	Yes	2
Eddie	No	Yes	No	No	No	No	1
Dave	Some	No	No	No	No	No	1
Albert	Some	No	No	No	No	No	1
Roy	Some	No	No	No	No	No	1
Terry	No	No	No	No	Yes	No	1
Melvin	No	No	No	No	No	No	0
Junior	No	No	No	No	No	No	0

Factors Associated with
Political Participation in Furntex

Anyone who wishes to induce the workingmen of Furntex to participate in politics should understand the factors that tend to inhibit their participation. One significant factor is political and structural in nature: registration rules and laws place a disproportionate burden on these working-class men relative to those of higher status. The impact of many background and attitudinal factors has been well documented in survey research, but the subject merits attention because not all of these factors play simple one-way roles. Some of those things that work *against* traditional political participation are prerequisites for being drawn into populist politics. This paradox must be understood if populist politics is to have any chance of success.

Demographic Factors

Education is perhaps the single factor that has been most associated with political participation. Nearly every study that attempts to explain participation finds education to be significant. This study of a microsample of the working class in a small-town southern setting is no exception. Even within this single social class and within a single occupational group, we find that education has a great impact. The four men who had the highest scores in overall political participation (see Table 1) average better than a high school degree (12.5 years completed), whereas the nine with the lower participation scores average almost two years less completed schooling (10.7 years).

Of course, the by-products of education, not education per se, cause increased political participation.[10] One by-product of successful completion of public schooling is an increased sense of control over one's environment. Those who are better able to cope with the demands and stresses of school are more likely to feel that they can meet other demands in life. This sense of personal effectiveness may have a spillover effect, giving one a sense of political effectiveness, a feeling that one may exert some significant influence into the political process.[11] I will shortly examine the impact of both these attitudes on political participation among workers of Furntex.

A second effect of education might be motivational in nature. Education may stimulate an interest in politics just as it helps to stimulate concern in many areas that are foreign to the immediate self-interests of day-to-day living.[12] Moreover, education may give the individual specific knowledge about the salience of politics to his daily life. He may learn that the seemingly remote actions of all levels of government confer upon him both rewards and punishments. He may discover links between government actions and inactions and the quality of life that he and his family lead. This knowledge along with other skills associated with increased levels of education (such as increased reading and comprehension skills, an increased ability to understand and deal with the complexities that surround modern political life) tend to make attention to the news media (especially newspapers, which give greater depth and more analysis than the electronic media) a more worthwhile and economic undertaking (in terms of understanding per unit of time expended).

Education may also instill a sense of civic duty. Those who have spent a longer period of time under the socializing forces of our educational institutions may have a firmer belief that one of the requirements of good citizenship is regular voting. Belief in this value then becomes a motivational force acting to increase the likelihood of voting independent of issue preferences.[13]

Among other background and environmental characteristics often utilized in attempts to explain political participation are income, social class, occupation, age, sex, party competitiveness, and region. Most of these factors are not relevant to the study of this small group of men because I have in effect controlled out most of their potential influence in selecting the sample. All of these men are relatively young, come from similar social backgrounds, make roughly the same wages (hourly if not family), are in similar occupations, and live in the same political environment.

These men vary on one demographic characteristic that is usually considered important—race. Blacks generally have lower participation rates than whites in any given community because society has been structured historically so as to bias all of these other socioeconomic factors against blacks.[14] In many southern communities, especially those having large black populations, the local political system was usually structured so that blacks were systematically excluded, at least until recently, when federal actions eliminated exclusionary laws and practices. Because Furntex does not have a particularly large black population and discriminatory voting laws have long been eliminated, one might expect the more subtle socioeconomic biases to explain most black/white differences in rates of participation, though because of past discriminatory voting laws blacks may not have caught up to and established as well as whites the habit of participation. But again I have in effect controlled for many of these subtle socioeconomic biases in selecting the sample, so that, if there are any significant differences in rates of participation, they probably are the vestiges of historical discrimination. Table 1 shows no apparent difference in the participation levels of the black and white workers in the group. Roughly half of the members of each race are in the upper half of the table.

Attitudinal Factors

We have noted that educational experience seems to be positively associated with political participation even within this small, relatively homogeneous group of workers. I will now examine the impact of several attitudes that may be associated with educational experience as well as some other attitudes that are often associated with political participation.

The first relevant attitude is the degree to which one feels personal con-

Table 2. *Political Participation and Associated Factors*

Name	Political Participation Scale	Personal Control	Political Efficacy			
			General	U.S.	N.C.	Furn†
Paul	5	4	16	2−3*	3	4−5
Rick	5	3	19	5	5	5
Brent	4	3	8	5	5	7
Jim	3	2	13	4	2	1
Mark	3	3	19	4	2	6
Kevin	2	3	19	1	1	3−4
John	2	3	8	1	1	1
Lewis	2	3	17	2	4	4
Eddie	1	4	15	4	4	5
Dave	1	2	18	1−2*	5−6*	5−
Albert	1	2	20	3	4	3
Roy	1	1	5	2−3*	1	1
Terry	1	1	6	1	2	4
Melvin	0	2	12	3	4	2
Junior	0	3	7	3	5	7

*Computed as follows: 1, if they mentioned nothing other than taxes; 2, if taxes and one other item such as police protection was mentioned; 3, if three or more items were mentioned.

*Each correct answer to the five questions was coded as "1" while incorrect answers were coded as "0". Each man was given an initial score of "1" so that the sum of possible scores range from "1" to "6."

trol over one's environment. Some minimal sense of personal control is necessary for any political involvement. The degree to which one believes in one's own personal control is a reasonably good predictor of the extent of political participation.[15] The workers of Furntex were asked a number of questions that together formed a five-point index indicating the degree to which they feel personal control.[16] Table 2 lists the scores of these men on the personal control index and their cumulative political participation scores. (See the first two columns of Table 2.) A comparison of their political participation scores with their scores on personal control indicates a positive association. Again, the reader should be reminded that the relationship can only be taken as suggestive and consistent with findings elsewhere in social science because the small size of the sample limits any statistical verification of this hypothetical relationship.

To explain their personal control scores, I attempted to explore the

Government Salience[c]	Political Knowledge[b]	Interaction[c]	Civic Duty	Tolerance of Ambiguity	Political Cynicism	Party Identification Strength[d]
2	5	160	1	47	27	0
3	4	228	1	45	18	3
3	4	96	2	37	32	3
3	5	195	3	47	20	1
3	3	171	2	29	29	2
2	3	114	0	33	25	1
2	3	48	1	40	28	0
3	3	153	0	37	17	2
3	3	135	0	38	27	1
3	3	162	2	31	22	0
1	1	20	3	32	18	1
1	1.5*	7.5	0	43	28	0
1	3	18	0	32	30	0
1	1.5*	18	1	33	26	1
1	1	7	0	23	19	1

[c] (General Political Efficacy) × (Government Salience) × (Political Knowledge).
[d] Scored as follows: 3, strong identifiers; 2, moderate; 1, weak; 0, independent or no identification.
* Indicates that the respondent either gave a range of answers or was given partial credit on an item.

backgrounds and experiences of these men. I asked them about the autonomy and responsibilities they were given as children, how well they are achieving their life's goals and ambitions, their work experiences, and similar questions. My findings bore little relationship to their scores.

Family background seemed to have the least explanatory power. Eddie had little autonomy, was severely punished whenever he broke rules, and came from a broken home. Yet he feels as much personal control as Paul, who had a good deal of childhood autonomy, was often treated leniently, and was raised in a relatively stable household.[17]

Life and work experiences seem to be more powerful explanatory factors. Those men who are most fatalistic toward life, who accept their life and work situation with little protest (men such as Dave, Roy, and Melvin), have low scores on personal control. Yet again the relationship is far from perfect for others with similar experiences have relatively higher scores (men such as Brent and Lewis). Of course, one must be very careful not to draw concrete conclusions from a microanalysis like this one, for theories that may be verifiable on a macro level in a statistical sense should not be expected to explain individual cases. Nevertheless, even in this small group, a strong sense of personal control does seem to contribute to a proclivity to engage in political action.

One substitute for personal control might be anger because one does not have personal control, as illustrated by Jim. He knows he lacks personal control over the direction of his life, yet he feels that he should have more control and is openly angry that it is denied to him by outside forces. He responds to this intense feeling of relative deprivation by engaging in political action when he perceives that his actions may alter the situation. When Jim said he could relate to Carter because of Carter's background—because Carter knows what it is like to be a workingman—Jim really meant he was responding to political forces that promise to increase the control he has over his own life. The difference between Jim, and Dave, Albert, and Melvin, all of whom scored low on personal control, is that Jim is angry and therefore ready to respond to political rhetoric that promises to increase his sense of control.

An attitude often closely related to a sense of personal control is a sense of political control or political efficacy. In this study I attempted to measure political efficacy in several different ways. First, four standard survey items were used to construct a twenty-five-point index that presumably indicates one's general sense of political efficacy.[18] I then asked each of these men how much effect he thought he could have if he really wanted some law or policy changed on the local, state, and national level of government. They were asked to rate themselves on a seven-point scale.[19] Their feelings of political efficacy on all these measures can be compared to their scores on political participation. (See Table 2.)

A careful comparison suggests a positive relationship between all the measures of political efficacy and political participation. If such a relationship does in fact exist, then once again the attitudes of these men of Furntex are consistent with those of people examined in other studies. The significance of this exercise, however, is not in discovering whether a relationship exists, but rather in exploring the feelings of these men about their perceived impact on government. The affect accompanying perceived political efficacy might prove useful to those who would wish to build a populist coalition. Just as populists might capitalize on anger over a sense of deprivation of personal control, they may also utilize the anger that exists over a sense of deprivation of political efficacy. Many of these men went beyond the mere acknowledgment that they feel they have little chance to have an impact on government. They expressed some anger and resentment over this perception. Junior was asked if he thought citizens should have more of a say about what government does.

JUNIOR: *Yes. We should have! They say we do when we write all these letters, [but] 90 percent of the time they'll send you a real nice answer and that's all you'll get. I think it should be considered through the whole governor or whoever goes through it. I think they should really take it into consideration, but most of the time you just get an answer and that's it. . . . That's what they're in there for is to help the problems and [they see it as] maybe that's your problem but it's not their problem. That's the way they look at it!*

The well-publicized efforts of Carter and other populist-style candidates to meet with and talk to average American citizens has a very obvious appeal to men such as Junior. Thus a low level of political efficacy may be a two-edged sword for a populist movement. It may be used to generate sympathetic support, but it is also a barrier to gaining the participatory support necessary to win elections.

While answering the efficacy questions, the men were quite realistic and pragmatic in their explanations. They recognized that individual actions would have very little effect at any level of government. Well over half the men in the group stipulated that their evaluations were based on the assumption that they were acting within and through an organized group. They were in effect estimating how effective they thought they could be in organizing and forming such groups. Thus these men, who for the most part are not involved in group activities but are oriented toward individual strategies, recognize the importance and necessity for group action to have any significant impact on politics at any level. This is a belief that would give some hope to those who would like to organize these otherwise staunch individualists into a political coalition.

Earlier in this discussion of participation, I mentioned that one possible effect of education is to show the individual citizen how government may affect his life either positively or negatively—to increase his sense of the government's salience. High salience would then become another motivation for political participation.

The men of Furntex were asked a number of questions designed to explore their perceptions of how government affects their lives. Their answers indicate that education is associated with high political awareness and that this awareness in turn motivates political activity. Of the six men with less than a high school education (Eddie, John, Albert, Roy, Melvin, and Junior), four see government as having little impact on them other than collecting taxes out of their paychecks. Eddie and John are atypical in that Eddie, from his rural background, is aware of the government's impact on farmers and John realizes that local government provides or fails to provide services that affect the quality of life in his neighborhood. Among those with high school educations or better, only one, Terry, perceives government impact to be as low as did most of those with lower educational levels. His answers to the questions are typical of those who do not see government as very salient to their daily lives.

QUESTION: *How does government affect your personal life?*
TERRY: *That goes back to taxes. I still think that they take too much out on taxes. Other than that I don't think they affect me.*
QUESTION: *How about your work life?*

TERRY: *No, none other than taking out too much taxes. Other than that the government don't have too much to do with me I guess.*
QUESTION: *How about in your community where you live? Does government affect you there in any way?*
TERRY: *I don't think government affects things [there] much.*

Considering that Terry is a veteran who has collected G.I. Bill educational benefits and who eventually hopes to be employed by the government as a prison guard, it is almost amazing that he consciously thinks only of taxes when asked these questions. The fact is that Terry and most of the others are unconsciously aware that government affects almost every aspect of their lives. In other parts of the interviews, they indicated awareness of the impact of government on their lives. But until this becomes conscious knowledge, it will not motivate political participation.

The others in the group with high school educations are much more conscious of the impact of government. They mentioned a large number of rewards and punishments, including taxes (on property as well as income), housing, health care, welfare benefits, the economy and how it affects their own jobs, job safety, wars and the draft, police and fire protection, recreation, and schools. But even those with a higher level of awareness almost invariably thought first of taxes. Thus if populist candidates wish to attract the attention of most of these men, they should make their number one priority an expression of interest in tax reform—the one area that seems salient to all of them.

From the content of the conversations, each of the men in the small sample was assigned a numerical score for perceived salience of government. (See Table 2.) A quick glance at these scores suggests that this variable also has a positive relationship with political participation.

Salience of government activity may depend on the level of government being considered. One national study has shown that state politics gets less attention than either local or national because it is not as visible and direct as local politics or as glamorous and well covered in the media as national politics.[20] The men of Furntex were asked what level of government they think is most important. Only Eddie was most interested in state politics. His interest can be explained by his close ties to farming that give him a keen interest in state agricultural policies. The significance of this observation is that populist-style candidates running for state-level offices may find it relatively more difficult to gain the attention of these men.

Earlier I hypothesized that education serves to increase knowledge about the workings of government. Increased knowledge might be interpreted as increased interest that would act as a motivator for gaining additional knowledge and for participation. As we have already discussed, some minimal knowledge of voting rules and regulations is a prerequisite for electoral participation.

A political knowledge index was constructed, ranking each man on the basis of answers to a five-question political quiz. They were asked the length of the terms of U.S. senators and the North Carolina governor, the party of President Eisenhower, the name of North Carolina's governor, and the number of justices sitting on the U.S. Supreme Court. The ranking given on Table 2 indicates that this variable also seems to have a positive relationship with political participation.

Interaction among the three factors just examined would multiply their individual impact on political participation.[21] The logic of this interaction is explained in the following proposition. If a person feels that government has an important impact on his daily life (political salience), has some knowledge of how government functions (political knowledge), and feels that he can have some impact on government (political efficacy), then he is much more likely to participate than a person who has none or only one or two of these qualities.

Given that measures have been constructed for all three of these factors, interactive effects can be computed by simple multiplication. The result is indicated in Table 2 in the column labeled Interaction. We should not be surprised that the interaction scores seem closely associated with political participation because they are the products of other factors that were also associated. The scores show only four deviant cases: Brent, who should have a higher score given his level of political participation, and Eddie, Dave, and Lewis, who should have lower scores given their low levels of political participation.

This somewhat redundant exercise is significant in explaining the four deviant cases. Brent's low score was obviously generated by his low score on political efficacy. But because he believed strongly that some issues in the 1976 election involved his self-interest, including the issue of his lack of political effectiveness, this liability of a low score on efficacy in effect became an asset. When asked what government ought not to do, he quickly answered that it should not show favoritism toward powerful special interest groups as it now tends to do. The other three men, despite relatively high scores on all three measures, did not choose to participate. Again, issues may be an explanation. Dave did not see any issues in the 1976 election that would affect the punishments and rewards government bestows upon him. Eddie thought that maybe Carter was not "whole hog" for school busing, a practice he opposes. But Eddie was not sure where Carter stood on busing and did not vote in 1976. Lewis, who is conservative on most social issues, expressed a strong preference for Carter only because of black pride. Carter was the candidate preferred by most blacks, and he gives blacks the credit for electing him. Had Lewis perceived the election in terms of the social issues that concern him, he likely would have supported Ford rather than Carter.

These results suggest some inadequacies in the measures used to calculate the interaction. The salience of government activities that may have an impact on issues of interest to each man should have been measured, not the salience of government actions in general. These men apparently act logically and consistently. If they perceive that a particular action on their part will have a beneficial impact on the activities of government affecting their own interests, they take that action. If not, they tend to remain inactive. Therefore, their political participation will be induced not merely by increasing their political knowledge or efficacy, but by convincing them that electoral choices and other political actions are relevant to the hurts and rewards of which they may already be aware. Political campaigns that define and raise issues are important!

One possible substitute for goal-oriented political activity is habitual political participation. One may vote out of habit or out of a sense of civic duty. Neither factor has any significant impact on these men. Only a few have participated enough to have formed any habit of political participation. Only about half have parents from whom they could have inherited the habit. Nor have many of them any sense of civic duty or obligation that involves public partisan political activities.

The men were asked several questions about civic obligations. They were asked to describe an "ideal good citizen." Their answers reflect their own individual private orientations. The attributes they valued were private morality, church attendance, giving to charities, being a good neighbor, and other, mostly private, individual activities. Some mentioned supporting groups that will work to improve the community such as the Jaycees, but only a few voluntarily mentioned any political activities. Terry argued that a good citizen would avoid any deep involvement in politics beyond voting. His comments reflect an attitude that politics is basically an immoral, selfish activity and that an important moral virtue is moderation in all things, including politics.

TERRY: He [the "ideal good citizen"] should have a level head and not really be for or against anything. He should be average on the deal, you know. He shouldn't go all out on anything. I don't think that he should get really wrapped up in politics, like those who on election day stay out of work and take people back and forth to the polls and pay them to vote. I know some people who have gone that far. They shouldn't offer 'em whiskey to vote either.

QUESTION: Would good citizens vote?

TERRY: Yes.

QUESTION: Would they get involved in campaigning in any other way?

TERRY: No, I don't think they should get involved in it.

Terry mentioned other ways good citizens should be involved in doing things for the community, but he did not include the somewhat tainted practice of politics. Terry was not typical in arguing that citizens should avoid politics, but most of the others agreed that political activities are not the most important element of good citizenship. Only six of the fifteen men volunteered political activity as an aspect of good citizenship. And of those six, three mentioned politics as an afterthought to private morality.

The men were also asked whether one has an obligation to vote if one does not care who wins an election, a question that should tap their sense of citizen duty to participate in politics. Their answers are consistent with their descriptions of good citizens. Seven of the men responded with a firm "no." Five hedged with a "maybe" answer, and only three said "yes."

Based on the answers given to these questions, civic duty scores were computed for each man in this small group. (See Table 2.) These scores reveal that this is another attitudinal factor that seems to be positively associated with political participation. The overall low level of felt civic duty (only two men had the maximum score) suggests that even though there may be a positive relationship, civic duty is not a very significant motivating force in their lives.

Tolerance of ambiguity is another attitude associated with political participation. Presumably, in order to participate in the uncertain process of democratic politics, one must be able to deal comfortably with complexities and uncertainties; otherwise the resulting frustration will become a significant barrier to participation.[22] Using a condensed version of a standard index that has been widely used to operationalize this attitudinal concept, a tolerance of ambiguity score was obtained for all the men in the small group.[23] Possible scores range from 8 (indicating a low tolerance of ambiguity) to 56 (a high tolerance).

Table 2 shows this attitudinal variable to be positively related to political participation as hypothesized.

Since our major concern is whether these men are potential recruits into a populist political movement, we might ask whether tolerance of ambiguity is a significant barrier to possible future political participation. The answer would be a very tentative no. Most of these men seem to realize that problems require more complex answers than a simple yes or no. If we assume 32 is a neutral point (a "4" response to each of the eight items), then their mean score of 36.5 is somewhat above the neutral point.[24]

Several studies have related political cynicism to political nonparticipation and have interpreted the level of political cynicism as a measure of the political health of our society. Recent rises in levels of cynicism have caused some alarm among political observers. Presumably, citizens who feel that they cannot trust their government, who feel that government is corrupt and wasteful and not concerned about their welfare, will be less likely to support government programs and laws designed to combat problems and more likely to support radical changes that may endanger the freedoms and rights we now possess.[25]

Attitudes of political cynicism are of central importance to this study, for the feeling that politics as usual does not serve one's interests is precisely what is necessary to attract an individual to the reformist-flavored politics of populism. Indeed, political cynicism would almost seem to be a prerequisite for populist politics. But once again there is the possibility of having to deal with a paradox. The same attitude that makes populism an attractive alternative may also drive men into apathy and away from all political participation.

To explore both these related issues, I asked the fifteen Furntex workers a number of questions designed to elicit any feelings of political cynicism they might possess. A standard five-item political cynicism index was employed to gain a general measure.[26] Three other indexes were employed to gain measures of political cynicism focused on different levels of government.[27] I also asked each of the men an open-ended question about how they would go about trying to get some law passed or action accomplished at the local level and whether they thought local officials would treat them fairly. This was followed by a similar question focusing on the local police.[28]

The scores of each of the men in the small group on the general five-item cynicism index are recorded in Table 2. Each item was scored on a scale of 1 to 7. Possible total scores could range from 5 (indicating very low cynicism) to 35 (high cynicism). Two observations are immediately apparent. First, there seems to be little relation between these scores and levels of political participation. Some of the men with high scores (Paul and Brent) are just as likely to participate as some of those with relatively low scores (Rick and Jim). The same is true of those in the bottom of the table. Thus general political cynicism does not in itself seem to have any direct impact on political participation in Furntex.

Second, if we assume that a score of 20 is a neutral point between political trust and distrust (responses scored as "4" to each of the five items), then we see that two-thirds of them as well as their average score (24.5) are above this neutral point. In sum, these men seem to be congruent with the image of high political cynicism that is said to characterize the United States in the 1970s.

Cynicism scores focused on each level of government and scores on how each man expects he would be treated by local government and police officials would give much the same result. There is no obvious relationship to political participation, and cynicism is high in almost all areas. The only level of government that fares at all well is state government, with a close to neutral score.

Their cynicism toward local government is based on their experiences with local officials. Those men who have engaged in political participation to the extent of dealing with local government officials (bureaucrats, police, and elected officials) tended to be cynical about what is required to get action. Most were realistic in realizing that long-term hypothetical plans of action might not get quick results and emphasizing the need for group action and petitions rather than merely individual contacts. A few of their comments follow.

PAUL: . . . the railroad crossing over by Frady Textiles, well, Christ, they need the flashing lights and the arms that come down and all they got is the little round sign. It says "Caution" with a little light that flashes. That's all they got out of it! At least they got something done. . . . I've read the paper and I see all the stupid things like when Edwin Sampson wanted to change Ramada Street to Nation Street, the whole stupid idea. And Harold Centers was complaining about that, you know. That's such a minute thing, you know, and it was such a big thing on the city council's agenda. That's why I take so little concern with the city government. Some of the things seem so ridiculous to me when we got all these other problems.

BRENT: First of all, they not gonna do anything for just one person. You'd have to more or less solicit names and more or less hire you a lawyer, probably, to present the petition to, uh, the city council or the traffic engineer. . . . You'd have to have some kind of organization, and even at that they would probably put you off until they just had to do it, or more or less they would probably refer you to the state. . . . Because that's the bureaucracy, that's the red tape you got to go through.

QUESTION: So do you think officials would listen to you?

BRENT: Yeah, they would be most courteous, especially during election time. "Come on in, sir. Why don't you have a seat." You know. Sure they'd listen. But then they'd—while they was listening they'd have a smile and probably have one hand up in the air like this [as if gesturing], and then tell you, "Well, you know, this problem's been presented to us before. We tried to do all we could, and operatin' on a low city budget, you know how the city"—they would come up with something that would sound sugar-coated, you know.

QUESTION: So do you think you would be treated fairly?

BRENT: That's too hypothetical. I doubt it very seriously. You talkin' about fairness. Would I be satisfied? Would I get any results? And the answer to that would be no. And if I did, it would be delayed, you know. . . . I'll tell you something else though, that a lot of people aren't aware of now. Now, this is more or less us [referring to people in Furntex]. This happened during racial riots, and all that. If you go up, say, neat, well dressed, nice suit, and go in speaking very intelligently and ask very intelligently about such and such change, they'll probably tell me very intelligently, "no!" But if I went up with a pair of dark shades on, a big "bush" [referring to a haircut style], with two bricks in my hand and tear up half the place, they would get on the phone. . . . History has proven that violence is usually what it takes to get something done.

LEWIS: For a street light I'd go to the city. And then if they act like they didn't want to listen to me, then I would feel like the next step would be to, uh, maybe get up a petition and go back to the city and say, "Hey, look. I'm not the only one that thinks so! It's a whole lot of other people that thinks so, too!" And then if he still, if the city still didn't see it my way, and I was right, then, uh, I would try to take it to somebody higher than him, try to make them step on his toes to get it done.

QUESTION: So do you think they would treat you fairly?

LEWIS: No. . . . Like my electric bill for this month is $76. And my next door neighbor, the black one, hers is $84 and she called up there and asked 'em how come her light bill was so high. [Utilities are city-owned in Furntex.] They told her, "Wait a minute, we're going to put you on hold and I'm going to get so-and-so to let you speak to them and ask them." And she waited and waited for some fifteen or twenty minutes and nobody came to the phone. See? And I complained to 'em one time. What had happened, I had been away from home for two weeks and I *didn't cut the fuse box off, but I wasn't using electricity, and my light bill was just as high for that month as it was for the month before. And I went up there and asked 'em how was that possible? I asked 'em to come out there and check my meter or something to see if there wasn't something wrong. And they said, "Well, all right. We'll send somebody out there." I didn't never see nobody come out there and it's still high, too.*

These men told other stories reflecting a strong feeling that local government officials and police are not responsive to their needs and do not treat them fairly. Junior, Lewis, John, and Roy all told of incidents where local police had unduly harassed them. Albert was unable to get police to do anything about destructive dogs in his neighborhood, so he himself took action and shot a number of the dogs. Kevin feels the local police tried to pin blame for an auto accident on him even though he was hit from the rear because the other person involved was an acquaintance of the police who investigated the accident. Dave claims to have walked into the local police station and been rudely treated by police who were drinking beer and playing poker while on duty. John sees the police as becoming involved in politics by letting all the drunks out of jail to vote at election time.

The fact is that most of these men have a low sense of subjective citizen competence that seems best explained by their experiences and resulting evaluations of government. Most do not know anyone of political influence, but feel that this would be the best way to get something accomplished. In fact, about the only man who was enthusiastic in evaluating local officials was Paul, who has relatives on the police force.

One of the essential ingredients of all populist campaigns is a style that appeals to feelings of alienation and separation from the political system. Effective utilization of such a style may be even more important than substantive issues, because cynicism, distrust, and inefficacy are more commonly shared than any specific issue positions.[29] Any good politician knows that being too specific on any issue or program is more apt to generate criticism and opposition than support. Perhaps the common thread to the campaigns of old-time populists such as Huey Long and more modern neopopulists such as George Wallace, Lester Maddox, Henry Howell (who won an upset victory in the 1977 Democratic gubernatorial primary in Virginia using a campaign theme of "Keep the big boys honest!"), and perhaps even Jimmy Carter, is a promise to give power to those who feel powerless, a common-man theme built on the premise that all men should be equal under the law and have equal access to and influence with the law. The heavy flavor of cynicism that permeates the attitudes of these men of Furntex toward all levels of government makes them potentially receptive to such appeals. Even if these appeals are coupled with appeals to racial hatred and resentments, the point is no less valid: cynicism is an attitude that binds these men together and must be a central target of any populist campaign. Furthermore, populists might take heart in the fact that cynicism does not seem to be a significant barrier to participation, given that those who participate are no less cynical and distrusting than those who fail to participate. Of course, such men as John, who feels the system is so corrupt that his vote will not even be counted, will always be difficult to lure to the voting booth. Beyond such extreme cynicism, however, the cynicism I found could be more of an asset than a liability to populist strategists.

One explanation of political cynicism is that it is a specific manifestation of a general attitude of distrust toward all people—misanthropy.[30] No doubt a generalized distrust of all of one's fellow man can contribute to a distrust of political and public man. An extensive experiential basis for political distrust exists among the men of Furntex. Thus there are two possible sources for political cynicism: experience with political institutions and a psychological predisposition toward distrust. Interaction may, of course, occur so that each reinforces the other. What is important here is the extent to which misanthropy is a source of political cynicism, for this type of political cynicism would seem logically much more of a barrier to participation in any kind of politics, even populist politics. Those who feel they can trust no man would have a very difficult time trusting even the different sounding populist-style politicians.

This is a very difficult judgment to make, but I will attempt it by closely examining the political participation and cynicism of those exhibiting the highest levels of misanthropy. A measure of misanthropy was obtained by administering a five-item index to each of the men in the group.[31] Melvin, Brent, and Lewis received maximum scores, indicating very high general distrust. From the content of the entire conversations, I judged three others also to be very distrusting of their fellow man: Kevin, Junior, and John. None of these men has many friends and distrust those they do have. (All of these scored three or higher on the misanthropy scale, indicating the general validity of the scale, though some others with scores of three or four I subjectively judged to be qualitatively less misanthropic.) Of these six men, the political cynicism scores of four were higher than the total group mean score, which tends to weakly confirm that extreme misanthropy may contribute to political cynicism. More important, only one of these six men had a score of three or more on political participation, whereas about half of the less misanthropic (four of nine) participated in politics up to and including registering and voting. Extreme misanthropy apparently tends to make political participation somewhat more difficult.

Given the nature of our voting procedures, misanthropy would seem an especially important factor for men who are liable to be in debt and who may live in fear of bill collectors. To place one's name in a voting registration book requires faith that the information will not be used for other purposes. Extreme distrust may breed irrational fears about giving personal information to anyone, as is attested by the difficulty I had in recruiting some of these men. Thus procedural voting reforms that reduce informational requirements may have an impact in reducing the barrier to participation of political cynicism born of misanthropy. This is yet another reason why such reforms are in the interest of those who would wish to see a populist coalition succeed.

The degree of party identification that one feels is an attitude that has been well documented as being associated with political participation.[32] Identification with a political party gives one a stake in the electoral process through the wish to see one's own group triumph over the opposition. Party identification helps one to sort out and process campaign information and serves as a decision rule when other cues are unavailable. That is, it makes choice easier by reducing information costs and therefore increases the likelihood of having a preference and voting that preference.

The workingmen of Furntex are more closely identified with the Democratic party than the Republican, as would be expected of southern blue-collar workers. But the strength of their identifications is relatively low. Each man was asked the identity and strength of his party affiliation. The breakdown is as follows: strong Democrats, two; moderate Democrats, one; weak Democrats, four; weak Republicans, two; moderate American Independent, one; independent, five. About twice as many are independents and weak identifiers as are moderate and strong identifiers. Party identification is not a very powerful motivator for these workingmen of Furntex.

Yet despite these low levels of identification, a relationship with participation exists. The men in the group were scored on the strength of their party identification. (See Table 2.) Comparing their scores to their rankings on political participation reveals a positive relationship.

Many studies have shown that party identification is often inherited from one's parents. By overhearing the political conversations of parents, children learn their parents' party identity, the differences between parties, and the value of partisan activity.[33] A more rational factor of self-interest also underlies inherited party identity. If children are of the same socioeconomic class as their parents, it is logical for them to take the same political identification if that identification expresses economic and social self-interest. In fact, children whose parents are incorrectly identified, such as black southern workers who are Republicans, are more likely to change their political affiliation than those whose parents are correctly identified. This tendency to correct identifications over generations is increased by education, which presumably increases the importance of the rational self-interest factor in transmitting party identity across generations.[34]

Many of the workers of Furntex followed their parents' party identification. In nine of the fifteen cases, whether Republican, Democrat, or independent, the men expressed the same party preference or lack thereof that their parents had. This ratio may underestimate the actual success of intergenerational transmission because several of the remaining six claim not to know their parents' identification.

This transmission process has other significant results. Even though consistent identifications were conveyed, intensity was lost across generations. Of those whose parents maintained some party identification, not one has a stronger identification than his parents, and five reported their affiliations to be weaker than those of their parents.

A movement was evident toward the Democratic party, which should be the normal choice of these workingmen. Besides Paul, who changed social classes and party identification (from Republican to independent) as a result of his downward social mobility, three others moved toward the Democratic party. Junior claims to have become a weak Democrat as a result of his support for Carter in the 1976 election. Lewis and Brent, who are both black, claim their parents were apolitical and identify themselves as moderate and strong Democrats, respectively. One member of the group moved toward the Republican party. Melvin, who claims his parents were apolitical, feels he is a weak Republican mainly because of his strong support for Richard Nixon. The net result is a two- or three-man gain for the Democrats, depending on how Paul votes in any given election.

The Democrats may have gained sympathy across generations, but they may have lost votes. If the reports of these men concerning the voting habits of their parents are accepted at face value, we find that the parents of about half the group vote regularly, whereas only a third of the offspring voted in 1976. Parental voting may be underestimated because three do not know whether their parents vote or not. Weakening party identifications across generations apparently has resulted in a lower level of political activity insofar as voting is concerned. Though this loss in activity may be explained by age differences (the young tend to vote less than their elders) and may be compensated for by the net movement toward the Democrats, these findings are consistent with contemporary trends toward the rise of the independent voter and a decline in voting participation.[35]

The significance of this change to those who would plan a populist strategy is twofold. First, party identifications are not strong enough among young southern blue-collar workers to bring them to the polls or give them clear-cut candidate preferences. Populist candidates must do more than merely emphasize party ties in campaign rhetoric if they wish to attract these men. Second, though party is a weak motivator, it must still be accounted for in a region of the country that has a large black population and is dominated by the Democratic party. Populist-style independents may be able to win statewide elections outside the South, but they would face an impossible task in the South. Any populist candidate would be wise to identify as a Democrat if he is to be successful (though he may fashion himself as a "maverick," which might help him). To do otherwise is to court the danger of writing off a significant proportion of one's natural constituency.

The last attitudinal factor is concern with morality. Morality brings into consideration a socializing institution that has had a great deal of influence on politics in the South—the church. The impact of religion on the political beliefs and behaviors of these men is a microcosm of its effect both in the South and in other parts of the country. Though only a few of these men are actively religious or attend church regularly, religion and the values it teaches have had a great impact on a large number of them.

Religion may have a political impact in drawing men away from politics, teaching them that the problems of this world are unimportant compared to the promises of afterlife. Such a belief leads men fatalistically to accept their economic and social conditions and pursue spiritual rather than material goals. Men who believe their powerlessness and deprivations are merely tests of spiritual worthiness are not likely to be drawn by the goals of populist reform. Such men consciously choose political apathy as an important value.

There is evidence that organized religion has had a negative effect on the political lives of some working-class people in Furntex. When Lewis was asked about his parents' party identification, he explained that their deep involvement in the Jehovah's Witness church precluded any political activities.

LEWIS: *My parents got baptized in 1955, and I was born in '53. . . . And every since they're been baptized they haven't had any political dealings, because one of the requirements of the religion that they belong to is that you, uh, just break off, if you have any, you just break off any political relationships. And if you don't have any, you don't get tied up in any.*

Though Lewis is no longer active in the church of his parents, he still follows many of the beliefs he was taught as a child, including avoidance of political activities involving anything other than informal group efforts to enforce moral codes of behavior.

Roy's religious beliefs also seem to reinforce his political impotence. His background is Baptist, and though he is not active in any church, he sends his children to a nearby fundamentalist church, watches a great number of revivalist religious programs on television, and seems to believe deeply that he should be more religious than he now is. In talking about the differences among religions, he revealed the fatalistic posture that defines most of his life: it is very important to be "saved," but all one can do is try to live right and hope, for only God knows who is and who is not saved. In fact, he was one of the most fatalistic members of the group. Roy resigns himself to living as best he can, "loving God and other people," hoping only secondarily that his endurance of hard and long work will bring him and his family a few more luxuries. His religion has taught him to be content with family relationships.

A second possible impact of religion is to promote political interest in the enforcement of moral codes rather than economic issues. Men who are preoccupied with the laws regarding the sale and consumption of alcohol and the public availability of pornographic materials are easily distracted from pursuing political strategies of economic self-interest. Evidence of this preoccupation and its religious foundation should be easy to find in one of the only two states in the country that as of 1976 prohibited sale of liquor by the drink. An abundance of concerns about individual morality was found among the workers of Furntex.

In describing the activities of an "ideal good citizen," Lewis included support for the strict enforcement of puritanical moral codes.

LEWIS: *He would be in the PTA, [be] member of at least one sports club, uh, kept a nice house, looked after his family, uh, [have] high moral standards. As far as political values went, he'd have only the strictest political values, you know. If he believed you should get rid of whore houses, you know, you should get rid of whore houses, you know, not put 'em outside the city limits.*

Later, in talking about how pornography could be controlled, Lewis was consistent with his conservative belief that government should be limited. He thought citizens might band together and use such devices as economic and social boycotts to force pornography peddlers out of business.

Mark and Jim are also motivated by their religious beliefs to support the enforcement of strict moral codes, but they endorse legal sanctions rather than merely private sanctions. Some of their statements in this area are so strong that a description of their interest as a "preoccupation" is not an exaggeration.

MARK: *Well, there's hardly anything they can do now because there's so many loopholes that they can get through. Now, back in the '20s and '30s, when, you know, they called 'em G-men. They almost stopped it, you know, speakeasies and back in the prohibition when liquor was coming out and everything and it was against the law and everything. They was breaking down on that. But now there's so many loopholes, like, you know, they legalized beer and wine and liquor . . . they should illegalize a lot of alcohol and, well, things like pornographic material and stuff like that. . . . [We have too much] freedom of the press, as far as pornographic materials go.*

JIM: *I think there should be restrictions on, uh, you talk about freedom, you talk about the free press . . . and I think about magazines and stuff like that, you know, being able to put what they want to in 'em. I think that a lot of times it can be harmful. . . . When it gets to the point where things that should be more controlled are open, then I think there should be a stopping place somewhere. There should be censorship. You know, it's not good for people to know everything. There's some things that people shouldn't know.*

These men represent a small minority of the group. Yet two of them are among the more vocal and more politically active members of the group. Because populists would at best be able to mobilize only a portion of this group, loss of even a small proportion of the politically active through distraction to morality issues would be serious.

A third impact religion has had in the South is to promote social and political conservatism. Churches often condemn any federal actions that interfere in any way with the teaching of their own beliefs and codes of morality, even in publicly supported institutions such as schools. The membership learn to distrust the power of the central government, the very power that could function to improve their economic lot. They learn that anything related to communism or even socialism is by definition evil and ungodly, thereby giving a powerful ideological weapon to those who oppose economic redistributive measures. Politicians who have cemented an alliance with churches on morality issues can use that alliance to gain religious sanction and support of their economically conservative views.

Once again we find ample evidence that these forces have had an impact in Furntex. Mark, Jim, and Junior bitterly complained that the national government had removed religion from the schools by banning prayer in public schools. All are more distrustful of government power as a result, though Mark and Jim would not hesitate to use it to enforce their own moral standards in literature. Lewis has learned that communists are atheistic and would force their views on others if allowed the freedom to do so. He is therefore alarmed by any measure that is labeled communistic. Junior is given literature in his church sent by North Carolina's ultra-conservative Senator Jesse Helms. The minister uses this literature as the basis for some of his sermons. The religious context in which these messages are delivered gives them a sanctity that overpowers and makes irrelevant Junior's economic self-interest.

JUNIOR: Well, [government] is trying to get together and stop all these churches from having all their own schools. Not because they can't get enough people to come to these schools, but because they'll learn to be a religious type of school instead of a school where you go learn about DeSoto one year and how to cut apart a frog the next year and all this. They just teach you how to learn about everything you need to know . . . plus be religious at the same time. [Ironically, Junior cannot afford to send his children to a private school.] And these big, uh, some government commission doesn't like it—we've seen papers that's been back from our senator that, uh, the child's going to, the child's momma and daddy tells him to do something and he gets a spanking for it, he feels like it is wrong, that he can take his own momma and daddy to court, which is legalized on paper in the government, which I didn't even know anything about. . . . I can get you one of the letters. It also talked about trying to stop taking your dues that you give to the Lord every week off your taxes. He's [the minister] got papers on that [and] about the communists, trying to take over all the religions.

Junior is unaware that North Carolina has two United States senators. He is aware only of his senator, Senator Helms, who writes letters to his church that are interpreted by the minister to warn the people about the ills of big government, tax reform, and creeping communism.

Organized religion may, however, teach values that might be conducive to political participation in a populist coalition. One such set of values would be a humanistic orientation teaching responsibility to participate in efforts to help one's fellow man. There was some evidence that this value exists and has a religious basis in Furntex.

Brent, who comes from a Baptist background, is not actively involved in any religious organization, although religion has played an important role in shaping his values. He described it as "the positive motivating force in my life. It keeps this thing inside of me that I talked about earlier, this compassion toward others, going." When asked why he included voting in his description of the "ideal good citizen," Brent responded, "I believe he would because he is morally correct and believes in God and church."

Jim, who is very active in the Baptist church he attends, also seems to have derived some of his social conscience from religious training. In talking about his idea of utopia and his philosophy of life, he said religion demands that he try to understand his fellow man, even those who are different from him, and also "try to help other people rather than oneself." Jim's concerns about housing, medical care, and salaries show that this feeling extends beyond looking after his fellow men's spiritual morality—he is also concerned with their material needs. At one point in the interview he criticized the churches in Furntex for not being more socially active in helping to secure better housing.

Religious training may have cultivated the social consciences of several other men in the group. Albert, Kevin, and Mark often couched their concern for the plight of their fellow man in terminology having a religious undertone.

In yet another way the common religious backgrounds of most of these men would place them in harmony with the chords struck by populistic rhetoric. In its history and nature, populist style is reformist, revivalistic, and moralistic. These men come from families that respond to the emotional appeals of religious revivals. They are not turned off by moralistic revivalist style. Quite the contrary—this kind of appeal is most likely to move them. The same emotions that bring them spontaneously to proclaim their sinfulness and pledge their lives to the Lord in sweaty tent meetings might get them to the polls on election day—if they do not have to plan too far ahead. For just as the exhilaration of being "saved" often quickly passes as they go back to the humdrum of their daily struggles to support their families, so, too, would pass the foolish hope that somehow their vote would notably improve their lot in life.

A more substantive commonality between the religious beliefs of these men and appeals of populism is a search for righteousness and integrity. Almost to a man, the workers of Furntex unashamedly spoke of the need for more integrity in both private and public life. This search springs from a combination of their religious backgrounds and the anguish of a society that has not yet recovered from Vietnam or Richard Nixon. This yearning for integrity in politics along with a familiar style helped make Carter's semireligious call for moral rectitude in politics appealing to these men. When Carter quietly talks about simply doing his best to do what is right, he strikes a harmonious chord with their religious-based public concerns.

BRENT: [In talking about the Russian wheat deal] The president [should be] president of all the people and not just the large wheat dealers! [He continued by saying the only way to change the country would be a religious sort of chain reaction beginning with one person and spreading to others through which man would rid himself of greed and selfishness.]

DAVE: [In telling why he liked Kennedy] Just, I always thought he was more truthful and really tried to help the U.S. out more . . . than most presidents I can remember.

EDDIE: [In discussing problems this country faces] A lot of 'em is, I think, the people has lost their trust really, in Congress, especially since the sex scandals came out. They've lost confidence in the men we've got up in Washington. . . . Well, I have thought about different things, but I would say anything we could do about it would maybe to get behind a group, and, I wouldn't say to run your own president or something like that, but kinda get, I don't know, maybe a group of people that you could, that really, police Washington, but just, you know, try to keep an eye out for things that was dealt under the table. If it didn't get so much that they couldn't stand it, then maybe they would back off of it a little. Right now I guess every little bit would help.

JIM: We voice our opinions when we vote, but there are a lot of things that we shouldn't have to voice our opinions on because it should be known what needs to be done . . . these are educated men, and they should know that it is wrong and do something.

JOHN: It is hard to say [about an ideal good citizen being in politics], because there are so many crooks and everything comes down to the dollar, so there would be a hard time in finding an ideal good citizen in politics because one rotten apple tends to spoil the bunch and he couldn't survive.

JUNIOR: Well, usually [when] somebody says "government" to me well, the first thing I think of is that they are making a bunch of money and they ain't gonna worry too much about what we're doin'. [They] say they're tryin' to help us do this and help us do that, and I say I bet 90 percent of 'em is interested in the money part of it. I know they say money is the roots of all evil and all. I'd say that's the truth. They're sittin' up there gettin' rich and they pretend to do this and pretend to do that and they swear they gonna do this and they swear they're gonna do that. When their time is gone they ain't accomplished anything.

KEVIN: I liked Carter best cause my mother told me to watch him, because he is a good Christian man, in his church and all. To me, you know, all of them is going to tell you what they're going to do. They might be lying. He might be lying. You don't know. But to me, I think the man's honest.

LEWIS: [In laying the blame for the energy crisis] I guess as a whole it *would be those who hold the high offices, sort of like, uh, not the president, you know, but like, uh, federal government, you know, people who intend to make a dollar off of it. Because, uh, I think that once you get so high and get so much, you stop looking out for the well-being of other people, you just look out for yourself. Any way you can make a buck, that's what you do.*

MARK: *Abe Lincoln was one of my idols, his honesty and integrity and how he thought everybody should be free and have their own thoughts. . . . One person can't do it [solve the country's problems] unless he's a very good speaker that can get the attention of the people to listen to him and show them that he's no hypocrite, that he is into his beliefs. But people is not like that. After they get up so far in success, they want to take more, and they can't be humble. Money's one evil thought. That's all it is. It's just evil.*

PAUL: *Everybody says to write your congressman, but I don't feel that people trust Congress anymore. I don't feel they trust government anymore. I do know that when Jimmy Carter got elected there was a sigh of relief around here.*

The search for integrity in politics gives these southern working-class men something in common with the middle-class Los Angeles suburbanites in Karl Lamb's study. They, too, "seek a political leader who is above politics, a man who will devote his efforts to the good of the whole."[36] It is noteworthy that many of the people in Lamb's study also came from strong religious backgrounds, and tend to make moralistic interpretations of public life.

How, then, can we evaluate the impact of religion on the attitudes of the workingmen of Furntex, for these attitudes also present a paradox to populist political candidates? Religion distracts these men from economic issues to somewhat authoritarian morality issues and places them in the grasp of those who combine moral conservatism with economic conservatism. But religion also tends to kindle a sense of compassion and sensitivity to social injustice that would make these men comfortable with the revivalist style of populist appeals. It tends to focus their interest on a search for integrity in politics, which lends credibility to the populist charge that politics has been corrupted by the powerful who seek only to maintain and strengthen their power. If this initial interest is abandoned in the face of self-interest, as Lamb found to be the case with his middle-class suburbanites, then so much the better for populism, for its programs are in the self-interest of these men.[37] Sparking some initial interest and attention with a call for integrity in politics in a style that naturally appeals to these men is precisely what is needed to overcome the prevailing barrier of political nonparticipation in Furntex. On balance, if aspiring populist political candidates are careful to avoid or straddle morality issues involving the strict enforcement of moral codes so as to not alienate their more liberal support (as Carter was able to do in 1976), they may capitalize on religiously based attitudes by their use of style and emphasis on integrity issues. Because credibility is of central importance, perhaps a southerner with a similar religious background would be best qualified to utilize this appealing style without appearing phony or foreign. Herein lies one of the many secrets of Carter's success in 1976.

Conclusion

These fifteen workingmen of Furntex are interested in politics to the extent that they engage in political discussions, but their participation does not extend far beyond conversation. Most do not register or vote, do not engage in other electoral-related behavior, hold memberships in formal groups, or have any contacts with elected public officials. Nonparticipation is inherited from their parents, and the habit of noninvolvement grows stronger—fewer of them are involved than their parents. They have little sense of civic duty involving political activity. They are moving away from the party identities of their parents toward a stance of partisan independence, which further reduces political participation. Their few contacts with public officials reinforce feelings of personal and political powerlessness along with feelings of political distrust and cynicism. Their contacts with government and views of citizenship confirm the picture already drawn of them as individual, private men who place family and personal success and happiness above public action aimed at improvement of their lot as a group. They do not see government as relevant to most aspects of their daily lives. Their life-style and distrust of people and public officials makes the physical and psychological actions necessary for voting registration difficult. Their religious concerns and preoccupations draw them away from the public realm except to call for sanctions against those who violate their moral codes of behavior. They share religious memberships and styles with social conservatives who turn them against all liberal ideas. Their underlying distrust of government is reinforced by their vision of government planning to undermine the religious and moral foundation of the country. All of these factors bode ill for those who would wish to recruit these men in a populist coalition.

Some signs of hope for populism did surface among the working class of Furntex. Race was not a factor affecting political participation. Laws and practices and past history no longer make political recruitment of working-class blacks much more difficult than recruitment of whites. Though these are essentially private men, they recognize the need for and importance of group actions in realizing political goals—they are surprisingly realistic in this sense. Their recognized personal and political powerlessness and their distrust of public officials are intensely felt deprivations—they do not feel this is the natural or just order of things. Therefore, these become issues around which to arouse interest. These concerns also suggest that the common-man style of populism is an effective means of arousing their interest. The interaction of salience, knowledge, and efficacy suggests that when issues are defined that interest these men and when they can see government to be relevant, they are attracted to political activities. One such issue may be anger at their lack of efficacy. Another issue important to all these men that is a natural part of any populist program is tax reform. Religious training and backgrounds may be a boon as well as a problem for populists. Religion tends to raise these men's sense of social conscience and compassion and raises their consciousness to another morality issue also of interest to populists—integrity in government. The familiar style of their religion is the natural style of populism. These men are also fairly tolerant of ambiguity and seem capable of sustaining the frustrations of long-term political participation.

All of this along with some of the other findings of my examination suggest a strategy for populists to overcome the problem of participation. First, they should utilize a style that appeals to these men by being both natural and containing a tone of high moral concern and integrity. This is the style in which they learned about religion. It is simple, fundamental, moralistic, emotional, unashamed, often quiet, and yet sometimes loud and revivalistic. In the past, only social conservatives have used this style in North Carolina. Social liberals may have difficulty using this style in such a way as to appeal to these men, avoid entanglement with authoritarian morality issues, and maintain support from liberal elements in the middle and upper classes. Carter's success suggests that, though it is a most difficult maneuver, it is possible.[38]

Second, populist candidates should emphasize issues of immediate interest that these men see as relevant to government action, such as tax reform and integrity in government. The integrity issue has the additional advantage of high compatibility with populist style.

The question of integrity raises a long-term problem for populists that Clotfelter and Hamilton mention in their evaluation of populist prospects in the South. It may be easier to be elected to office than to be reelected.[39] The prevalent cynicism and resentment toward those who hold power might turn against populist politicians who are bidding for reelection. No doubt Carter's withdrawal of the $50 tax rebate proposal of 1977 will cause him problems among the workingmen of Furntex when he runs for reelection in 1980. Several of them mentioned that proposal as one reason why they liked and supported Carter in 1976. A few even talked about how they would spend the money. Carter's voluntary withdrawal of the plan without effectively placing blame on others will cause some of these men to question both his allegiances and his sincerity. The best way to avoid this problem may be to lay the blame for failures to deliver on powerful enemies, such as "special interests."

The popularity of the North Carolina politician who comes closest to being a populist may be explained in this way. John Ingram, the commissioner of insurance in North Carolina, has maintained a high degree of support in the state and won reelection even though he has not delivered on all promises to lower insurance rates and did not have the support of the establishment of the state Democratic party. His tactic was to run against the hated insurance companies rather than against primary or general election opponents. Though he may be viewed by some liberal-leaning progressives as irresponsible and though his programs may not be in the best interests of consumers, his position of laying blame for his substantive failures on powerful special interests serves as an important lesson.

Finally, populists should seek to implement political structural reforms that would ease the mobilization of their working-class constituency. Automatic or post card voter registration might be the most important of all possible reforms, for it would lower the physical and psychological costs of voting.

Had all those in this small group who had a preference in the 1976 election voted, Carter would have received ten of thirteen votes rather than the five votes he actually balloted. Even though this may be a small net increase, it could have a decisive impact in any otherwise close election if enough workingmen feel as do these fifteen furniture workers of Furntex.

CHAPTER SIX

Conclusion

Survival in Rose Hill is a matter of holding your job, which means you take what they pay you and you go on home. "If they don't like workin' for me," laughs Nash Johnson, "they can always leave." . . . No amount of personal will, let alone accountability, has the slightest effect. When He is ready, the spirit will claim us. But only at the whim of the Lord. It is a whim that is capricious and not to be questioned, silent and immutable as the big old houses on Main Street, the Democratic executive committee, the relationship between tenant and landlord, chicken catcher and Nash Johnson. The preacher passes the basket, the deputies haul the voters. And all for a greater purpose beyond our understanding. "I've never been so ignorant as to express my opinion," says housewife Tippy Murray. . . . But it is Ben Harrell, the mayor, who has the decisive word. "There are," he told me, "no politics in Rose Hill." [Reed Wolcott, Rose Hill, pp. 17, 21–22.]

    The central purpose of this exploration into the lives and beliefs of these fifteen southern furniture workers has been to evaluate the possibility of biracial cooperative action that would strive to improve the economic condition of these men and their families. Their opinions about such issues as jobs, wages, opportunities, and health care, beliefs and prejudices about race, and a number of factors that bear upon their propensity to participate in politics, such as education, group memberships, personal attitudes, citizen duty, and party identification, have been examined.

    The interviews uncovered several factors that have a negative impact on the potential for a populist coalition and may be a large part of the reason why such a coalition has not happened—though, of course, one can never fully explain a nonevent. The men of Furntex do not believe that government has an unlimited responsibility to provide all men with high-quality jobs. Politicians who would appeal to them on issues of unemployment and underemployment must understand that these men view the right to a job as limited and something that must be earned. It is limited in that the government should provide jobs only when almost all other opportunities have been exhausted, and it must be earned by showing a willingness to work at any available job rather than seeking government aid and welfare. This somewhat self-defeating belief with its "catch-22" quality best serving employers who offer low wages and poor working conditions is rooted in a strong sense of rugged individualism

195

that these men have learned from their parents, peers, and their own struggles for survival. They are essentially private men who pursue individual strategies for the moderate upward mobility that most feel is possible for themselves and, if not, for their children. Their lives are dominated by private satisfactions and private goals, family pleasures, and new cars. They fail to see many links between their daily personal problems and the political choices offered them. They exhibit enough racial prejudice so that they could be separated from their black working-class peers on a number of issues.[1] The most important of these issues evolves from the negative stereotype of the "lazy, shiftless" black apparently held by most of these white men. Blacks are seen as threatening because they wish to use the powers of the national government to change the rules of meritocracy to gain an unfair advantage in jobs and promotions. This stereotype embitters white workers toward all government power, especially that of the national government, and threatens to alienate whites from blacks, who generally feel that they are discriminated against. For a number of other reasons, any political participation is difficult for these men. Consistent with their private, individualistic outlooks toward life, they are involved with few formal organizations through which they might gain a sense of group interest, political information, or strategies for group advancement through political action. The church, which is the organization that has the most impact on their lives, reinforces their propensity to cope individually and privately with whatever situation life deals them. Religion concerns them with issues that are irrelevant or even detrimental to their economic well-being (Jim, for example, feels he cannot take a job in a high-paying local brewery because of his religion). Their few contacts with public officials further reinforce the belief that individual, private coping actions serve them better than public action. This finding is congruent with their belief that government is largely irrelevant to their daily lives. They possess no real sense of citizen duty motivating public political activities. Their notions of good citizenship also revolve around private and individual actions. Severe misanthropy may prevent some of the men from trusting any politician. Their sense of partisan identification is weak, even weaker than that of their parents, and this further depresses the likelihood and salience of political action.

The picture, however, was not totally bleak for those who would hope to bring these men together in coalitions pursuing economic self-interest. These fifteen workingmen share a number of strong issue concerns and beliefs that might be used to build such a coalition. Most expressed definite feelings of relative deprivation with respect to wages. They do not feel their hard and persistent work is paying off as it should. They tend to blame the rich and corporate interests for this deprivation of rewards and, to a lesser extent, opportunities. Furthermore, they feel that these same groups deprive them of political power, use government to gain unfair tax advantages, and reap undeserved profits from such underhanded acts as the Russian wheat deal and the coffee and energy shortages. This anger manifests itself in a strong political cynicism and seems to have helped develop a surprisingly profound, though as yet unsophisticated, sense of class awareness and consciousness. Study of the interaction among salience, knowledge, and efficacy, as well as examination of the beliefs of those who did and did not vote, showed that issues do count and are important if they are seen to be relevant to the concerns of these men and if meaningful choices are offered. The challenge for aspiring populist candidates is to define and offer these choices. Though these men tend to pursue private, individual strategies, they are surprisingly realistic in their theoretical understanding of the necessity to organize. Union organizers must appeal to this understanding. Populist candidates could provide the opportunity and leadership to engage them in an organization, especially if no more time and effort were required than voting. One significant barrier to voting—registration—must be lowered to reduce the physical and psychological costs of this important mode of participation. Although actual participation levels were low, the men indicated a widespread interest in talking about politics. Intolerance of ambiguity was not so great as significantly to depress the participation of most of these men. Though they are divided along racial lines on some questions, both races share similar goals with respect to important economic and social issues. Both would support a minimum income for all those who are willing to work as long as it is not defined in a way that does damage to the ideal of meritocracy. Both races want better health care, housing, and tax reform and would support strong government actions in all these areas. Both also accept some important norms of racial justice: public facilities and schools should be integrated. Busing is not a potent issue for most of these small-town white men. The depth and quality of the racial prejudice that did surface involved only a few of the white workers who would be psychologically prevented from joining their black working-class peers in self-interested action. Populist candidates face the problem of defining economic issues in such a way as to emphasize common interests and avoid coalition-splitting issues of reverse discrimination. Though religion has some negative impact, it suggests a style and tone that has natural appeal to these men and has developed in them some sense of social responsibility.

Thus the situation in Furntex is very complex, and the prospects for populism are possible and conditional. If populists are to succeed, they must choose and define their issues carefully, beginning by working for procedural reforms. They must avoid battles on racial and morality issues. The dangers of regionalism must be avoided, for these men resent the fact that workers in the North earn more money than they do. Blame and resentment of the rich and corporations could easily be displaced by resentment of unions and workers in the North, both of whom are perceived to be selfish.

Some quantitative evidence suggests that the citizens of Furntex may choose to vote their class interests when the issues are properly defined. An analysis of precinct returns was performed on two 1976 electoral contests, one of which had a strong flavor of populism and the other the odor of racial prejudice.

The first contest was in the 1976 state Democratic primary and involved the office of commissioner of insurance. The incumbent, John Ingram, had built a reputation as an opponent of large insurance corporations and welcomed and promoted a public image as champion of the average consumer. His challenger, Joseph Johnson, was seen as a responsible, business-oriented candidate. He had greater support within the state Democratic party organization and received significant financial contributions from insurance companies. Ingram made a good deal of political hay with this latter fact.

The voters of Furntex seem to have perceived this contest as one involving issues related to economic class. This can be shown by comparing the returns in a dominantly middle- and upper-class white precinct with those from a working-class racially mixed precinct (about 50 percent black). Democrats in the middle- and upper-class white precinct gave the establishment candidate a majority by a slight margin, while both of the working-class precincts gave Ingram about a two-to-one majority. (See Table 3.) In this contest, working-class blacks and whites joined forces and "voted their pocketbooks." Ingram won in the state as a whole.

The second contest was a 1976 Democratic runoff election following the state primary. A well-known moderate black liberal who had worked his way up through the party ranks, Howard Lee, was running against a con-

Table 3. *The Impact of Class and Race on Voting*

1976 Democratic Primary for Commissioner of Insurance

	Precinct Description		
Candidate	Middle- and Upper-Class White	Working-Class White	Working-Class Mixed
Ingram	48% (110)	66% (109)	73% (140)
Johnson	52 (115)	34 (55)	27 (53)
	100% (225)	100% (164)	100% (193)

1976 Democratic Runoff Primary for Lt. Governor

	Precinct Description		
Candidate	Middle- and Upper-Class White	Working-Class White	Working-Class Mixed
Lee	25% (41)	17% (21)	76% (131)
Green	75 (164)	83 (102)	24 (42)
	100% (205)	100% (123)	100% (173)

servative white who had been a Democratic party leader in the state legislature, Jimmy Green. Though race was not openly an issue, there were obvious racial overtones. Neither candidate stressed any differences on substantive issues. Lee was well known as the first serious black candidate for a statewide office in this century. He openly courted the black vote through the churches and other community organizations. Green made several statements about the dangers of "block voting." The real issue was not defined as liberal versus conservative or who would best represent the "little man," but whether North Carolina was ready to elect a black to a state-level office.

The voters of Furntex apparently perceived the contest as involving race rather than class. This time working-class whites formed a coalition with middle- and upper-class whites to defeat Lee soundly (he also lost in the state as a whole). The middle- and upper-class white precinct gave Green a three-to-one margin, and the working-class white precinct voted even more heavily for Green, better than a four-to-one margin. On the other hand, the working-class racially mixed precinct voted for Lee by a three-to-one margin.

Perhaps the greatest obstacle to populist success is the fatalistic, individually adjusting and coping stance that these men take toward most of life's situations. Though they are less fatalistic than were the workers in Lane's study, what they lack in simple acceptance they seem to make up for in their ability privately to cope, adjust, and survive and then to take a stubborn pride in this small accomplishment. The same attitudes that allow them to cope with faits accomplis thrust upon them by the government with respect to the integration of public facilities allow them to cope with everyday survival problems. The angers they feel and express may be only momentary happenings overshadowed by daily coping and adjusting.

In an analysis of why and how populism failed in the South at the turn of the century, W. J. Cash pointed to a similar but exaggerated mental state in the ancestors of these men:

> We need to recall how simple these people were—that they had no training in, and no power of analysis, no notion of the social forces affecting their lives. We need to remember that they approached the situation . . . within the frame of a pattern accepted as in the nature of things. And that really to suppose them breaking out of it, we have first to suppose them acquiring a whole new habitus of thought and a new complexity of mind. . . . Instead of anger and resentment, the dominant emotion of the white cropper or tenant toward the more fortunate neighbor on whose land he found himself planted, under whose mastery he found himself lodged, was likely to be gratefulness. . . . Grumble at him, hate him spasmodically—you would of course. But you would never get up tenacious resentment enough to even keep alive the co-operative stores the [Farmers'] Alliance was setting up against him.[2]

Another important factor obstructing the cooperative mobilization of these men is the very same factor that helped make inoperable the Marxist prediction of the inevitable uprising of the working classes in industrialized capitalist nations. W. J. Cash also saw this factor impairing the populist movement at the turn of the century.[3] Though opportunity and upward mobility are not equally available to all, they are available to enough so that some of the brightest and the most capable, the would-be leaders of any workers' revolt, do advance and lose their motivation for group betterment. Those who do not advance blame their failures on misfortune, bad luck, or lack of education and hope for a brighter day for their children. Those in this small group who are most competent and most angry (Rick, Jim, Mark, and Paul) are also the most likely to leave the furniture factories of Furntex or at least to move into higher paying blue-collar jobs. Indigenous leadership is drained off. The socioeconomic system is designed so that some opportunity for upward social mobility viewed through a meritocratic, individualist belief perspective tends greatly to reduce the chances of disruptive working-class uprisings. If populism is to have any chance of success, the working-class empathy of these men must be retained at least insofar as voting is concerned, and the momentary angers must burn long enough to sustain them through the act of voting.

The organization of labor unions has a potential role here. Studies have shown that a tradition of union involvement may stimulate political participation among the working class.[4] The successful organization of the labor force could serve to retain the allegiance of the firebrands and eventually stimulate greater political involvement of all workers.

On balance, it would seem that though the issues, rhetoric, and style of populism may be used to unite these men to vote their economic self-interests in any given election, there are so many impediments to the stability and success of a biracial coalition that the conclusion must be pessimistic to those who would wish to resurrect this ancient and almost forgotten movement. Though some populistic electoral victories are possible, significant and difficult changes must take place before they become very probable except in isolated cases.

The potentially explosive and divisive racial issues surrounding affirmative action programs must be resolved and become another issue of the past, as did school integration. Until this is accomplished, the old racial hatreds and fears may still be ignited by those who would wish to separate the races.

Barriers to the widespread political participation of these men must be lowered. They experience many social, psychological, and political disincentives to political activity relative to those in the middle and upper classes. Procedural changes such as automatic universal voter registration might significantly lower these barriers. Though such reforms are being given serious national consideration, they do not seem any more likely in the near future than the success of the movement to unionize the mills and factories of the South. Their opponents apparently realize what is at stake.

Until these changes come to pass, these workingmen of Furntex and their peers will continue privately to cope and adjust in their daily lives, and there will be no "public" politics in Furntex.

Epilogue

Since the original writing, two events relevant to my findings have occurred. First, the citizens of Furntex were offered an electoral choice between a modern populist and an ultraconservative. Second, the Teamsters began a massive drive to organize the factories of Furntex.

In 1978, John Ingram, the popular and populist-flavored insurance commissioner of North Carolina, narrowly won the Democratic nomination for the United States Senate over several more establishment-oriented Democrats. The coalition he put together was similar to that seen in his race for insurance commissioner: blacks and working-class whites along with some liberals. The nomination won him the right to face North Carolina's incumbent Republican senator, Jesse Helms. Helms was mentioned in the discussion of political participation in the context that his literature on the danger of big government was finding its way into the sermons given at some of the churches attended by these workingmen.

In the November Senate race the middle and upper classes faced a choice between a Republican whom they considered to be a social conservative and a Democrat whom they saw as an economic radical. Blacks faced an easy choice. They would vote for the man who possessed the right party label, was a liberal on civil rights questions, and strongly advocated economic policies that favored the working poor. The alternative, a Republican economic conservative who has a long and consistent anti-civil-rights reputation would not fare well among blacks. Working-class whites were forced to choose between moral principles of rugged individualism with anti-civil-rights overtones on the right and appeals to class-based economic self-interest on the left.

In terms of candidate styles, those with a taste for populism were probably confused. Both candidates sounded antiestablishment and both had something of an evangelical flavor in their appeals. Helms was more successful in presenting this flavor for two reasons. First, his campaign was better financed, resulting in more exposure. Second, he was a better orator than his opponent. He also unabashedly advertised his religious fundamentalist beliefs. In correspondence with one of Ingram's campaign managers, I learned that the Ingram organization was very bitter because Helms made religion a litmus test for electability. The findings of my study leave little doubt that this maneuver helped Helms to increase the potency and authenticity of his appeals on other issues to the white workers of Furntex.

Table 4 indicates how the citizens in three different precincts in Furntex cast their votes when faced with these issues. These are the same three precincts examined earlier in the Democratic primary in which Ingram ran for the office of insurance commissioner. For comparative purposes, included in brackets are the percentages of voters who supported the other Democrat running for national office in Furntex in that 1978 election, an incumbent congressman who had no serious Republican opposition.

To carry the entire county, Ingram needed to run extremely strongly in the normally Democratic precincts of Furntex in order to offset the normally Republican precincts of the outlying areas. This is precisely what the incumbent Democratic congressman was able to do. The margins he built up in Furntex allowed him to carry Duane County with 55 percent of the vote. As can be seen in Table 4, Ingram did carry the Furntex precincts, but not with large enough margins to carry the county as a whole, as he had done in 1976 in a different contest against a much weaker Republican opponent.

The numbers reveal where Ingram failed and where the rebirth of Populism was aborted. Ingram was able to accomplish the necessary margin of victory in the racially mixed working-class precinct. But he failed in the white working-class precinct, where he ran 10 percent behind the other Democrat running for national office. The well-financed campaign of Helms, advertising social and moral conservatism, drew enough working whites away from their black economic peers and their normal party identification to frustrate an effective electoral alliance. Ingram did no better here than he did among upper- and middle-class whites in Furntex, where he also mustered 10 percent less votes than the incumbent Democratic congressman.

The lesson seems clear. The working classes will not be able to form an effective biracial alliance until more of them avoid entangling themselves in morality issues and begin to vote in a more self-interested way on eco-

Table 4. *Populism versus Moral Conservatism in the 1978 General Election*

	Precinct Description		
Candidate	Middle- and Upper-Class White	Working-Class Mixed	Working-Class Mixed (about 50% Black)
Ingram	57% (269)	59% (239)	82% (279)
the incumbent Democratic congressman	[67%]	[69%]	[84%]
Helms	43 (202)	41 (166)	18 (61)
	100% (471)	100% (405)	100% (340)

nomic matters as do the relatively more affluent. The white workingmen of Furntex have not yet overcome the fears and hatreds that bind them.

In late 1978, the Teamsters came to Furntex and launched a drive to organize the labor force. They wisely began in plants that were relatively new to the area, where the work force was relatively young, where there was no tradition of paternalism, and where management was more likely to be composed of transplanted northerners who were not as vitriolic in their hatred of unions. Even so, the struggle was bitterly and fiercely engaged, involving a multitude of unfair labor practice charges and becoming entangled with issues of personal morality. In one instance, the woman who was the chief union organizer was sued for causing "alienation of affection" in a local marital dispute. The suit was later dropped.

The organizing effort has achieved some successes, but these have been limited. Five plants voted in favor of organization, and, as of the fall of 1979, two contracts have been successfully negotiated and signed. At one company, however, a long strike was broken without any contract being signed. Shortly thereafter, the union voluntarily withdrew from that plant. Another plant is still pursuing legal challenges of the 1978 election that led to NLRB certification of the Teamsters as bargaining agent for employees. At the last plant, the union was dissolved after several failures to negotiate a contract. A majority of workers at that plant, which is the oldest and strongest locally based of the five, signed a petition to decertify the Teamsters as their bargaining representative. Foreseeing a loss, the union withdrew without a new election. All efforts to organize the more well-established textile and furniture factories of Furntex have been unsuccessful.

Management tactics have capitalized upon the attitudes I uncovered among the fifteen young workers in this study. The emphasis these men place upon individual coping and adjustment results in a scarcity of the patience and organizational loyalty necessary for long and difficult contract negotiations. Their individual fears of security have been fueled by a well-publicized case of a worker who was fired at one plant and denied employment at other plants for union activity, despite the fact that she won an administrative judicial ruling and an NLRB decision. The case is now in its third year, and a company appeal to the federal circuit court seems likely. The message to these men is clear. You may be fired and be unable to find work elsewhere in Furntex if you engage in union activity. You may eventually win in court, but in the meantime you will need substantial savings to survive. Justice delayed is justice denied.

As long as companies are able to utilize tactics of delay in legal proceedings and in bargaining, the workers of Furntex will remain prisoners of their own stubborn individual pride. The freedom individually to make one's own way translates into the freedom to work for low wages and to be afraid of losing one's job.

APPENDIX A
Tables

Table A-1. *Economic Liberalism*

Name	Economic Liberalism Score*	Race	Hourly Wage	Education (number of school years completed)
Paul	27	W	3.38	13
Junior	26	W	4.50	10
Rick	26	B	3.00	12
Brent	25	B	3.38	12
Jim	25	W	3.77	13
Albert	24	B	3.55	9
Dave	24	W	4.50	12
John	24	B	5.18	10
Mark	24	W	2.70	12
Terry	24	W	4.25	13
Eddie	21	W	4.68	9
Roy	21‡	W	3.20	8
Kevin	20‡	W	3.86	12
Melvin	20‡	W	2.70	9
Lewis	14	B	3.40	12

* Total scores are the sum of scores over the four items, each of which has a seven-point Likert response set ranging from "strongly agree" (coded as 7) through "don't feel either way" (coded as 4, the neutral point) to "strongly disagree" (coded as 1). The last item was reverse scored. Higher scores indicate greater economic liberalism. The mean score is 22.9.

Personal Control Score	Voted in 1976	Presidential Preference in 1976†
4	Yes	C/ST
3	No	C/MOD
3	Yes	C/ST
3	Yes	C/ST
2	Yes	C/ST
2	No	C/MOD
2	No	F/WK
3	No	D.K.
3	No	D.K.
1	No	C/MOD
4	No	C/WK
1	No	F/MOD
3	Yes	C/ST
2	No	F/ST
3	No	C/ST

†Symbols: C/ST—strong Carter; C/MOD—moderate Carter; C/WK—weak Carter; F/WK—weak Ford; F/MOD—moderate Ford; F/ST—strong Ford; D.K.—don't know.

‡These scores may have been affected by some acquiescence response set bias and as a result may be artificially high.

Table A-2. *The Impact of Class Consciousness and Anxiety over Class Status*

Name	Class Consciousness* (0–11)	Voted in 1976	Presidential Preference 1976	Party Identification and Strength	Union Support (0–4)†	Economic Liberalism Score (7–28)
Brent	10	Y	C/ST	D/ST	4	25
Mark	10	N	D.K.	AM. IND.	3	24
Rick	10	Y	C/ST	D/ST	4	26
Jim	9	Y	C/ST	D/WK	4	25
Junior	8–9	N	C/MOD	D/WK	3	26
Albert	8	N	C/MOD	D/WK	4	24
Eddie	8	N	C/WK	R/WK	1	21
Kevin	8	Y	C/ST	D/WK	4	20‡
Paul	8	Y	C/ST	IND	3	27
Terry	7–8	N	C/MOD	IND	0	24
John	7	N	D.K.	IND	4	24
Lewis	5	N	C/ST	D/MOD	0	14
Roy	3–5	N	F/MOD	D.K.	3	21‡
Dave	3	N	F/WK	IND	0	24
Melvin	2	N	F/ST	R/WK	3	20‡

* The class consciousness score for each man is the summation of the coded answers he gave to the questions concerning concepts of class and class differences, class self-identification, social mobility and opportunity, the issue of blame, tax inequities across classes, perception of class conflict, and the relative happiness of the rich.

Each worker was scored as 0, 0–1, or 1 on each of the above questions, with the exception of the question of class conflict. Here, each individual was scored as 0, 1, or 2, since there are three categories. Therefore, on these seven questions, a maximum score would be 8. One additional set of questions was added to complete the index. These questions were designed to tap the extent to which the worker sympathizes with the working class. Each was asked three questions: (1) Do you think that working people are treated fairly and squarely by their employers, or do employers sometimes take advantage of them? (2) In strikes and disputes between working people and employers, do you usually side with the working people or with the employers? (3) Would this be a better country if working people had more power and influence in government? Adding this subindex of working-class sympathy, on which scores can range from 0 to 3, to the class consciousness index, the range of possible scores is from 0 (indicating low consciousness and little anxiety and therefore little attraction to a populist political movement) to 11 (indicating high consciousness, high anxiety, and much greater attraction).

† Scores are interpreted as follows: (4) yes; (3) leaning toward; (2) don't know; (1) leaning against; (0) no.

‡ Possible error due to acquiescence response set bias.

The Questionnaire

1. I'd like to begin our discussion with you telling me about your family and background—a kind of brief life story. Beginning with your grandparents, tell me what your family did for a living, where they lived, what kinds of things they were interested in, and so on. [Probe for the following:] How strict were the rules in your family when you were growing up? What kind of things were you able to decide for yourself? When you were growing up, who seemed to make most of the family rules? Did you help or participate in making the rules? Did your mother or father seem to be consistent in the application of these rules, or did you sometimes get punished for breaking a rule and sometimes not, depending on the circumstances? How many of your parents were around while you were growing up? Everyone has good points and bad points and problems. In thinking about your parents, what were their good and bad points? What were some of their problems? What did they worry about? How did you get along with your brothers and sisters? How old are they in relation to you? Where are they now? What do they do? How do you get along with them now? Do you see them often? What do you talk about when you do see them? What did you worry about when you were growing up? What did you enjoy doing most? least? What were your ambitions, dreams? What were your major problems?

2. What major illnesses and accidents have you suffered in your lifetime? What kind of health problems do you have?

3. How many years of school did you complete?

4. Remembering back to when you were in school, how well did you do in comparison to most of the rest of the kids? Would you say that (a) you were not really successful at it, not "cut out" for school; (b) you were not quite as good as most kids; (c) you were about the same as the rest; (d) you did a little better in school than most; (e) you were a very successful student?

5. Most people feel quite differently about the place in which they live. I should like to find out how you feel about living in this area. Is there anything you particularly like about living here? Explain. What are some of the bad things? [Probe for explanation.] How do you think this area compares to other places you've been or heard about? If your job made it necessary for you and your family to pack up and move to some other city, how would you feel about leaving here? Whom or what would you miss most? Do you think North Carolina is the best state in America? Why? If you could choose to live anywhere you wish— anywhere—where would you choose to live?

6. What do you think are the major problems facing America today? [Probe for each problem.] What do you think the government should do about it? What should ordinary citizens like us do about it? Who is to blame for this situation?

7. What are the major problems facing this community today? [Same probes.]

8. What are the major problems facing North Carolina today? [Same probes.]

9. Of all these problems we have been talking about, which do you think are the most important? Why?

10. Is there anything in the news in the past two years that really made you mad? Can you remember why? Whose fault was it, if anyone's? Did you do anything about it? Could anything be done? Was there anything else?

11. Has there been anything in the news in the past two years that gave you a lot of satisfaction? Can you remember why? Who gets the credit?

12. How do you feel about what the government has done to promote school integration? What percentage of blacks (whites) would you be willing to accept having in the school your children attend? 10, 25, 50, 75, to 90 percent?

13. What do you think about school busing?

14. How do you feel about Medicare? national health care? How far should government go? Should it make all doctors government employees with fixed salaries? Would this be socialism? Would that bother you if it was?

15. What do you think about our income tax system? Does it seem fair?

16. How about the Communist party? Should they be allowed to operate legally just like any other political party?

17. How about the Ku Klux Klan? Should they be outlawed? Or is it a necessary organization?

18. Do you think that the government should provide jobs for those who can't find any work and who want to work? Do you mind having some of your tax money spent on this kind of thing?

19. What do you think causes wars? Will there always be wars?

20. What do you think causes people to be poor—to be in poverty?

21. How about inflation, what do you think causes that?

22. Generally speaking, what would you like to see different in this country? [Probe.] Why?

23. Many people talk about liberals and conservatives. What do you think is the difference between liberals and conservatives? Which term do you think comes closer to describing the way you feel? Why?

24. Do you often change your opinion on political issues, or don't you change your opinions very easily?

25. Do you happen to belong to any organizations that sometimes take a stand on housing, better government, school problems, or other public issues? [If yes, ask] What organizations?

26. When you get together with your friends, would you say that you discuss public issues like government regulation of business, labor unions, taxes, or racial problems frequently, occasionally, or never? [if frequently or occasionally] How would you describe the part you yourself take in these discussions with your friends? In which of the following categories do you fall? Even though I have my own opinions, I usually just listen. Mostly I listen, but once in a while, I express my opinions. I talk as much as anyone in the conversations. I do more than just hold up my end; I usually try to convince the others that I am right.

27. Have you ever written to your congressman or senator or any other public officials to let them know what you would like them to do on some public issue you were interested in?

28. In the last four years, have you ever worked for the election of any political candidate by doing things like distributing circulars or leaflets, making speeches, or calling on voters?

29. Probably you can't remember, but how many times do you think you have gone to the polls and voted in the last four years?

30. Whether you voted or not, I would be interested to know who you liked best in some of the past elections. If you remember, back in 1968, Nixon ran for the presidency as the Republican candidate; Humphrey ran as the Democratic

candidate; and Governor Wallace of Alabama ran as a third-party candidate. Do you remember who you liked best out of those three? Do you remember why? In 1972, Nixon ran for reelection as the Republican candidate and George McGovern was the Democratic candidate. Wallace ran in the primaries but did not run in the general election because he had been shot in an assassination attempt. Whether you voted or not, do you remember who you liked best among these three? [Probe.] Do you remember why? More recently, in March of 1976, North Carolina held a presidential primary. On the Republican side, Governor Reagan of California ran against President Ford. There were many candidates for the Democratic party. Among them were Jimmy Carter, George Wallace, Morris Udall, and some others. Do you remember whether you voted? Whether you voted or not, do you remember who you liked best among all of these candidates? [Probe.] Do you happen to remember why? In the presidential election held this year, Ford ran against Carter. Do you remember whether or not you voted? Whether or not you voted, which one of these candidates did you like the best at the time of the election? [Probe.] Do you happen to remember why? [whites only] Although George Wallace ran in the primaries for the Democratic nomination, he chose not to run as a third-party candidate this year after he was beaten by Carter in some of the primaries. Suppose Wallace had chosen to run as a third-party candidate. Do you think you might have supported him? [Probe.] Why or why not?

31. (a) Which one of the following statements comes *closest* to describing the way you felt the last time you went to the polls and voted? [If the respondent has not voted at all], the way you think you might feel if you did go to the polls and vote? I get a feeling of satisfaction out of it; I do it only because it's my duty; I feel annoyed; it's a waste of time; I don't feel anything in particular. (b) If you don't care who wins an election, do you still feel a duty to vote? Why or why not?

32. Think for a minute about what an ideal "good citizen" would be like in a democracy. Regardless of whether or not such a person really exists, what kinds of things do you think he would do? How do you think he would feel about politics? How close do most people come to this ideal? How close would you say that you come?

33. What do you think of when you think about the term "government?" [Probe for several things.] What kinds of things do you think government ought to do? Ought not to do? What part of the government do you think is most important: the president, Congress, or the Supreme Court? [Probe.] Can you tell me why? Would you say you were more interested in international affairs, national affairs, state affairs, or local affairs when you follow the news? [Probe.] Can you tell me why —— interests you more? Thinking about government, how does it most affect your personal or family life? your work life? your community or neighborhood?

34. I'd like now to ask you a few questions that you may or may not be able to answer. Do you happen to recall whether President Eisenhower was a Democrat or a Republican? Which? Do you happen to know who (is or was just elected) governor of North Carolina? How long a term does a governor serve in North Carolina? How many years does a U.S. senator serve between elections? Do you happen to recall how many members there are on the U.S. Supreme Court?

35. If there were something that you wanted to get done in Furntex, like having a traffic light put on a dangerous corner or getting a street paved, how would you go about it? Would officials listen? Would you be treated fairly? Do you happen to know anybody with political influence who might help you get such things

done? Who? Suppose you went to the police with a problem? Would they treat you fairly?

36. Generally speaking, do you think of yourself as a Republican, a Democrat, an Independent, or what? [if Democrat or Republican] Would you call yourself a strong —— or a not very strong ——? Has there ever been a time when you thought of yourself as being in the —— [other party]? When did this change occur? [if Independent] Do you think of yourself as closer to the Republican or Democratic party? Was there ever a time when you thought of yourself as a Republican or Democrat? [If yes] Which party? When did you change? Do you think there are any important differences between what the two parties stand for, or do you think that they are about the same? [Probe.] What kinds of differences?

37. Do you remember how your parents felt about the Republican and Democratic parties? Which one do you think they identified with? [Probe for possible differences between mother and father.] Do you remember ever hearing them talk about presidential elections or candidates? What do you remember them saying? [Probe to find preferences.]

38. Right now there is high unemployment in many parts of the country, and it has been suggested that government ought to help business create more jobs to improve the economy and reduce unemployment. Do you think improving the economy and reducing unemployment is something that can be done immediately, or will it take a while? How long? How long are you willing to wait?

39. Now I'd like to read you some statements. After you've listened to each statement, I'd like you to tell me which answer on this card [show card with seven-point agree/disagree scale] best describes how you feel about that statement. The feelings range from strongly agreeing through not caring or feeling one way or the other to strongly disagreeing. Feel free to comment on or explain how you feel on any of the statements—if you want to do more than agree or disagree. Here's the first. (a) What young people need most of all is strict discipline from their parents. (b) There are many difficulties a person cannot overcome no matter how much will power he has. (c) A few strong leaders could make this country better than all the laws and talk. (d) Insults to our honor are not always important enough to bother about. (e) In the long run, it is better for our country if young people are allowed a good deal of personal freedom and are not strictly disciplined. [Follow up.] Which do you think is better, strict discipline or a good deal of personal freedom for children? (f) Most people who don't want to get ahead just don't have enough will power. [Follow up.] Do you think it's more *a lack of will power* or *obstacles* and *luck* that keep people from getting ahead? (g) It is more important for a country to have a just legal and political system than to have strong and courageous political leaders. [Follow up.] If you had to choose, which would you rather have of the two? (h) An insult to your honor should not be forgotten. [Follow up.] Do you remember insults to your honor, or don't you bother with them?

40. Some people say that most people can be trusted. Others say that you can't be too careful in your dealings with people. How do you feel about it: most people trusted; can't be too careful. Would you say that most people are more inclined to help others, or more inclined to look out for themselves: help others; look out for themselves. How do you feel about these next statements? [Show seven-point card.] If you don't watch yourself, people will take advantage of you. [If agree, ask] How did you come to that conclusion? Experiences or what? When you get right down to it, no one is going to care what happens to you. Is human nature basically cooperative or uncooperative?

41. Now I'd like to read you some *pairs* of statements and I'd like you to tell me which statement in each pair you most agree with. Here is the first pair.

1. a. I have often found that what is going to happen will happen.

   b. Trusting to fate has never turned out as well for me as making a decision to take a definite course of action.

2. a. What happens to me is my own doing.

   b. Sometimes I don't feel that I have control over the way my life is going.

3. a. When I make plans, I'm almost certain I can make them work.

   b. It's not wise to plan too far ahead because many things turn out to be a matter of good or bad fortune.

4. a. In my case, getting what I want has little or nothing to do with luck.

   b. Many times, we might as well decide what to do by flipping a coin.

42. Here are some more statements that I'd like you to tell me whether you agree or disagree with. [Show seven-point card.] (a) An expert who doesn't come up with a *definite* answer probably doesn't know too much. (b) A good job is one where what you have to do and how you're supposed to do it is always clearly explained. [If agree, ask] Is that the kind of job you like personally? (c) What we are used to is always better than things that are unfamiliar. [Follow up.] Do you prefer things that are familiar or do you like to experience things, persons, and places that are strange and unfamiliar? (d) The sooner we all acquire similar values and ideals the better. [Follow up.] Do you really think it would be a better world if we all had the same ideals and values? (e) People who fit their lives to a schedule probably miss most of the joy of living. [Follow up.] Do you like living on a schedule or would you rather live a life where your time is mostly unplanned? (f) It is more fun to tackle a complicated problem than to solve a simple one. [Follow up.] Which would you rather do? Tackle a complex problem that maybe you can't solve or solve a simple one? (g) People who insist on a "yes" or "no" answer just don't know how complicated things are. [If agree, ask] Do you think a "yes" or "no" answer, a more simple answer like that, is better than complex "maybe" and "sometimes" answers? (h) Teachers or supervisors who hand out vague assignments give a chance for one to show initiative and originality. [Follow up.] Would you rather be told exactly what to do or have a vague assignment?

43. Here are some statements dealing with the sexual revolution that many people say has occurred in this country. Once again, I'd like you just to indicate how much you agree or disagree with each of the statements. Feel free to comment on them if you wish. Here is the first: (a) Most people have some kind of sexual problem. (b) There is more sexual perversion than most people think. (c) Movies and the news have too much sex. (d) The younger generations are just as moral as the older ones were. [If disagree, ask] How are they less moral? (e) Most people are sexually inhibited. (f) Most women are sexually cold. (g) Not many people are sexually promiscuous. (h) Homosexuality and prostitution are not as bad as most people think.

44. Now I'd like you to tell me how much you agree or disagree with a few statements dealing with government and politics. (a) I don't think public officials care much about what people like me think. [If agree, ask] Do you think *any* public officials care? [If yes, ask] Which ones? (b) Voting is the only way people like me can have a say about how the government runs things. (c) People like me don't have any say about what the government does. Do you think we *should* have a say? How much? How should the government get it? (d) Sometimes politics and government seem so complicated that a person like me can't really understand what is going on.

45. (a) In order to get nominated, most candidates for political office have to make basic compromises and undesirable commitments. [If agree, ask] Is that good or bad? (b) Politicians spend most of their time getting reelected or getting

reappointed. [If agree, ask] Do you think that is good or bad? (c) Money is the most important factor influencing public policy. (d) A large number of city and county politicians are greedy opportunists. (e) Politicians represent the general public interest more frequently than they represent selfish special interests. Which would you rather see them represent—the general public interest or special interests?

46. Now, if you don't mind, I'd like to talk to you a little about religion. Do you belong to any organized religious groups? Which ones?

47. Do you think it is possible to be religious without going to church?

48. Are you active in your church? [Probe.] What do you do?

49. Do you have many friends in church? Do you see them at other times?

50. What does your religion mean to you?

51. Is it important in your daily living?

52. Does religion help a person to stay honest and stay on the right track, or doesn't it make much difference?

53. How do you feel about people who belong to other religions? Do you feel that they are a little bit different in any way?

54. Is it easy to change from one religion to another?

55. How do you feel about blacks and whites going to church together? (Ask about the incident at Carter's church in Plains, Georgia.) Are there any blacks [whites] in your church? How would you feel if one tried to join?

56. Do you think it helps a man to get ahead to belong to your religion or doesn't it make any difference? Where you work, does it help to get a job to belong to a church? [If yes, probe.] Explain.

57. About the way men think in this community, do you think people think more or less of someone who belongs to your church or religion?

58. What about the special beliefs in your church? How important are they? How about gambling, card playing, and drinking? How about the Bible: do you think that everything in it is absolutely true or that some of the things in it may be in error?

59. How do you feel about this statement? [Show seven-point card.] I'd be very happy in life if I could always count on enough money for food, clothes, house payments, and so on, the basics. Which of the following best describes your family's financial life when you were a child: always had everything we needed; sometimes we lacked things, but we were about as well off as most; we were not as well off as most people; we were very poor—sometimes we didn't have enough to eat.

60. How do you feel about these statements? [Show card.] (a) The biggest cause of happiness is being able to *know* what you are going to be doing next month, next year, and in ten years. [If agree, ask] Do you think it would make *you* happy to know? Why? (b) It is better to buy what you can of the good things in life than to put your money into the bank. [If agree, ask] Have you been able to buy any of the good things? What for example? (c) It is better to have good friends than money in the bank.

61. (a) It is possible to be very happy in love. (b) Basically, the world we live in is a pretty lonesome place. [If agree, ask] How did you come to that conclusion? Experiences? (c) [Take down card.] Compared to other people that you know, how many friends do you think you have? More, less, or about the same? (d) Which of the following describes your family life as a child: very happy; happier than most; about the same as most; not as happy as most; very unhappy.

62. (a) [Show card.] The most important satisfaction in life is being able to do something so well that everyone looks up to you. (b) It really makes you mad because you rarely get any appreciation for a job well done. [If agree, ask] Where

would you like to get more appreciation? [If disagree, ask] Where do you get appreciation shown to you?

63. (a) How do you feel about this statement? [Continue to show card.] If cities and towns around the country need help to build more schools or water treatment facilities, the government in Washington ought to give them the money they need. (b) The government in Washington ought to see to it that everyone who wants to work can find a job. (c) The government in Washington ought to help all people get doctors and hospital care at low cost. (d) The government should leave things like energy and housing for private businessmen to handle. (e) If blacks are not getting fair treatment in jobs and housing, the government ought to see to it that they do. (f) [Remove card.] Do you think that working people are treated fairly and squarely by their employers, or do employers sometimes take advantage of them? (g) In strikes and disputes between working people and employers, do you usually side with the working people or the employers? (h) Would this be a better country if working people had more power and influence in government? [Follow up.] Why? (i) Do you think labor unions might help workers around here in getting better pay and benefits? How do your fellow workers feel about unions?

64. Sometimes people talk about the idea of "social class" like when they use the terms "middle class" or "working class." What do you think people mean by these terms? [Probe for such things as income, life-style, education, friendships, race, or birth.]

65. Would you say that you were upper class, middle class, working class, or lower class? How so?

66. How important do you think social classes are in America today?

67. Do you think it is easy or hard to go from one social class to another? For example?

68. [If they can think of themselves as being in a social class] How do you feel about being in the —— class?

69. Some people say that the various social classes want different things and come into conflict with each other. How important do you think this class conflict is in America? Have you come across any evidence of class conflict of this kind?

70. We've now had racial integration here in the South for several years, and it's important for people to know how southerners have adjusted to it. In general, how many of the white people in this area would you say are still opposed to integration—all, most, about half, less than half, or very few? How about yourself? How about the blacks (whites)? Do you prefer strict segregation, integration, or something in between? Have your views changed over the years at all? How so?

71. Have you ever known a (black or white) well enough that you would talk to him as a friend? How did you come to think of this person as a friend? Do you come into a lot of contact with (blacks or whites) with: people at work; people who live nearby; people where you shop or trade; where else?

72. (whites only) By and large, do you think that white people are more dependable than blacks?

73. (whites only) In general, do you think that whites behave better than blacks, blacks better than whites, or are they about the same?

74. (whites only) On the whole, do you think that white people try to get ahead more than blacks?

75. Here in the South, as in many parts of the world, different races of people are living together in the same communities. Now I would like for you to think about the very *best* way that blacks and whites could live in the same place

together. In other words, what would be the very best kind of race relations, the most perfect, you could imagine? Take your time—such things are not very easy to put into words. [Use "anything else" as a probe.]

76. Now, taking the other side of the picture, what would be the very *worst* kind of race relations you could imagine a community having?

77. Now [show the ten-step ladder], think of the top of this ladder, the tenth step, as representing the best kind of race relations that you have just described, and the bottom step, the first step, as representing the worst. Now think of race relations in Furntex about ten years ago. Where on this ladder would you put the race relations of Furntex ten years ago? Where would you put race relations now? Thinking ahead, where would you expect race relations to be about ten years from now, where on the ladder?

78. Now I'd like to find out a little bit about the work you do for a living. In the plant where you work, what would you say are the most respected and sought-after jobs—other than supervisory jobs? What are the least respected and desired jobs? What kinds of things determine the differences? [Probe for things like pay.] Where would you say your job ranks? Would you mind telling me about what your hourly wage is? How large is the plant? your department?

79. I'd like to know a little more about exactly what you do in your job. Suppose I were a new worker who you were training to do your job on another shift. How would you explain your job to me so that I could do it? [Probe in the following areas] How long would it take to learn the job? How does your job fit in with other jobs in making the product? Repetition—How long does it take you to do each task? Does it seem like you do a lot of different things or does it sometimes seem like a never-ending process? How many different things do you do? Can you control the rate at which you work—can you slow down when you want to? Can you take breaks when you want—like to go to the john? What kinds of problems come up that you have to handle or decide for yourself? What kinds of decisions do you have to make? Who is your supervisor? How closely does he supervise what you do? How do you get along with him?

80. Would you say that your job involves getting very dirty compared to other production jobs in the plant? How so? How about the air? Is there any dirt in the air that bothers you? How noisy is it where you work? Are you able to carry on a conversation with others without shouting? Do you talk with others while you work—or is there no opportunity for this? How physically difficult would you say that your job is—could someone weaker than you possibly handle it? Do you get any kind of bonuses for high production or profits? Are you paid according to production? How about fringe benefits? Retirement? Medical insurance? Sick pay? Vacation? Holidays? How secure would you say that your job is—have you ever been laid off? Have others you know been? Do you worry about that? What are your chances for promotion? How long have you worked there and how long will you have to work for promotions?

81. Now I'm going to read some words and phrases that people often use to describe their work. Answer "yes" or "no" according to whether or not the word describes *your* job.

fascinating	useful
routine	tiresome
satisfying	healthful
boring	challenging
creative	frustrating
respected	simple
hot	endless
pleasant	gives a sense of accomplishment

82. Answer "yes" or "no" according to whether or not these next words and phrases describe your *supervision*.

asks my advice	tells me where I stand
hard to please	annoying
impolite	stubborn
praises good work	knows the job well
doesn't supervise enough	intelligent
quick-tempered	leaves me on my own
lazy	around when needed

83. These next words and phrases might describe the people you work with. Again, answer "yes" or "no."

stimulating	talk too much
boring	lazy
ambitious	smart
stupid	unpleasant
responsible	narrow interests
easy to make enemies	loyal
hard to meet	

84. This next group of words and phrases might describe your pay.

income adequate for normal expenses	good fringe benefits
can barely live on the income	good vacation and paid holidays
provides some luxuries	
insecure	
less than I deserve	
highly paid	
underpaid	

85. The last group might describe your promotional opportunities.

good opportunity for advancement
somewhat limited opportunity
promotions on ability
dead-end job
good chances for promotion
unfair promotion policy
infrequent promotions
regular promotions

86. Thinking about all of these different things and any others that you might have in mind, in your opinion, what are the most important things that go into making a job good or bad?

87. Do you like to "talk shop" when you're away from the job?

88. Do you feel that you are "cut out" for this kind of work?

89. Have you ever thought seriously about changing to some other kind of job? Under what conditions might you change?

90. How did you get into this kind of work? How long have you had your present job?

91. When you were a child, did your parents have any special ideas about what you ought to be when you grew up? [Probe.] What ideas?

92. [If parents are living] What do they think of the job that you have now? How do you feel about your job?

93. What kind of work would you like for your children to do when they grow up? Would you mind if they do the same kind of work as you?

94. Does your wife work [if married]? What does she do? How do you feel about her working? about women working in general?

95. What is your understanding of the meaning of democracy?

96. What are the advantages of democracy compared to other systems?

97. What kinds of things would you consider undemocratic?

98. If there were a war with threat of atomic bombing, would you approve of a temporary dictatorship in the hands of the president?

99. Do you think that democracy creates confusion and prevents important things from getting done? What things?

100. Are the organizations and groups that you belong to democratically run? (for example, civic clubs, social clubs, church, family, work)

101. In general, do you think that the people or the elected leaders are more likely to know what is best for the country? [Probe.] Why?

102. Democracy, according to some people, means that everyone, no matter how ignorant or careless, should have an equal vote. Do you agree with that?

103. Do you think it is right for the government to force people to do things against their will? Why?

104. What do you think the future of democracy will be in this country?

105. What is your understanding of the phrase "all men are created equal"?

106. In your own personal life, are there some people whom you regard as not equal to you? Who? In what ways?

107. How would you feel if everyone received the same income, whatever his job was? How about if incomes were just made a lot closer than they are now, but perfect equality was not achieved? Would people work as hard, or wouldn't that matter? Do you think that people get pretty much what they deserve right now the way things are?

108. Suppose you were a member of a club or group that was just getting started. How do you think the club or group should organize so that it can decide things? How would it decide things like how much dues would be or how it should spend the dues?

109. Suppose people paid dues according to how much they could afford with a rich man paying, say, $100 a year and a poor man paying $10 a year. Do you think the man who pays more in dues should have more say or votes when the club is deciding things? Why or why not?

110. How do you think the club should decide who can be a member?

111. It has been said that the people of our generation have lived through a sexual revolution. If you don't mind talking about it, could you tell me when you first learned about sex? If you can remember, would you mind telling me about the circumstances surrounding your first sexual experience?

112. How much effect do you think you could have if you really wanted to change some law or policy here in the United States? How about in North Carolina? How about in this community? On a scale of 1 to 7 with 1 meaning no effect and 7 meaning a lot of effect, where do you think you would rank yourself with respect to the United States? With respect to North Carolina? With respect to this community?

113. How effective do you feel the national government is at this time in responding to the needs and wishes of the American people? Where would you rank the responsiveness of the national government on a scale of 1 to 7 with 1 meaning not responsive and 7 meaning very responsive? How about the North Carolina state government, how responsive is it to the needs and wishes of North Carolinians? Where on a scale of 1 to 7? How about the local government here? Where would it rank on a scale of 1 to 7?

114. Here are some other statements that I'd like to get your feelings about. (a) How important is it for you to feel that you run your own life without depending on other people who are older and more experienced than you: not at all; slightly; somewhat; very; extremely. (b) How often do you find that you can carry

out other people's suggestions without changing them any: rarely; sometimes; often; very often; almost always. (c) How much do you usually want the person who is in charge of a group you are in to tell you what to do: not at all; a little; somewhat; quite a lot; very much. (d) If you have thought about something and come to a conclusion, how hard is it for someone else to change your mind: not at all hard; somewhat; quite; very; extremely. (e) How much do you dislike being told to do something by a superior that is against your wishes: not at all; a little; somewhat; quite a bit; very much.

115. Are there groups in America that you think have too much power? [Probe on the following: minorities, the rich, the poor, labor unions, business, lawyers, politicians, bureaucrats, farmers.]

116. Do you think all races and religions should mix socially in this country? Which ones? Why (or why not)? Should any group be kept out of important decisions?

117. What does the word "freedom" make you think of? What kind of freedom is most important to you?

118. Some people think there should be more freedom than we have now; other people think there should be less. What do you think? [Follow by probing.] What kinds of freedom do you mean?

119. What are the dangers of too much freedom in a country like ours? of too little freedom? What happens when people feel too free?

120. Are there any groups in this country that may go a little too far if they have too much freedom? Who? What will they do?

121. Do you sometimes feel that listening to all the different points of view on a subject is too confusing and that you would like to hear just one point of view from somebody who knows? For example?

122. Do you think there is any special way of bringing up children in a democracy in which there is the kind of freedom we have here? How?

123. Are there any kinds of things you think might better be discussed privately instead of in the newspapers and on the air where anybody can see and hear them? [Probe.] What kinds of things?

124. Some people say that those who talk about "freedom of speech" usually turn out to be radicals of one sort or another. Do you think this is true or not?

125. A famous man once said: "Man is born free and everywhere he is in chains." What do you think he might have meant by this?

126. Can you remember the last time you lost your temper? [Probe.] What happened? Impatience? Frustrations when you were a child? Reactions to drinking a little too much? How often do you drink?

127. Are there any recent events that made you feel very unhappy or feel like crying? What was that? [Probe—does he turn to other people, to solitude, or to action when unhappy?]

128. What are your worries? What kinds of things do you worry about? For example? Do you lie awake at night worrying? Do you worry about things that aren't likely to happen.

129. Some people think they can plan their lives and shoot for long-range goals—like what they will be doing ten years from now. Others, in the words of the song, say "whatever will be will be," and take things as they come. What do you think of this? [Probe.] Have you ever made any long-range plans for yourself or for a group of people? How did they work out?

130. How important are friends in a person's life? [Probe.] Can you explain a little more?

131. What attracts you to a friend? For example?

132. How do you go about choosing or finding friends?

133. What sorts of things do you enjoy doing with your friends? [Probe.] For example? Is there anything else?

134. Are you the sort of person with a few close friends, or do you have a lot of friends, or what? Which do you think is better?

135. Think back to the last time you were out in the evening and had a good time. What was it that made it a good time for you? How about the last time you had a bad time? What made it a bad time?

136. Think of yourself now in a group of friends. How would you describe yourself: life of the party, a good listener, or what?

137. About how much do you think your income will be this year? How much more will other members of the family contribute?

138. Is your income better or worse than last year? than five years ago?

139. How much better do you think it will be five years from now?

140. What do you miss most that your present income doesn't permit you to buy? How important are those things?

141. What is the most important thing that money can give a person?

142. Some people like to take chances: win a lot, lose a lot—others are more cautious and try to save a lot of money. What is your attitude about this? How much are you able to save out of each paycheck? Are you having to pay a lot of bills for things bought on time or credit? How do you feel about buying things on credit?

143. Do you think that people who are very rich are happier than people who are just average? Why is that?

144. What do you think is the best way to teach a child how to handle money?

145. What do you think the perfect society—utopia—would be like?

146. How would people behave there?

147. What would people do for a living? Would they have to work?

148. What kind of government, if any, would there be?

149. Who would run things?

150. What kind of things that you do now would you not have to do in an ideal society?

151. Are we getting any closer to this ideal society?

152. Now I should like to find out the things you have found important in your life. Many people gradually develop some sort of philosophy of life, a general way of looking at things, though they may not know if they have one, or may find it hard to talk about it. I would like you to tell me a little about yours. Have you had much of a chance to think about such things? [Wait for a short answer and then ask] Well, let me begin by asking you this question—it might be worth it to take the time to think about it a little now. What would you say the most important lessons of life have been for you?

153. What makes people happy?

154. What are the things you believe in most, or think most important?

155. What was the most important event in your life?

156. What would you say is the point in living—why are we here?

157. What kind of people would you like your children to be when they grow up?

Notes

Preface

1. John Shelton Reed, "The Southern Quality of Life," p. E5.
2. John Dollard, *Caste and Class in a Southern Town.*
3. Robert Coles, *Migrants, Sharecroppers, Mountaineers,* pp. 25–26.
4. Abraham Maslow, *The Psychology of Science,* especially pp. 102–19.
5. Karl A. Lamb, *As Orange Goes.*
6. Robert E. Lane, *Political Ideology.*

Chapter 1. Introduction

1. Bureau of Labor Statistics, *Employment and Earnings, States and Areas, 1939–1978.*
2. H. Brandt Ayres, "You Can't Eat Magnolias," p. 8.
3. Chandler Davidson, *Biracial Politics,* pp. 186–207.
4. V. O. Key, Jr., and Alexander Heard, *Southern Politics in State and Nation,* pp. 655–70. Also see Alexander Heard, *A Two Party South?* p. 248.
5. Numan D. Bartley and Hugh D. Graham, *Southern Politics and the Second Reconstruction,* p. 200.
6. Richard F. Hamilton, *Class and Politics in the United States,* p. 408; James W. Loewen, *The Mississippi Chinese,* p. 105; Gordon Allport, *The Nature of Prejudice,* pp. 11–12; and Davidson, *Biracial Politics,* p. 179.
7. Hamilton, *Class and Politics,* pp. 408–9.
8. V. O. Key, Jr., *Public Opinion and American Democracy,* pp. 103–5.
9. Donald R. Matthews and James W. Prothro, *Negroes and the New Southern Politics,* pp. 115–18.
10. Heard, *A Two Party South?* p. 248.
11. W. J. Cash, *The Mind of the South,* pp. 177–83.
12. Liston Pope, *Millhands and Preachers,* pp. 9–12, 58–62.
13. Bureau of Labor Statistics, *Employment and Earnings.*
14. In his history of blue-collar workers in New Haven, Lane also offered a small fee for participation. He drew much the same conclusion about the impact of this inducement on his study (Robert E. Lane, *Political Ideology,* pp. 5–6).

Chapter 3. Economic Liberalism

1. V. O. Key, Jr., *Public Opinion and American Democracy,* pp. 104–5, 170.
2. Richard F. Hamilton, *Class and Politics in the United States,* p. 284.
3. James R. Clotfelter and William R. Hamilton, "Beyond Race Politics," p. 247.
4. Numan V. Bartley and Hugh D. Graham, *Southern Politics and the Second Reconstruction,* p. 141.

5. Ibid., pp. 109–10.

6. Gabriel Almond and Sidney Verba, *The Civic Culture*, pp. 17–18.

7. Karl A. Lamb, *As Orange Goes*, p. 110.

8. W. J. Cash, *The Mind of the South*, p. 34.

9. John P. Robinson and Philip Shaver, *Measures of Social Psychological Attitudes*, pp. 105–7.

10. Several political scientists have developed this idea as a theoretical concept. For an excellent summary utilizing a vast number of findings in the area, see Ted Gurr, *Why Men Rebel*.

11. Frank Parkin, *Class Inequality and Political Order*, p. 97.

12. Robert E. Lane, *Political Ideology*, pp. 57–81.

13. Ibid., pp. 73, 78.

14. Ibid., p. 77.

15. Parkin, *Class Inequality*, p. 88.

16. Lamb, *As Orange Goes*, pp. 173–80.

17. Lane, *Political Ideology*, p. 76.

18. Bureau of Labor Statistics, *Employment and Earnings, States and Areas, 1939–1978*.

19. Liston Pope, *Millhands and Preachers*.

20. Angus Campbell, Philip E. Converse, Warren E. Miller, and Donald E. Stokes, *The American Voter*, pp. 170–74.

21. Clotfelter and Hamilton, "Beyond Race Politics," p. 148.

22. Lamb, *As Orange Goes*, p. 179.

23. Theodore R. Marmor, *The Politics of Medicare*.

24. Lane, *Political Ideology*, p. 399.

25. Parkin, *Class Inequality*, p. 90.

26. Almond and Verba, *The Civic Culture*, pp. 17–18.

27. Lane, *Political Ideology*, p. 398.

28. Ibid., pp. 61–62.

29. Ibid., p. 261.

30. See Bernard Hennessy, "A Headnote on the Existence and Study of Political Attitudes," and Herbert McClosky, "Consensus and Ideology in American Politics."

Chapter 4. The Social Issue—Racial Prejudice

1. Richard F. Hamilton, *Class and Politics in the United States*, p. 408; Chandler Davidson, *Biracial Politics*, p. 179; James W. Loewen, *The Mississippi Chinese*, p. 105; and Gordon Allport, *The Nature of Prejudice*, pp. 11–12.

2. Arthur Miller, "Rejoinder to 'Comment' by Jack Citrin."

3. These items were borrowed from a slightly longer scale utilized to measure racial stereotypes. See Donald R. Matthews and James W. Prothro, *Negroes and the New Southern Politics*, pp. 294–96, 513.

4. Ibid., pp. 294–96.

5. Allport points out that prejudice structures the view of whites so that they perceive what is really individual competition for jobs as group competition: "It is often said that Negroes constitute a realistic threat to the lower class white people, since both are competing for lower class jobs. Strictly speaking, of course, the rivalry is not between group and group, but between individuals. It is never the colored *group* that prevents a white laborer from obtaining a job, but only some person (white or colored) who got there first. To say that the conflict is 'realistic' in this case means nothing more than that the contestants *view* the

rivalry as an ethnic matter" (Allport, *The Nature of Prejudice*, p. 223). Of course, discrimination against blacks as individuals because of their group membership and affirmative action plans that whites view as reverse discrimination make the perception that group conflict is taking place all the more likely, regardless of how prejudice structures one's perceptions.

6. Karl A. Lamb, *As Orange Goes*, p. 179. This also tends to confirm Bartley and Graham's conclusion that lower income whites are much closer to affluent whites than they are to lower income blacks on the issue of the federal government taking an active role in the area of jobs (Numan Bartley and Hugh D. Graham, *Southern Politics and the Second Reconstruction*, p. 141).

7. Allport, *The Nature of Prejudice*, pp. 250-67.

8. Ibid., p. 351.

9. Allport makes this point in his examination of prejudice (ibid., p. 354).

10. Lincoln quoted by Allport, ibid., pp. 354-55.

11. James McEvoy III, *Radicals or Conservatives*, p. 145.

12. James Clotfelter and William R. Hamilton, "Beyond Race Politics," p. 152.

13. This theme appears in several works that attempt to explain the Wallace appeal. See, for example, Clotfelter and Hamilton, "Beyond Race Politics," p. 149, and Garry Wills, *Nixon Agonistes*, pp. 56-61.

14. Allport, *The Nature of Prejudice*, p. 15.

15. Allport argues that this threat may be suppressed from its actual target and merely be displaced on the target group. The validation of such judgements is beyond the scope of this study. See ibid., pp. 373-74.

16. Ibid., p. 50.

17. Clotfelter and Hamilton, using mass survey data, came to a similar conclusion ("Beyond Race Politics," pp. 154-55).

18. See, for example, Davidson, *Biracial Politics*, pp. 186-207; V. O. Key, Jr., and Alexander Heard, *Southern Politics in State and Nation*, pp. 655-70; and Alexander Heard, *A Two Party South?* p. 248.

19. Bartley and Graham, *Southern Politics*, p. 200.

20. Clotfelter and Hamilton, "Beyond Race Politics," pp. 156-58.

21. See, for example, Matthews and Prothro, *Negroes and the New Southern Politics*, pp. 116-20, and Clotfelter and Hamilton, "Beyond Race Politics," p. 154. They found increased Wallace support in counties with relatively greater black populations.

Chapter 5. The Problem of Participation

1. Matthews and Prothro used a similar definition in their study of black participation in the South (Donald R. Matthews and James W. Prothro, *Negroes and the New Southern Politics*, p. 37).

2. Kelley, Ayres, and Bowen made a similar argument using survey data. Much of this inquiry was inspired by their findings. See Stanley Kelley, Jr., Richard Ayres, and William G. Bowen, "Registration and Voting."

3. In a widely read and thoroughly criticized study of urban poverty, Banfield views the poor as being "present oriented." I have borrowed his terminology, but applied a slightly different meaning to the term. He views this time orientation as a *cause* rather than a *result* of life's conditions (Edward C. Banfield, *The Unheavenly City*).

4. Matthews and Prothro used a similar Guttman Scale. My scale differs slightly yet significantly from theirs in that I separated registration from voting (*Negroes and the New Southern Politics*, p. 53).

5. Verba and Nie argued that political scientists are remiss in considering political participation to be unidimensional along an electoral dimension. They argued that there are other equally important dimensions that may be related to different skills and abilities than campaign-related activities require. See Sidney Verba and Norman Nie, *Participation in America*. I will draw upon their ideas in what follows.

6. Many studies could be cited here. See, for example, V. O. Key, Jr., *Public Opinion and American Democracy*, pp. 500–503.

7. Ibid., p. 502.

8. Ibid., p. 504.

9. Samuel H. Barnes, "Participation, Education, and Political Competence."

10. In mass survey studies, one reason years of education has such a great impact is that it serves as a substitute variable for social class. That is, those in the higher classes tend also to attain higher levels of education. But social class has some independent effects that enhance the influence of education, such as the greater expectations middle- and upper-class parents have for their children to participate in all areas of life. In this study I in effect controlled out the impact of class by choosing a small sample within a single class, except for the case of Paul, whose greater participation was no doubt influenced by the norms and expectations that are a part of his middle-class family background. For an excellent discussion of the impact of education on political participation, see Angus Campbell, Philip E. Converse, Warren E. Miller, and Donald E. Stokes, *The American Voter*, pp. 475–81.

11. See, for example, ibid., p. 517.

12. Matthews and Prothro, *Negroes and the New Southern Politics*, pp. 271–75.

13. Campbell et al., *The American Voter*, pp. 105–6, 480.

14. Matthews and Prothro, *Negroes and the New Southern Politics*, pp. 323–24.

15. Stanley Allen Renshon, *Psychological Needs and Political Behavior*.

16. The items are "forced choice" pairs of statements. The following pair is typical. (1) What happens to me is my own doing. (2) Sometimes I don't feel I have control over the way my life is going. See John P. Robinson and Philip Shaver, *Measures of Social Psychological Attitudes*, pp. 148–49.

17. Renshon argued that childhood autonomy, rule enforcement, household stability, and many other factors in one's early background are related to personal control (*Psychological Needs*).

18. This scale was constructed using four standard survey items, each of which was scored along a seven-point agree/disagree scale. See Angus Campbell, Gerald Gurin, and Warren E. Miller, *The Voter Decides*, pp. 187–89.

19. This approach was taken from a very interesting study of political alienation that used a causal modeling approach to predict political behavior, David C. Schwartz, *Political Alienation and Political Behavior*.

20. David R. Berman, *State and Local Politics*, pp. 13–14.

21. Renshon suggested that an interaction takes place between two of these factors, saliency and efficacy (*Psychological Needs*, p. 192). I added a third factor, political knowledge, on logical grounds.

22. Jeanne N. Knutson, *The Human Basis of the Polity*, p. 143.

23. This scale is composed of items selected from a sixteen-item scale developed by Stanley Budner, "Intolerance of Ambiguity as a Personality Variable."

24. The assumption that a neutral score on this or any other attitudinal index is indeed neutral in meaning is tenuous at best because we are not dealing with ratio data that have a natural zero or neutral point. Therefore the reader should

keep in mind that being above or below some arbitrary neutral point on any index is intended only to be suggestive.

25. This view is by no means unanimous. Some regard expressions of cynicism as merely ritualistic responses that have become fashionable. See Jack Citrin, "Comment: The Political Relevance of Trust in Government."

26. This scale was taken from a six-item scale developed by Robert Agger, Marshall Goldstein, and Stanley Pearl, "Political Cynicism: Measurement and Meaning." One of the items was eliminated for the sake of economy and because it was judged to be redundant.

27. These are borrowed from Schwartz (*Political Alienation*) and are similar to the items measuring personal political efficacy focused on each level of government, except here the emphasis is on trust focused on each level.

28. These two questions were originally utilized by Gabriel Almond and Sidney Verba (*The Civic Culture*, pp. 68–69) and were designed to measure expectation of fair treatment by police and government officials. Obviously, the lead question in which I asked the respondent how he would go about getting action taps political efficacy, which is often related to political cynicism.

29. James Clotfelter and William R. Hamilton made this argument in their analysis, "Beyond Race Politics," pp. 140–58.

30. Some evidence has been found in mass survey research to support this hypothesis. See Morris Rosenberg, "Misanthropy and Political Ideology."

31. I used Rosenberg's five-item scale ("Misanthropy and Political Ideology"). Possible scores ranged from 0, indicating low misanthropy, to 5, indicating high misanthropy.

32. Campbell et al., *The American Voter*, pp. 120–45.

33. Ibid., pp. 146–49.

34. See Kent L. Tedin, "The Influence of Parents on the Political Attitudes of Adolescents."

35. One possible explanation may be found in extending what political scientists call the theory of "critical elections." According to this theory, party allegiances are established in elections where great emotional issues are at stake, and these loyalties remain intact until the next critical election rolls around. The last critical election in the United States took place in either 1932 or 1936, when the country was in the depths of the Great Depression and Roosevelt swept the country, establishing the Democratic party as the party of the blacks and working classes. Since then no crisis elections have occurred to reaffirm these loyalties. A full generation has passed, and the primary way in which party loyalty has been learned is through inheritance. This is a very imperfect process that is not nearly as effective as personally experiencing involvement in great emotional issues. Thus we should not be surprised that the children of the children of the Depression are relatively weaker in their party identifications. For a more detailed description of critical election theory, see Walter Dean Burnham, *Critical Elections and the Mainspring of American Politics*.

36. Karl A. Lamb, *As Orange Goes*, p. 252.

37. Ibid., p. 257.

38. In a syndicated newspaper article written before Carter was nominated by his party, Michael Novak argued that Carter's evangelical style had an appeal that extended far beyond the Bible-belt South. He estimated that about two-thirds of all white Protestants have evangelical backgrounds. This style, however, was seen as somewhat different from the style of populism that Novak also gave religious roots. He saw populism as springing from the "purifier" tradition of the great Prairie Protestants such as William Jennings Bryan, George McGovern, and

Fred Harris. The emphasis of this style was seen as more punitive and threatening. Novak distinguished Carter from these populists, saying, "he does not wish to 'purify,' but to heal and bring 'love'" (Michael Novak, "Carter Tapping Religious Power Base," pp. A1, 10–11).

39. Clotfelter and Hamilton, "Beyond Race Politics," p. 158.

Chapter 6. Conclusion

1. Herbert Shapiro argues that in North Carolina, the populists of the turn of the century never really did separate themselves from racist issues as was the case in most other southern states. If this were so, then in North Carolina there is less historical basis for working-class whites to repudiate racist politics than in other areas of the South ("The Populists and the Negro").

2. W. J. Cash, The Mind of the South, pp. 166, 171.

3. Ibid., p. 168.

4. Gerald Johnson, "Research Note on Political Correlates of Voter Participation."

Bibliography

Aberbach, Joel D., and Walker, Jack L. "Political Trust and Racial Ideology."
  American Political Science Review 64 (December 1970):1199–1219.
Agger, Robert, and Goldstein, Marshall. "Political Cynicism: Measurement and
  Meaning." *Journal of Politics* 23 (August 1961):477–506.
Allport. Gordon. *The Nature of Prejudice*. Garden City, N.Y.: Doubleday Anchor
  Books, 1954.
Almond, Gabriel, and Verba, Sidney. *The Civic Culture: Political Attitudes and
  Democracy in Five Nations*. Boston: Little, Brown, and Co., 1963.
Ayres, H. Brandt. "You Can't Eat Magnolias." In *You Can't Eat Magnolias*; edited
  by H. Brandt Ayres and Thomas Naylor, pp. 3–24. New York: McGraw-Hill,
  1972.
Ayres, H. Brandt, and Naylor, Thomas, eds. *You Can't Eat Magnolias*. New York:
  McGraw-Hill, 1972.
Banfield, Edward C. *The Unheavenly City*. Boston: Little, Brown, and Co., 1968.
Barnes, Samuel H. "Participation, Education, and Political Competence." *American Political Science Review* 60 (June 1966):348–53.
Bartley, Numan V., and Graham, Hugh D. *Southern Politics and the Second Reconstruction*. Baltimore: Johns Hopkins Press, 1975.
Berman, David R. *State and Local Politics*. Boston: Holbrook Press, Inc., 1975.
Budner, Stanley. "Intolerance of Ambiguity as a Personality Variable." *Journal of
  Personality* 30 (1962):29–50.
Bureau of Labor Statistics. *Employment and Earnings, States and Areas, 1939–
  1978*. Bureau of Labor Statistics Bulletin 1370–13, forthcoming.
Burnham, Walter Dean. *Critical Elections and the Mainspring of American Politics*. New York: W. W. Norton and Co., Inc., 1970.
Campbell, Angus; Converse, Philip E.; Miller, Warren E.; and Stokes, Donald E.
  The American Voter. New York: Wiley and Sons, 1960.
Campbell, Angus; Gurin, Gerald; and Miller, Warren E. *The Voter Decides*. Evanston: Row, Peterson, and Co., 1954.
Cash, W. J. *The Mind of the South*. New York: Alfred A. Knopf, 1941.
Chandler, David Leon. *The Natural Superiority of Southern Politicians: A Revisionist History*. Garden City, N.Y.: Doubleday and Co., 1977.
Citrin, Jack. "Comment: The Political Relevance of Trust in Government." *American Political Science Review* 68 (September 1974):973–88.
Clotfelter, James, and Hamilton, William R. "Beyond Race Politics: Electing
  Southern Populists in the 1970's." In *You Can't Eat Magnolias*, edited by H.
  Brandt Ayres and Thomas Naylor, pp. 136–59. New York: McGraw-Hill,
  1972.
Coles, Robert. *Migrants, Sharecroppers, Mountaineers*. Boston: Little, Brown, and
  Co., 1967.
Davidson, Chandler. *Biracial Politics: Conflict and Coalition in the Metropolitan
  South*. Baton Rouge: Louisiana State University Press, 1972.

Dollard, John. *Caste and Class in a Southern Town*. Garden City, N.Y.: Doubleday Anchor Books, 1937.

Earle, John R.; Knudsen, David D.; and Shriver, Donald W., Jr. *Spindles and Spires: A Re-Study of Religion and Social Change in Gastonia*. Atlanta: John Knox Press, 1976.

Easton, David, and Dennis, Jack. "The Child's Acquisition of Regime Norms: Political Efficacy." *American Political Science Review* 61 (March 1967):25–38.

Erbe, William. "Social Involvement and Political Activity." *American Sociological Review* 29 (April 1964):198–215.

Federal Writers' Project. *These Are Our Lives: As Told by the People and Written by Members of the Federal Writers' Project of the Works Progress Administration in North Carolina, Tennessee, and Georgia*. Chapel Hill: University of North Carolina Press, 1939.

Gaither, Gerald H. *Blacks and the Populist Revolt: Ballots and Bigotry in the New South*. University, Ala.: University of Alabama Press, 1977.

Greenstein, Fred I. *Personality and Politics: Problems of Evidence, Inference, and Conceptualization*. Chicago: Markham Publishing Co., 1969.

Gurr, Ted. *Why Men Rebel*. Princeton: Princeton University Press, 1970.

Hamilton, Howard D. "The Municipal Voter: Voting and Nonvoting in City Elections." *American Political Science Review* 65 (December 1971):1135–40.

Hamilton, Richard F. *Class and Politics in the United States*. New York: John Wiley and Sons, Inc., 1972.

Heard, Alexander. *A Two Party South?* Chapel Hill: University of North Carolina Press, 1952.

Heberle, Rudolf. "Social Consequences of the Industrialization of Southern Cities." *Social Forces* 27 (October 1949):29–37.

Hennessy, Bernard. "A Headnote of the Existence and Study of Political Attitudes." In *Political Attitudes and Public Opinion*, edited by Dan D. Nimmo and Charles M. Bonjean, pp. 27–40. New York: David McKay, Co., Inc., 1972.

Jennings, M. Kent, and Niemi, Richard G. "The Transmission of Political Values from Parent to Child." *American Political Science Review* 67 (March 1968):169–84.

Johnson, Gerald. "Research Note of Political Correlates of Voter Participation: A Deviant Case Analysis." *American Political Science Review* 65 (September 1971):768–76.

Katz, Daniel. "Attitude Formation and Public Opinion." In *Political Attitudes and Public Opinion*, edited by Dan D. Nimmo and Charles M. Bonjean, pp. 13–26. New York: David McKay Co., Inc., 1972.

Kelley, Stanley, Jr.; Ayres, Richard E.; and Bowen, William G. "Registration and Voting: Putting First Things First." *American Political Science Review* 61 (June 1967):359–76.

Key, V. O., Jr. *Public Opinion and American Democracy*. New York: Alfred A. Knopf, Inc., 1961.

———. "A Theory of Critical Elections." *Journal of Politics* 17 (February 1955):3–18.

———, and Heard, Alexander. *Southern Politics in State and Nation*. New York: Alfred A. Knopf, Inc., 1950.

Knutson, Jeanne N. *The Human Basis of the Polity*. Chicago: Aldine Atherton, 1972.

Lamb, Karl A. *As Orange Goes: Twelve California Families and the Future of American Politics*. New York: W. W. Norton and Co., 1974.

Lane, Robert E. *Political Ideology: Why the American Common Man Believes What He Does*. New York: Free Press, 1962.

Langton, Kenneth P., and Jennings, M. Kent. "Political Socialization and the High School Civics Curriculum in the United States," *American Political Science Review* 62 (September 1968):852–67.

Levitan, Sar A., ed. *Blue-Collar Workers: A Symposium on Middle America*. New York: McGraw-Hill, 1971.

Litt, Edgar. "Political Cynicism and Political Futility." *Journal of Politics* 25 (May 1963):312–23.

Loewen, James W. *The Mississippi Chinese: Between Black and White*. Cambridge, Mass.: Harvard University Press, 1971.

Marmor, Theodore R. *The Politics of Medicare*. Chicago: Aldine, 1970.

Maslow, Abraham. *The Psychology of Science: A Reconnaissance*. New York: Harper and Row, 1966.

Matthews, Donald R., and Prothro, James W. *Negroes and the New Southern Politics*. New York: Harcourt, Brace, and World, 1966.

McClosky, Herbert. "Consensus and Ideology in American Politics." In *Political Parties and Political Behavior*, edited by William J. Crotty, Donald M. Freeman, and Douglas S. Gatlin, pp. 155–89. Boston: Allyn and Bacon, Inc., 1966.

McEvoy, James, III. *Radicals or Conservatives: The Contemporary American Right*. Chicago: Rand McNally and Co., 1971.

Miller, Arthur H. "Political Issues and Trust in Government." *American Political Science Review* 67 (September 1974):951–72.

―――. "Rejoinder to 'Comment' by Jack Citrin: Political Discontent or Ritualism?" *American Political Science Review* 68 (September 1974):989–1001.

Novak, Michael. "Carter Tapping Religious Power Base." Greensboro *Daily News*, 4 April 1976, pp. A1, 10–11.

Orum, Anthony. "Religion and the Rise of the Radical White: The Case of Southern Wallace Support in 1968." In *Political Attitudes and Public Opinion*, edited by Dan D. Nimmo and Charles M. Bonjean, pp. 474–88. New York: David McKay Co., Inc., 1972.

Parkin, Frank. *Class Inequality and Political Order: Social Stratification in Capitalist and Communist Societies*. New York: Praeger, 1971.

Pope, Liston. *Millhands and Preachers: A Study of Gastonia*. New Haven: Yale University Press, 1942.

Prothro, James W., and Grigg, Charles M. "Fundamental Principles of Democracy: Bases of Agreement and Disagreement." *Journal of Politics* 22 (May 1960):277–94.

Reed, John Shelton. *The Enduring South: Subcultural Resistance in Mass Society*. Lexington, Mass.: D. C. Heath, 1972.

―――. "The Southern Quality of Life." Greensboro *Daily News*, 16 February 1975, p. E5.

Renshon, Stanley Allen. *Psychological Needs and Political Behavior*. New York: Free Press, 1974.

Repass, David E. "Issue Salience and Party Choice." *American Political Science Review* 65 (June 1971):389–400.

Robinson, John P.; Athanasiou, Robert; and Head, Kendra B. *Measures of Occupational Attitudes and Occupational Characteristics*. Ann Arbor: Institute for Social Research, 1969.

Robinson, John P.; Rusk, Jerrold G.; and Head, Kendra B. *Measures of Political Attitudes*. Ann Arbor: Institute for Social Research, 1969.

Robinson, John P., and Shaver, Philip. *Measures of Social Psychological Attitudes*. Ann Arbor: Institute for Social Research, 1969.

Rosenberg, Morris. "Misanthropy and Political Ideology." *American Sociological Review* 21 (December 1956):690–95.

Scammon, Richard, and Wattenberg, Ben. *The Real Majority.* New York: Coward-McCann, 1970.

Schwartz, David C. *Political Alienation and Political Behavior.* Chicago: Aldine Publishing Co., 1973.

Shapiro, Herbert. "The Populists and the Negro: A Reconsideration." In *The Making of Black America: Volume II, The Black Community in Modern America,* edited by August Meier and Elliot Rudwick, pp. 27–36. New York: Atheneum, 1969.

Tedin, Kent L. "The Influence of Parents on the Political Attitudes of Adolescents." *American Political Science Review* 68 (December 1974):1579–92.

Templeton, Fredric. "Alienation and Political Participation: Some Research Findings." *Public Opinion Quarterly* 30 (Summer 1966):249–61.

Verba, Sidney, and Nie, Norman. *Participation in America.* New York: Harper and Row, 1972.

Warren, Roland L. *The Community in America.* Chicago: Rand, McNally, and Co., 1963.

Weisberg, Herbert F., and Rusk, Jerrold G. "Dimensions of Candidate Evaluation." *American Political Science Review* 64 (December 1970):1167–85.

Westie, Frank R. "The American Dilemma: An Empirical Test." *American Sociological Review* 30 (August 1965):527–38.

Williams, T. Harry. *Huey Long.* New York: Knopf, 1969.

Wills, Garry. *Nixon Agonistes: The Crisis of the Self-Made Man.* New York: Signet, 1969.

Wolcott, Reed. *Rose Hill.* New York: G. P. Putnam's Sons, 1976.

Woodward, C. Vann. *Origins of the New South: 1877–1913.* Baton Rouge: Louisiana State University Press, 1951.

———. *The Strange Career of Jim Crow.* New York: Oxford University Press, 1955.

———. *Tom Watson: Agrarian Rebel.* Savannah: Beehive Press, 1938.

Index

Affirmative action. *See* Reverse discrimination
Albert (fictitious name of respondent), 20–22; empathy of, 61; individualism of, and on government providing jobs, 61–62; on unemployment, 67; on working a swing shift, 73; on discrimination, 79, 137; on equality in wages, 84–85; on social mobility, 111; on school busing, 135; on integration, 139–40, 148; on police, 182
Alcohol. *See* Drinking
Allport, Gordon, 145–46, 148, 157–58
Almond, Gabriel, 57
Ambiguity, tolerance of, 179
Articulation levels, 14–15, 50
Ayres, H. Brandt, 3

Bartley, Numan D., 5
Belief system. *See* Ideology
Black Panthers, 153
Blacks: population density and prejudice, 7, 161–62, 225 (n. 21); and jobs, 12–13; and housing conditions, 144–45; on race relations, 150–52. *See also* Integration; Ku Klux Klan; Race; Race relations; Racial prejudice; Racial stereotypes; Reverse discrimination
Brent (fictitious name of respondent), 22–24; on taxes, 61; on individualism, 64; on unemployment, 68; on equality in wages, 80; on health care, 98; on social class, 109, 111, 113, 117; on poverty, 113; on crime, 117; on school busing, 134–35; on race and sexual relations, 148; and political participation, 177; on local government, 181; on integrity in politics, 190
Busing, 127–36

Campbell, Angus, 91
Carter, Jimmy: reasons for supporting, 3–4, 29–30, 32, 35–36, 38, 46, 48, 53, 59; reasons for opposing, 24, 44; economic liberalism tied to support, 57; compared to Ford, 90–91; image as a populist, 123; and religious integration, 139–41; compared to Wallace, 155; identification with the working class, 174; and integrity in politics, 189–90; evangelical style of, 193, 227 (n. 38); and taxes, 193
Cash, W. J., 65, 199–200
Chandler, David Leon, 124
Civic duty, 171, 178–79
Civil rights movement, 49
Class consciousness, 121–23. *See also* Social class
Clotfelter, James R., 54–55, 161, 193
Coles, Robert, xii
Compassion. *See* Empathy
Comprehensive Employment and Training Act, 62
Congress, 68, 190
Conservatism. *See* Populism; Economic liberalism; Religious fundamentalism
Corporate profits, 81. *See also* Energy crisis
Couch, W. T., 20
Crime, 51, 94
Critical elections, 227 (n. 35)

Dave (fictitious name of respondent), 24–25; on government providing jobs, 58; on unemployment, 58–59, 66; on wages, 70, 83–84; on health care, 97–99; on fringe benefits of job, 103; on social class, 108, 118; on energy crisis and oil companies, 113–14; on integration, 131, 141–42, 146–47, 149–50, 152; on Ku Klux Klan,